ALTGELD'S AMERICA

Altgeld's America

THE LINCOLN IDEAL

VERSUS

CHANGING REALITIES

BY

RAY GINGER

NEW VIEWPOINTS
A Division of Franklin Watts
NEW YORK | LONDON

Contents

"The history of reform is always identical, it is the comparison of the idea with the fact."

Ralph Waldo Emerson

"It is from the realities of life that the highest idealities are born."

Clarence S. Darrow

"In a democracy there can be but one fundamental test of citizenship, namely: Are you using such gifts as you possess for or against the people?"

Louis H. Sullivan

Prologue: From Lincoln to Altgeld

> The fact that you met with an accident or got your legs
> broken, your neck twisted and your head smashed is not
> equal to a delivery of the goods.
>
> —John Peter Altgeld [*]

ABRAHAM LINCOLN for four years served his country as a great
president; for a much longer period he served it as a great
symbol. Nowhere was this more true than in the Midwest,
and in his home state of Illinois. When an ordinary man
dreamed of the future of his son, he thought of Lincoln as embodying everything he wanted his own boy to be.

Of all the qualities of Lincoln's character, the most appealing was simply his humanity. His greatness did not consist in
any unique abilities that he had; it consisted, rather, as Jane
Addams said in 1894, in his possession of "the largest share of
the common human qualities and experiences." He was a
humble man. He did not set himself above the crowd, but
sought to cultivate his ties to the crowd. The White House
during his residence was a swirl of common people coming
and going—more open than during the tenure of any other
president. He always thought of his own career as an example
of what an ordinary citizen could achieve.

From this came his remarkable compassion. He could put
himself in the shoes of others, grasp their problems, sense their
hopes, know their anguish and their joy. He had the same capacity for deep sympathy which would make Clarence Darrow
a great lawyer, Theodore Dreiser a great novelist, and John

[*] Commencement address at the University of Illinois, June 7, 1893.

1

Peter Altgeld a great governor. Lincoln's concern, during the Civil War, for military necessities did not keep him from using his pardon power freely to save deserters from the death penalty.

His compassion was universal. He was speaking his deepest feeling when he prayed: "With malice toward none, with charity for all. . . ." In spite of the intensely anti-Negro environment in which he was reared, he was able to see that the fatal weakness of the proslavery argument was simply its discrimination, its effort to set up categories of men with different sets of rights and duties. In telling Joshua Speed that he was not a Know-Nothing, he asked:

> How could I be? How can anyone who abhors the oppression of negroes be in favor of degrading classes of white people? Our progress in degeneracy appears to me to be pretty rapid. As a nation we began by declaring that "all men are created equal." We now practically read it "all men are created equal except negroes." When the Know-Nothings get control, it will read "all men are created equal except negroes and foreigners and Catholics." When it comes to this, I shall prefer emigrating to some country where they make no pretense of loving liberty, —to Russia, for instance, where despotism can be taken pure, and without the base alloy of hypocrisy.

Lincoln insisted that ideals must relate to reality, that they must set the standard toward which we try to shape reality. And his ideals he took from the Declaration of Independence and from Jefferson, whose principles he called "the definitions and axioms of free society."

This side of Lincoln's morality looked toward love, toward an acceptance of all men no matter what their errors and failings. As Billy Herndon wrote, Lincoln's heart was "as gentle as a woman's and as tender." But Lincoln's ethics also looked in another direction, toward duty. He felt keenly that, as Altgeld would insist, men should "deliver the goods." One of the finest indexes of his manhood lies just here: he felt his own duty more keenly than he felt the duties of others. This fatal sensitivity accounts for much of the torment he knew as president.

On taking office, he swore to maintain the Union and preserve the Constitution. That was his duty. He clung to it with an iron will. Beside it, nothing mattered (except, of course, the heartaches of individual people). He left no doubt about his position. When Horace Greeley protested to him in 1862 because the slaves of rebels had not been freed, Lincoln replied: "My paramount object in this struggle is to save the Union, and is not either to save or to destroy slavery. If I could save the Union without freeing any slave, I would do it; and if I could save it by freeing all the slaves, I would do it; and if I could save it by freeing some and leaving others alone, I would also do that. . . . I have here stated my purpose according to my view of official duty, and I intend no modification of my oft-expressed personal wish that all men, everywhere, could be free."

Personal feelings were one thing, official duty another. (When Clarence Darrow was a member of the state legislature in 1903, he voted against an appropriation for Altgeld's widow because he thought it a misuse of public funds, and he was crying honest tears when he got up to explain his vote.)

But love was not unrelated to duty. In all but five states, slavery was in fact ended by the Thirteenth Amendment. Lincoln used all his power to line up the necessary two-thirds vote in the House of Representatives. The measure passed by three votes. Even Lincoln's conviction of the overriding need to save the Union was dependent on what he thought the Union meant. It meant popular government, which was both a form of political rule and a set of social institutions. He told Congress early in the war:

> This is essentially a people's contest. On the side of the Union it is a struggle for maintaining in the world that form and substance of a government whose leading object is to elevate the

condition of men—to lift artificial weights from all shoulders; to clear the paths of laudable pursuit for all; to afford all an unfettered start, and a fair chance in the race of life. . . .

Lincoln saw life as a race, and each man ran that race alone. Thus, if love and duty were not contradictory, neither did regard for others rule out a keen regard for one's own interests. Lincoln himself was a man of fierce desire for political office; quite possibly until he reached the White House that desire was the most important element in his life. "He was always calculating and planning ahead," wrote Herndon. "His ambition was a little engine that knew no rest."

Lincoln never thought this self-regard was improper. He believed in private property, and in the right of any man to accumulate wealth and to use it as he wished. For him the key test of democracy was whether it opened up this chance to everybody. He thought like, and spoke for, the men who had started as he had, in a humble station, and had risen by their own efforts to become wealthy farmers and businessmen and professional men. He spoke even more for the men who still had this ascent to make. His philosophy was the philosophy of individualism and self-help. "The prudent, penniless beginner in the world," he said, "labors for wages awhile, saves a surplus with which to buy tools or land for himself, then labors on his own account another while, and at length hires another new beginner to help him."

If a man keeps this up long enough, perhaps he will have five hundred or a thousand men working for him for wages, and Lincoln had no objection to this either. He was precise in stating his ideal:

> I take it that it is best for all to leave each man free to acquire property as fast as he can. Some will get wealthy. I don't believe in a law to prevent a man from getting rich; it would do more harm than good. So while we do not propose any war upon capital, we do wish to allow the humblest man an equal chance to get rich with everybody else.

Here, then, is what Lincoln represented to the generation that followed. He stood for an open society in which all men would have an equal chance to accumulate wealth and prestige. "I am a living witness," he told a regiment of soldiers, "that any one of your children may look to come here as my father's child has." By this vision, the worthy goal is to improve your status and to do so by your own efforts—and yet to remain a human being who has deep regard for the material and intimate needs of other human beings. Lincoln seemed great because, while doing the first, he had also done the latter. He never became puffed up with success. He never became arrogant or tyrannical. Quite the contrary. After his election he lost his personal ambition. Instead of being exhilarated by his power as president, he was humbled by his responsibility. Of his tenure at the White House he said: "So long as I have been here, I have not willingly planted a thorn in any man's bosom."

From the Civil War to 1900, Abraham Lincoln dominated the visions of the good society which were being projected to exonerate the successful and to inspire the young. To know what was good, men looked at Lincoln. But during those very decades—it is one of the ironies with which history is fertile—the social realities that had shaped the Lincoln ideal were being chipped away, and the ideal itself was being twisted beyond recognition.

The Lincoln ideal was rural. The image was of Abe the rail-splitter, not of Abe the machinist. But Illinois was rapidly ceasing to be rural. No city in the history of the world had grown more rapidly than Chicago grew then. In 1840, it had fewer than five thousand residents. For the next fifty years, its population more than doubled in every decade but one—the decade of the Great Fire of 1871. By 1890, more than a million people lived in Chicago. From 1880 to 1910, the population rose by a half-million every ten years.

The Lincoln ideal was intensely individualistic. It pictured each man alone succeeding in life by his personal efforts. But Chicago by 1890 was a city of organizations, where the efforts of an individual man counted for little. It was a city of monopolies, which closed off the former precious opportunities for ordinary men. A man could not gather together a few dollars and set out to compete with the McCormick reaper works, which employed more men than the city had held people fifty years earlier. It was still possible for men to start from modest origins and rise to the top, but most of them did so in peculiar occupations: Clarence Darrow in law, Theodore Dreiser in literature, John Dewey in teaching, Altgeld in politics. And these were men of great ability and great luck. Thousands of men worked hard all their lives and got nowhere. "Land of opportunity, you say," sneered a Chicago laborer. "You know damn well my children will be where I am—that is, if I can keep them out of the gutter." Countless businessmen and lawyers came to feel the same way as they lost their business to great corporations that could undersell or outmaneuver them.

The Lincoln ideal of popular government was also undermined. As industry in Chicago expanded, it drew thousands of immigrants to man the unskilled jobs. By 1890, fully 68 percent of the population had been born abroad, and another 10 percent were the children of foreign-born. The great majority of these immigrants had been peasants in Europe, and they had had no experience with government except that it had tyrannized over them. Understanding nothing about democracy, many of them saw no reason not to sell their votes; desperately needing the essentials of life, they had good reason to sell their votes if they could get a little money in return.

Many businessmen had their own reasons to corrupt the political processes. As the city grew violently, there was need for sewers to be dug, street-car lines to be operated, electric companies to furnish power. These were natural monopolies: if one company got the right, nobody else could have it. The right was worth a fortune, and who got it depended on public officials. Aldermen in Chicago sold franchises as continuously and efficiently as Marshall Field sold dry goods, and if a businessman occasionally developed a queasy conscience—well, that was just the way things were done. None knew this better (or rested easier about it) than Charles Tyson Yerkes, the Chicago street-car king, who by 1893 was a power in both major political parties, in the city council of Chicago, and in the legislature of Illinois. When Theodore Dreiser modeled his novel about a traction magnate after the career of Yerkes, he made painfully obvious how far the state had departed from the type of popular government that Abraham Lincoln had known in Sangamon County.

The fact was clear: when Altgeld became governor in 1893, many aspects of reality in Chicago had become a mockery of the Lincoln ideal. But the men who benefited from the new realities had been revising the ideal to make it fit the realities. The balanced paradoxes of Lincoln were gone. In their stead was the single goal of Success. All that counted was practical results. "If you are sent to bring something, bring it, and not an explanation," Altgeld told the graduating class of the University of Illinois in 1893. "If you agree to do something, do it; don't come back with an explanation. Explanations as to how you came to fail are not worth two cents a ton. Nobody wants them or cares for them."

Here was doctrine that Chicago's millionaires could endorse with full hearts. It was the doctrine that had powered the expansion of Field's dry-goods company, of the packing plants of Philip D. Armour and Gustavus F. Swift, of the metal-products factory of Charles R. Crane, of the locomotive works and steel mills. It could become the doctrine that guided the sweatshop operators of the Nineteenth Ward to grab what they could from the wretched lives of their employees (who were also their neighbors and usually their fellow countrymen). It was the doctrine that moved Governor Altgeld to tell Jane Addams in 1893 that the erection of the $500,000 Unity Building in Chicago had given him more satisfaction than anything else he had ever done. It was the doctrine behind the burst of energy that created the grounds for the Columbian Exposition that same year.

But while the Columbian Exposition disclosed incredible abilities to deliver the goods, it also revealed that almost nobody in Chicago knew what sort of goods should be delivered. By its imitativeness, its vulgar display, its lack of any esthetic standards of its own, it raised for thoughtful men and women the question: What are we doing?

They looked around them and were appalled. The Exposition was a White City on the lake front; all around it were filth and squalor and the evidence of greed. The well-to-do lived in mansions that were exercises in bad taste; the poor lived in slums that were wretched and disease-ridden. The city for three decades had been living in an orgy of money-making. Anything was permissible, as long as somebody could make a profit from it. The natural beauties of the city had been defaced, the air above it was heavy with stench, the waters that flowed past it and through it had been polluted.

Polluted too were the lives of the people who lived in it. Chicago had become a city of intolerable extremes. At the top were men like Marshall Field, who could spend $75,000 on a birthday party for his son. At the bottom were innumerable families where ten-year-old children had to work along with their mothers and fathers to scrape together the necessities for the most miserable existence. Field had piled up his fortune while thousands of women clerks in his store earned less than a living wage. Swift had made his, but if a worker in his packing house broke a leg, the man was turned into the street and forgotten and another hired in his place. George Pullman built a model factory town and made many inventions and a great fortune—but in doing so he goaded his workers into striking, and the strike set off one of the most violent labor conflicts in American history. When the demand for meat declined, Armour might turn out thousands of men with no notice at all; if their families starved, that was no concern of the company. Such were the inexorable laws of trade. Men who could not rise to the top were smashed underfoot.

Something somewhere had miscarried. The city had surged

ahead—and some now saw that it had been surging toward madness. At the commercial heights and in the social depths life had become brutalizing drudgery. A prominent woman doctor in Chicago contended that women in both the lower class and the upper class were unfit to be mothers: the former had exhausted themselves by toil, the latter by foolish (but socially obligatory) dissipation. She went further to point out that the excessive work and the excessive idleness were complementary: the wealthy exploited the poor but did not themselves find sanity or happiness. Philip D. Armour confessed rather plaintively that he had no interest except business. Marshall Field neglected his family and everything else except his store, only to discover late in life that he had nothing except money, and it was not enough. In gaining his wealth, he had lost his humanity, the humanity that had flowed out of Abraham Lincoln into the Gettysburg Address. The President's own son, Robert Todd Lincoln, became president of The Pullman Company, but he could never have written his father's letter to Mrs. Bixby. The father was a great man; the son was pompous and almost empty of feeling.

The Lincoln ideal? What of that now? True, Lincoln had been a self-made man, a poor boy who rose in life by his own efforts. But in the process of getting ahead he had developed the gentle and generous qualities in his own nature. He had not just achieved something—he had become a better man. No perversion of his significance could be worse than to substitute unalloyed greed for his bleeding compassion.

Yet that was what had happened. An English tourist said of Chicago that "everybody is fighting to be rich, is then straining to be refined and nobody can attend to making the city fit to live in." A local clergyman was even blunter: "Chicago people are money and pleasure mad. In other cities the question is 'Does reform help the city?' In Chicago it is 'Does it pay?' "

A part of the Lincoln ideal had come to do duty for the whole: the vision of his life as an instance of man's triumph over hardships and temptations had been distorted into a wholehearted worship of material success. A whole city had run after false gods. As a result the ruthless had won out over the compassionate, the practical over the philosophic, the readily marketed item over the perfectly executed, the mass-produced over the unique, the derivative over the creative. The quality of life itself had become thinner and less various.

The gap between the vision and the fact became too great, and men found that they could not live this life. Then protest came. The old ideal was reasserted, and men insisted that reality should be molded to its dictates. They declared anew that the final purpose of mankind is to help each individual to develop his powers in a full and balanced way. These reformers were not ascetics who scoffed at material goods; they well knew that a man's belly cannot be empty if his soul is to thrive. But they also demanded that the values of men must reach beyond the concrete and the quantitative to embrace the intangible and the qualitative. What they sought was a sufficiency of goods and a blossoming of spirit. Their concern was the kind of life that man lived—and the kind of man that life shaped.

Thus Altgeld, in stressing the importance of practical results in 1893, did not allow his exposition to end there; he elaborated it so that he turned away from the creed of brutal efficiency, turned back toward Lincoln's humanism. Men and women must succeed, he said, at some constructive and noble work. They must work in accord with "the sunlight of eternal principles." Just as Altgeld would later title one of his books *The Cost of Something for Nothing*, so now he said that "dishonesty rots a man down, limits his usefulness and shortens his career, and therefore he is a fool who will follow that path."

Altgeld could speak with feeling, for he had just learned in torment and solitude how tempting that path could be. When he took office, three men were in prison. He became convinced that they were confined unjustly. But to pardon them would be to jeopardize his own future in politics. For months he lived in anguish, while his ambition and his ideals fought for control. Then he wrote a pardon message that was a savage indictment of class favoritism in the administration of justice. There must be, Altgeld proclaimed, one law—for rich and poor, for conservatives and radicals. What Altgeld began, Clarence Darrow continued. Year after year, in case after case, Darrow made his penetrating, eloquent protests against callous treatment in the courts of workingmen and lunatics and deviates. Gradually, out of their endless labor, they made the criminal law into a more flexible and humane instrument.

The same humanism moved Jane Addams and her associates as they virtually invented the profession of social work. For a model they looked to Lincoln (when Lincoln was president, Florence Kelley's father was in Congress, and the fathers of Jane Addams and Julia Lathrop were in the Illinois legislature). Their ideals were old; their techniques novel. Hull-House in 1889 became the second settlement house in the country. Four years later Florence Kelley directed a thorough study of the surrounding slum—the first social survey of an American city. Altgeld appointed her state factory inspector, and she used her position to press for safer working conditions, prohibition of child labor, laws requiring children to attend school. In 1899 she became the head of the National Consumers' League, which led the campaign to abolish child labor in the United States. Altgeld appointed Julia Lathrop to the state board of charities, and she later became the first director of the United States Children's Bureau; the second was another woman from Hull-House, Grace Abbott. Grace's sister Edith, an authority on immigrant laborers, became dean of the new School of Social Service Administration at the University of Chicago. Another woman who came under Jane Addams' tutelage was Alice Hamilton, whose priority in industrial medicine made her a professor at the Harvard Medical School. Alzina Stevens was the first probation officer of the first juvenile court in the United States. Eight years after the court was founded, Julia Lathrop prompted its pioneering in psychiatric diagnosis and guidance.

Chicago was being remade, piecemeal, and its reformers were setting examples that other cities might follow. When John Dewey set up the Elementary School at the University of Chicago, he planned it as a laboratory to devise a type of schooling that would be valid for modern industrial society. Dewey's colleague Thorstein Veblen watched with delighted irony while high society in Chicago acted out its elaborate rituals, but he went beyond that to write a sweeping critique of the standards by which the American people distinguished good from bad.

Each of these reformers had his own specialty; each toiled in his own vineyard. But almost every effort at reform finally arrived at a common question: Were the people of Chicago to govern themselves, or were they to be governed by Yerkes and other capitalists and corrupt politicians? For a decade Altgeld summoned the voters to do battle against the monopolies, and the voters came through—then one night the city hall was surrounded by angry crowds bearing nooses of rope and demanding that the aldermen vote honestly. The aroused citizens drove most of the boodlers out of public office, and made Chicago unsuitable for Yerkes. But the problem still was not solved, and men like Darrow mounted a dramatic campaign for city ownership of the street-car lines.

As these visionaries sought to reshape society to the Lincoln ideal, they learned more about the nature of reality. Their new knowledge revealed flaws in the Lincoln ideal itself, so they revised that too. The philosophic harvest was rich. They learned new insights into men and society and how change occurs in both. They learned that man is not infinitely plastic, that all men have certain needs that must be met if the man is to keep his health. (Had Lincoln hinted it when he said that "you cannot repeal human nature"?) Where Lincoln's philosophy had shuttled between determinism and individualism, Veblen and Dewey arrived at better notions of the interactions of the individual and society, while Louis Sullivan and Frank Lloyd Wright reached toward deeper expressions of the idea of free will. They learned, all of them, that man is a total organism, and that his potentialities need to develop in a balanced way. Man cannot be Economic Man, like Marshall Field, or purely Social Man like Mrs. Potter Palmer. He must be Man.

Dewey, Veblen, Darrow, Dreiser—they made profound use of their realization that all change is a matter of cause-and-effect; that where you can get to depends largely on where you start from. (Had Lincoln hinted that, too, when he said, "If we could first know where we are and whither we are tending, we could better judge what to do and how to do it."?) If a person is to achieve any goal, he must start from the existing possibilities, and he must know the material realities he is dealing with. He must not turn away from the objective facts. But neither can he turn away from subjective needs—including his own. Veblen was never more incisive than when he explained why the women of the upper class were available for reform causes. Jane Addams said the same thing when she spoke of the "subjective need for reform"; she knew that the bewildered and crushed residents of the Nineteenth Ward symbolized the objective need for reform, but she knew too that she needed to be a reformer.

So did Eugene Debs, who wandered through the model town of Pullman when the strike there was just beginning. So did Upton Sinclair, who toured the stockyards for seven weeks and wrote *The Jungle*, which hastened the passage of the Federal Pure Food and Drug Act of 1906. (Sinclair admitted ruefully that his effort had miscarried: "I aimed at the public's heart," he said, "and by accident hit it in the stomach.")

If Sinclair's artistic aim was faulty, that of Theodore Dreiser was masterly. Dreiser pondered over the deeper realities that would be slow to change. They could be conquered in only one way, by the imagination, and by the writer's craft. He brooded for years over the pocked careers of the residents of Chicago, and out of his brooding came characters in novels: George Hurstwood, a haunting portrait of man separated from work; Carrie Meeber, the inane shopgirl whose vitality carries her to the top; Jennie Gerhardt, the mother as saint.

What Dreiser did in fiction, Louis Sullivan did in architecture. But where Dreiser was depressed by the realities around him, Sullivan exulted about the possibilities within. His Getty Tomb, his Gage Building, his department store for Schlesinger & Mayer—they have originality and rhythm and proportion and personality. Sullivan's pupil Frank Lloyd Wright achieved these same qualities and expressed them in the elegant simplicity of the Charnley house and the superbly flowing space of the Robie house.

Here is the story of these men and women, of the city they lived in, the visions they had, and of their efforts to remake the city. But it is not the story of Chicago alone; for it tells of how industrialism came to the world, arm in arm with the search for profit, and of the troubles the marriage made, and of how people of noble purpose labored to overcome those troubles.

CHAPTER 1

White City in the Muck

Chicago asked in 1893 for the first time the question whether
the American people knew where they were driving.*

I

THE YEAR 1893 would mark the 400th anniversary of Columbus' voyage, and a mammoth jubilee seemed appropriate.
When Congress in 1890 was seeking to designate a site, no city
pushed its claims more vigorously than Chicago, with a brashness born of success. Chicago had arrived, and she lusted for
recognition. Congress gave it to her.

She immediately set out to insure that the rest of the world
would too. A magnificent White City would be flung up in
Jackson Park, on the shores of Lake Michigan five miles south
of the business district. The chief planners of the grounds and
buildings were Burnham and Root, the city's foremost architectural firm. John Wellborn Root, the designer for the partnership, ripped off countless sketches on bits of brown paper:
all sorts of buildings, every architectural style known to man,
from mosques and pagodas to Romanesque towers.

And thus, at the starting gate, Chicago's brashness stumbled.
Root was a young man with an original mind. He had designed

* *The Education of Henry Adams* (New York: Modern Library, 1931), p. 343.

superb office buildings in the city, culminating in the seven-teen-story Monadnock, an all-masonry structure that seemed slender in spite of its massive walls, graceful in spite of its austere freedom from ornamentation. Here Root perfected the use of precisely spaced vertical rows of projecting bay win-dows, a characteristic of Chicago buildings. The city had other capable architects, especially that poet in stone and words, Louis Sullivan, and his engineer-partner Dankmar Adler, and a craggy young draftsman, Frank Lloyd Wright, who was mastering his trade in their office. But now, with a chance to show the world what Chicagoans could create, Root's mind froze, and he could think only of copying.

Daniel Burnham was hardly an architect at all, but an execu-tive and promoter. He had gone bankrupt in Chicago just before the Great Fire of 1871. The Fire gave him an opening (the entire center of the city had to be rebuilt)—the Fire plus his partnership with Root. Burnham found the clients, Root did the designs, Burnham saw that the building was finished on time and properly. Burnham was a better judge of food than of designs for buildings, and each year he sent a keg of Ma-deira wine twice around the world so that it would age before going into his cellar. But he was no architect.

Burnham and Root had already decided that a national proj-ect such as the Exposition must have national collaboration in its design. Sullivan was given the Transportation Building, and for the others the call went to the top firms in New York and Boston and Kansas City. Frederick Law Olmstead, who had designed Central Park in New York and the parks of Washington, was given charge of the landscaping. Summons also went to sculptors and painters. When the men assembled at a luncheon in Chicago, Augustus St. Gaudens remarked that it was the greatest gathering of artists in five hundred years. A few days later, Root died suddenly. Then the other archi-tects still further diluted his watery conceptions; Louis Sulli-van, who knew better, lacked the influence to stop them. Architects in the nineteenth century had been increasingly drawn to the findings of archeologists, and the style of classicism had long been threatening to swamp originality. Now it did so in the designs for the Columbian Exposition.

While the artists worked at drafting boards and in studios, Burnham worked at Jackson Park. His job was to build what amounted to a substantial city in two and a half years. All that now existed was beach and bog. He made his headquarters at Jackson Park and slept there. He had seven thousand men working for him, and he drove them mercilessly. They worked through rainstorms, through blizzards. Horses sank to their bellies in the mud of springtime. The work went forward regardless of frequent strikes, of frozen ground, of heavy snows that accumulated on the roofs and crushed the skylights. In Chicago, they got things done. But they paid the price. In the single year 1891, some seven hundred accidents took place, one for every ten men. Seventeen men were killed.

While Daniel Burnham pursued his vision at Jackson Park, Alderman Johnny Powers saw opportunity of another kind. Notable for his thieving even in a legislative body where excellence in this respect was common, Powers introduced an ordinance into the city council by saying: "Why not pipe into the city of Chicago during the World's Fair good, clear, cool spring water from the famous springs at Wisconsin's Waukesha?" Other aldermen could immediately see the merits in Powers' proposal; Waukesha was eighty miles from Chicago, and a construction project of such magnitude was sure to offer many chances for graft (or boodling, as the language of the day had it). But an opposing member asked venomously: "How many men supporting the ordinance ever drink water? What one of those aldermen drinks water?" Nonetheless, the ordinance was passed; the majority of the Chicago council worked ceaselessly to deserve their name, "the gray wolves." Powers even lobbied the bill through the Wisconsin legislature. But his scheme ran afoul in the executive branches: the governor of Wisconsin and Mayor Hempstead Washburne of Chicago both vetoed it.

Through the winter of 1892 the work at Jackson Park went forward. Mud flats became lawns, wooded islands, and lagoons. The dozen main buildings for exhibits covered twenty acres each. More than two hundred smaller buildings were scattered among the huge halls. But all were based on the same heresy. After the steel frames of the great buildings had been erected, each was concealed by elaborately ornamental walls of some derivative style. The walls were coated with stucco, an absurd surfacing in a Chicago climate. As a final exquisite touch, the stucco was painted white, with gold for trim. The idea was to copy, and to decorate in a way that had little or no relation to the structure—and no relation at all to the life of the city. Here was enormous energy, but no vision. Here was incredible building, but no creation. Only Louis Sullivan, with his Transportation Building, achieved that.

For months the approaching Fair was discussed all over the country. In Marion, Indiana, a man mused about the coming mayoralty election in Chicago and about the reputation of the Democratic candidate, and concluded: "If Old Carter Harrison's elected mayor, I'm goin' to Chicago to the Fair, but I'm going to wear nothing but tights and carry a knife between my teeth and a pistol in each hand." In New York, the society dictator Ward McAllister thought it strange that the Exposition was to honor Columbus: "In a social way Columbus was an ordinary man." He also warned that Chicago, well known to him for the "sharp character" of its financiers, should not presume to rival the East "in matters of refinement."

The opening was May 1, 1893, when a rude wild crowd estimated at nearly half a million people massed somehow into the Court of Honor and gazed at the dome of the Administration Building. (It was higher than the dome of the National Capitol. Quantity above all.) They looked at the fountains, the statues. They shrieked and shoved. Husbands held their children, even their wives, in the air above the ruthless mob. The air was rent with shouts of protest, with pleas, with screams of anguish. In the crowd was Jane Addams, young mistress of

Hull-House. She felt her purse seized by a pickpocket. An officer of the Columbian Guard used his sword to trip the rogue and then hustled him away.

At last came the dignitaries in carriages, headed by President Grover Cleveland, cabinet members, generals, royalty from Spain, the new governor, John Peter Altgeld. Spectators, the lucky few, looked down from the dome of the Administration Building or from the top of Machinery Hall. The President gave a speech: "Stupendous results of American enterprise . . . proud national destiny . . . exalted mission." He pressed a button, and thousands of flags unfurled. On warships out in Lake Michigan, the guns boomed.

The ponderous President was the antithesis of Governor Altgeld, a slight man who seemed to be always fighting to control a twitch that, once started, would shake his entire body. The two, although both Democrats, were not affable together. They held to the proprieties, but no more.

The coolness between Cleveland and Altgeld was nothing to the chill exuded by the visiting Infanta Eulalia of Spain, who balked at being guest of honor at a reception given by the acknowledged leader of high society in Chicago, Mrs. Potter Palmer. Upon learning that Palmer, while immensely wealthy, was a real estate man and hotel owner, the Infanta said: "I prefer not to meet this innkeeper's wife." (A few years later when Mrs. Palmer was in Paris, she was invited to a fête for the Infanta. She declined, saying: "I cannot meet this bibulous representative of a decadent monarchy.") Other members of the Spanish nobility were more sociable. Two lineal descendants of Columbus himself attended a breakfast at the Union League Club, where they were treated to oysters, roast woodchucks, veal chops with Castilian sauce, chicken, eggs with rice, olives, fried peppers, tomatoes with onions, sherbet, and strawberry shortcake with kirsch. The beverages served were sherry, Chateau Leoville, Pommery sec, Malaga, coffee, and cognac. This was breakfast.

All summer at the Union League Club the champagne

flowed. One member went to the wine clerk and suggested that he plug a watermelon, scoop out the center, pour in a whole bottle of champagne, replug it and let it stand in the ice box. This became very popular. The Club also installed a machine to freeze champagne into champagne ice.

These exoticisms were for the rich, but the Exposition offered others to the poor. They could see a map of the United States made of pickles or a Krupp cannon weighing 130 tons. For the artistic there were Sèvres porcelains and Gobelin tapestries, and, exhibited three and four deep on the walls in any location where they chanced to fit, were nine thousand paintings, nearly all of them mediocre. But some of the industrial displays were stunning: the telescope that Charles Tyson Yerkes, the local street-car king, had donated to the new University of Chicago for an observatory that was not yet built; the "high-tension currents" of Nikolá Tesla; a long-distance telephone to New York; prize livestock; shows of grain and food, including grapefruit, which thus got its start on American menus.

During May fifty thousand people paid the fifty-cent admission to the Fair. The next month a financial panic struck the country. A dangerous run started on the Chicago banks. Depositors stood in line before the tellers' windows and shouted for their money—and they got it. A few banks failed; the others hung on and paid cash. One night the Illinois Trust and Savings Bank stayed open until three o'clock in the morning and paid everybody who wanted to be paid. Marshall Field and Philip D. Armour came to the bank and talked reassuringly to the crowds. Harlow Higginbotham, head of the committee that had charge of the Exposition, deserted his duties at Jackson Park to appear at a bank, where he was seen holding a baby for a tired mother in the line.

In other cities the panic carried into depression. Workers were laid off. Businesses went bankrupt. But in Chicago the panic was stopped for a time as the Exposition drew a swelling stream of visitors to spend their money in Chicago stores. The crass magnificence of it pulled them in. People who had never seen a large city thought of the Fair as an escape from their stunted lives on the farm. All over the Midwest men mortgaged their land to raise money for the trip. School teachers spent every cent of their savings on it. Even a sophisticate like Hamlin Garland, a young writer on the way up, wrote to his aging parents on their Dakota farm: "Sell the cook stove if necessary and come. You *must* see this fair." At Jackson Park an old man was heard to comment to his wife: "Well, Susan, it paid, even if it did take all the burial money."

What they sought was the sensational, the saccharine, the easily understood. Theodore Thomas, conductor of the Chicago Symphony Orchestra, had planned two series of concerts for the Exposition. Every day at noon all comers were admitted free to hear popular music. The crowds there were big and enthusiastic. But Thomas—a conductor who took himself seriously when he said: "Mediocrity is the curse of art. It should be wiped out, not encouraged!"—also arranged a series, for a fee, to present a wide selection of classical works by the great composers. This series did so badly financially that the Exposition canceled all appearances by visiting artists. Early in August, Thomas resigned his connection with the Fair.

Several reform congresses were held in conjunction with the Exposition. The leading suffragettes gathered to agitate for their cause. Prohibition of alcoholic beverages, juvenile delinquency, crime prevention, pauperism—each had its special meeting. But none was more timely, in view of the growing unemployment in the country, than the Labor Congress. By late August, when the Congress met, so many workers had been laid off in Chicago that the trade unions were demanding a program of public works. A single meeting outdoors on the Lake Front drew 25,000 people to hear speeches by President Samuel Gompers of the American Federation of Labor, the single-tax leader Henry George, and the railroad lawyer Clarence Darrow.

The Fair continued for another two months, and when it closed on October 30 it had drawn a total attendance of more than 27 million—more than any earlier world's fair. But what else had it done? Doubtless it had spread knowledge of many useful pieces of machinery, of superior plants and animals. But was that enough? Henry Adams found the Fair a chaos; to him it asked whether the American people had any notion what their purpose was, what the purpose of man in general was. Where are we going? Adams asked. Backward, Louis Sullivan replied, in an eloquent obituary on the buildings at Jackson Park: "Thus architecture died in the land of the free and the home of the brave—in a land declaring its democracy, inventiveness, unique daring, enterprise and progress. . . . The damage wrought by the World's Fair will last for half a century from its date, if not longer."

A speaker at the Columbian Exposition had made even more disturbing pronouncements. Appearing there at the meeting of the American Historical Association, Frederick Jackson Turner asserted that the chief influence on three centuries of American life had been the existence of unoccupied land beyond the western border of settlement. The frontier had given to humble men a chance to go west and get ahead. Thus it had nurtured democracy and equality. It had made the Lincoln ideal a reality. But now, said Turner, the frontier line had disappeared. The country was settled. No matter what the future might be, it could not be a repetition of the past.

II

If visitors to the Exposition proved indifferent to classical music, they were captivated by other amusements. Along the Midway, to the almost constant throbbing of a cannibal drum, the freak shows and dime museums made money with their monstrosities. The flowing tides of people were able to see natives of nearly every culture in the world. And three miles away, on the Levee of the near South Side, even greater thrills could be found. Everybody knew that the customers had come to town, and that big money could be made, and the police abandoned their customary gestures at repressing vice. The gambling halls were open all night, for stud and roulette, chuck-a-luck and piquette. The marks could lose their money slowly or quickly, and for many it did not take long at all; a syndicate headed by Tom O'Brien, King of the Bunko Men, netted more than $500,000 in a few months. The prostitution was more startling yet. Cheap whores and pimps went into the streets to campaign. Lavish new houses were built. On every bordello the shutters came down. Vina Fields, formerly the leading madam in town with forty girls, now offered seventy or eighty. At the ornate brownstone showplace of Carrie Watson, sixty girls paraded in their clothes of shining silk while a parrot at the door croaked: "Carrie Watson. Come in, gentlemen." Everywhere the girls worked double shifts, the corks popped, the pianos pounded. Free-born Americans were having fun. All night it lasted, and the crowds swept out of the theaters where some of the greatest artists in the world were playing, and into the gambling halls and saloons and brothels, and out again, and rode in carriages along the broad boulevards singing, "After the Ball."

Some of these streets, such as West Monroe and West Washington, were lined with excellent residences. The North Side had more lavish mansions near the Lake: the ridiculous Romanesque of Franklin MacVeagh, head of the Board of Trade; the Tudor of Potter Palmer, with a glass porte-cochère and a lovely lawn. Chicago had more than two hundred millionaires, nearly all men who had made their own fortunes in the booming city, and they were not hesitant to wear, or to live in, badges of their status. But even in the wealthy areas there were signs of another Chicago: the filthy, brutal, squalid Chicago where lived the working poor. At times of falling barometer and southwest wind, members of the Union League Club itself, as they consumed their champagne ice, could not escape the stench from the manure and decaying flesh at the stockyards. The Chicago River was likewise fetid, the grease so thick on its surface that it seemed a liquid rainbow as it crossed the center of the city to the Lake, carrying with it garbage, human excrement, refuse, dead animals. In most districts the streets added their small but innumerable sources of nausea: manure, garbage. Small wonder that the city's water supply was contaminated, and that the death rate from typhoid was twice as high as in New York or Boston.

Chicago had two thousand miles of streets. Fewer than a third were paved, mainly with huge blocks of wood, but also with macadam, with gravel, asphalt, cinders, cobblestones, or with great blocks of granite which in winter sweated a cold slime: treacherous footing for the draft horses with their metal shoes. The unpaved streets were dust or mud, unending bogs where wagons sank to the hub, horses to the knee, while the mustached drivers strained and cursed and plied the whip. Many thoroughfares had street-car lines: steel rails and rattling swaying cars. These were the cable cars, successor to animal power and predecessor of electric street cars. A stationary steam engine was used to revolve an endless steel cable that ran in a slot between the rails. On each car was an arm that could reach down to grip the cable. In the open air, on the front of the car, stood the gripman, a burly giant who drove the arm down when he wanted to move, raised it up when he wanted to stop.

The cable car was twice as fast as horse railways had been. But it cost more to install and more to maintain. Thus it was unprofitable unless the traffic load was heavy. Passengers crammed into the cars had cause to envy the cattle coming in relative comfort to their death at the stockyards. The cable car hurled its cargo first this way, then that; for it could move only at the speed of the moving cable; each start was a wrench, each stop snatched at the windpipe. The stops were frequent, and often seemed interminable, for when the cable broke the entire system jammed. Noise, stench, heat, lack of air, bruising congestion: existence in a cable car was difficult. But it was far more so in some of the buildings that the cable cars passed.

In one Chicago precinct, a newborn baby had only two chances in five of surviving his first year of life.

Scene: *Estate at Lake Forest of a grain broker named Poole*

> Three hundred children from the Half Orphan Asylum in Chicago are present for a day-long outing. Young Ernest Poole and his brother make friends with some of the boys and lead them to the beach and ravines. Ernest becomes friendly with one boy, showing him all of the special hiding places, showing him fishhooks and a bow and an air gun. The boy returns what he hears, talking of his own secret places in the asylum, defiantly taking from his pockets a top, marbles, a small broken knife. He boasts all day of the pleasures he finds in the city.
>
> The day ends. It is time to go. The boy says to Ernest: "Golly, it must be fine to live here!"
>
> Ernest: "Sure it is, but you said it was fine in your place, too."
>
> The boy spins sharply away. He clenches his fists. Ernest swallows hard. He understands. Impulsively he asks: "Want this air gun?"
>
> "Hell, no!" fiercely. "Jesus Christ, but it's hell to be poor!"
>
> He turns and runs.

In Chicago the Nineteenth Ward, where Hull-House stood, was one of the worst. During the summer when the Columbian Exposition was going gaily forward, Florence Kelley was directing a survey of living and working conditions in an area a mile square. What the investigators found was the diseased underbelly of Chicago's growth, the muck out of which rose the white and gold at Jackson Park. The growth of the city had been driven by a single-minded pursuit of profit. The way to make money was to build factories and warehouses and street-car lines, not homes for people to live in, parks for them to play in. The capital and labor power of Chicago was spent on "productive" facilities. There was no profit in erecting decent homes for workingmen. The factories went up, and wage earners poured into Chicago from all over Europe and clustered around the factories like calves around the mother cow. The shacks around the factory were placed on wheels and hauled away; a solid tenement of three or four stories, with no light, no air, often no plumbing, went up. Still more workers came, and the small yards behind the tenements became sites for more shacks, until no empty space was left. Still more workers came, and the population rose, but the living facilities remained the same.

In such areas the family was hardly a distinct unit. Often a family did not take its meals together; many had no table at all. It was common for several families to share a kitchen. About the most that could be said was that members of a family shared an apartment, at least at night. Often they shared it, not only with each other, but with outsiders or other families.

Quite a few residences in the ward were not occupied by families at all. Houses candidly reported themselves in the census as brothels, women as prostitutes who listed their incomes as varying from $5 to $50 a week. Nearly all of them were American, mainly born in the region from Virginia to Georgia. Many were Negroes, often living in the same house with white women. Here, if nowhere else, Chicago was unsegregated. Efforts at "helping" these women faced real difficulties. One who was enticed away from the bordello and provided with light work in a factory lasted there only a week before going back to her old trade. She explained to the civic worker: "It is easy enough for you with all your fine clothes and your soft food to preach to a girl like me, but I just cannot stand working all day and going home at night to a miserable little hall bedroom where I cannot even see to read, and I am going back where at least I will have some comfort and companionship." In addition to the declared whores, the census takers were dubious about some women who said they were "dressmakers."

But of course real dressmakers and clothing workers were more common than prostitutes—and often exploited as badly. The area around Hull-House, with its thousands of desperately poor immigrants, was peculiarly the locus of the so-called "sweating system" in the clothing trades.

The manufacture of clothing was controlled by the wholesale firms, whose large factories clustered in a small area in the First Ward near the center of Chicago. The garments for the entire trade were cut in these. Many of them were complete factories, doing all the processes of clothing manufacture: the garment, after being cut, went to the operator who stitched the seams, to the buttonholer, to the woman who did the hand finishing, to the presser who also cleaned it. Such "inside shops" were fairly sanitary and well lighted. Electrical power was often furnished for the sewing machines. Working conditions and wages were tolerable; for the skilled cutters, they were quite good.

But the sweating system repeatedly undermined the working standards in the inside shops. If the employees in a factory became too vocal in their demands for shorter hours or higher pay, the employer might respond by transferring work outside of the factory altogether, to the dank tenements of the Nineteenth Ward. By 1893, many wholesalers had entirely closed their inside shops. Others, while producing some garments themselves, gave out others to individual employees to be made at home. Or they gave them to the sweaters.

The sweaters of the Nineteenth Ward were Russian Jews or Bohemians, more than a thousand of them, who offered themselves to the wholesalers as agents for the completion of garments that had been cut. Each of the sweaters, in order to get contracts, underbid the others. There was no standard price for the making of any garment. The sweater bid as low as necessary to get the job, and he then made his profit by driving down even lower the piece rate paid to those who did the actual work. Sometimes he gathered these garment workers into one filthy, littered room in a tenement house, or he might let each worker take the garments "home." The operators who stitched the seams were the same nationality as the sweater, but the hand finishers were invariably Italian, peasant women whose sole economic virtue was their ability to crudely ply a needle in sewing on buttons or finishing buttonholes, the wives and daughters of the ditch-diggers and workers on railroad construction gangs and street sweepers who were so numerous in the ward. All through the district, at dusk, these women could be seen staggering home, bowed under the weight of countless pairs of trousers, small reeling mountains of fabric swaying along through the dusk, homeward, to the home that was also a factory except that no employer had to pay the rent.

In one such home a small girl, with dirty face and matted unkempt hair, lay on a bed covered with newspapers. The only light in the windowless room came from a candle on a chair by the bed. Beside the candle was a chunk of bread, the girl's food for the day. She held in her hands a long iron spike on which she wound and rewound a soiled strip of paper. This was her doll.

Elsewhere in a bedroom two men were at work. The room held a sewing machine, a chair, a reeking lamp, and a bed, where lay a mass of bedclothes, two overcoats, two hats, and nine magnificent tan capes trimmed with ecru lace. A tenth cape was being stitched on the sewing machine. The premises were swarming with vermin.

The front flat on the ground floor of a brick tenement on Bunker Street seemed very clean. Here a tailor sat at a table, working on a broadcloth dinner jacket of the best quality, part of an evening suit to sell for $70 to $100 (the tailor himself might earn as much as $450 a year). About five feet from the table, on a bed, lay the tailor's son dying of typhoid fever. The next day the boy died, and soon thereafter the coat was finished and delivered to the customer without being fumigated.

Disease flowed through these tenement workshops like a soughing wind: diphtheria, typhoid, scarlet fever, smallpox, to pass under the marquees and into the ballrooms of the best hotels in town.

But if the custom tailors often delivered disease, they also delivered the coat—on time. It took from 45 to 50 hours for a tailor to make a dress coat. During the busy season, he might complete one at a single sitting, staying awake somehow, anything to keep the needle moving. A man had to work when there was work to be done; during prosperous times a cloakmaker worked only eight months in the year, and in bad years he might work only half that. In an average year, the off-season of three to five months inevitably found the sweater's victims applying for public relief.

One of the largest clothing firms in the world, located in Chicago, was headed by a millionaire philanthropist who gave generously to a local hospital. Every winter many clothing workers suffering from disease or malnutrition went to this hospital. The manufacturer was asked why he did not lighten the load on the hospital by refusing to give out garments to the sweaters for finishing. Why didn't his firm employ directly the workers who made his goods and furnish them steam power to run their machines? "So far," he said, "we have found leg power and the sweater cheaper."

Reduced by their employers to desperate poverty, the garment workers were easy victims for others. In one case a family borrowed $25 with its household furniture as security. The interest was $2 per week—a yearly rate of 416 percent. When the women of Hull-House intervened to buy up the mortgage, the family had paid $42 in order to have the use of $25 for five months.

But men cling desperately to symbols of decency and self-respect, and in the Nineteenth Ward few families were so beaten that they did not seek to honor their dead by munificent funerals. The agents of the burial-insurance companies went their way from tenement to tenement, collecting their premiums week by week so that the amount seemed, if not trifling, at least possible. But when a man is down on his luck, it may desert him altogether, and even those who sought most zealously to honor their dead were sometimes frustrated. Doubtless others suffered the torment of the newly bereaved mother who exclaimed in bewilderment: "And to think that this child I've lost was the only one that wasn't insured!"

The Jewish garment workers were poor, terribly so, but their poverty did not result from personal vices. They worked hard. They were thrifty. They had no experience with drunkenness. Florence Kelley, who knew them well, said that they were "probably more temperate, hard-working, and avaricious than any equally large body of wage-earners in America."

III

Avarice. In order to survive, the poor man had to forget all else and scramble always for money. This easily became greed, and the chief victims of a slum dweller's greed were often his own children. An investigation of 200 working girls found that only 10 of them had the use of their own earnings, and that 124 turned every penny they earned over to their mothers. Many fathers were disabled while their children were still young: garment workers who were permanently exhausted, ditch-diggers stricken with rheumatism, railroad workers or construction workers who had lost a limb. In these situations, since society had made no other provision for the support of the occupationally disabled and his family, the labor of the child was necessary to survival.

But children were forced to work for other reasons also. Especially among Italians, Bohemians, and Germans, a father would often seek to lift himself financially by buying a tenement house and would then drive all members of his family into paid employment so that he could pay off the mortgage. Sometimes the children, who spoke English, were more employable than the parents, who did not. One Italian father, thirty-three years old, went to Hull-House in grief over the death of his twelve-year-old daughter. "She was the oldest kid I had," he exclaimed. "Now I shall have to go back to work again until the next one is able to take care of me." A peasant from southern Italy who had picked olives and packed oranges from earliest childhood could see nothing wrong with child labor and failed to notice that he had worked under far better conditions than those surrounding his children.

Thus a fourteen-year-old boy was found running, by foot-power, a heavy buttonholing machine. Medical examination showed him to be suffering from rachitis and a double curvature of the spine. The boy had two grown brothers who were able-bodied, and his father was not in straitened circumstances.

Children were scarce in the trades where unions were strong and working conditions comparatively good; they clustered in the unorganized industries. As a result, their work was often unsanitary or unsafe in addition to being underpaid. At the stockyards, boys, standing ankle deep in the water used to flush away refuse from the floors in the drains, and breathing air that was sickening, cut up the animals as soon as the hide was removed. Ventilating machines and deodorizers to remove the fetid air were expensive, and no force existed to make the companies install them; so they did not do so.

At a stamping works an endless chain revolved over a trough filled with molten solder. The chain dragged cans through the solder. At each end of the trough stood a boy with a small iron poker. His job was to keep each can in its place in the line and to lift it out at the end. But he was not always deft enough to keep his hand clear of the molten fluid. The entire arrangement had been replaced in some factories by an automatic machine, but the machine cost money, and boys' hands did not. Within two years two boys were killed in this plant, and several others were mutilated.

Illinois did not have a law that provided compensation for industrial accidents. The only recourse open to parents of injured boys was to bring an individual suit for damages, and such suits were involved and expensive. They were also unlikely of success, especially so since companies like Illinois Steel required a release form: "I . . . parent as aforesaid fully recognize the hazardous nature of the employment in which my said son is about to engage, but nevertheless I, the said parent . . . consent to the employment of said minor, and in consideration thereof . . . I do hereby release and forever discharge the Illinois Steel Co. of and from all claims . . . for loss of service of said minor on account of any personal injuries he may sustain while in the employ of said company."

The largest employer of child labor in Chicago was a caramel factory in the Nineteenth Ward. Here, during the rush season for several weeks before Christmas, as many as two hundred young girls sat in a six-story building, wrapping and packing the caramels. There was no fire escape, and a single wooden staircase led from one floor to the next, even though steam used in boiling the caramels was a constant fire hazard. The girls were paid a few cents for every thousand caramels packed. They worked from 7 A.M. to 9 P.M., with twenty minutes for lunch and no time for supper—a work week of eighty-two hours.

In the West Side stores, many young girls worked thirteen hours a day for five days a week, and fifteen on Saturday.

Scene: *West Side of Chicago*
Time: *December 23*

> A thirteen-year-old girl notices in the evening paper an advertisement for six girls to work in one of the large candy chains. Candidates are to apply at 7 A.M. on Christmas Eve at a branch store on the West Side, a mile and a half from the girl's home.
>
> She spends five cents in carfare to get there. There are several applicants but only one vacancy, not six. She is hired, and told to go to a downtown branch, over two and a quarter miles away. She walks there to save carfare. She buys her own lunch and goes without supper. She works until midnight. At that time she is paid fifty cents and discharged, being told that she was needed only for the one day.
>
> No street-cars are running at this early hour on Christmas morning. She walks home alone through the First Ward where vice stands at attention twenty-four hours a day. At 1 A.M. she is back in the arms of her terrified mother.

This company is one of the most generous donors of Christmas candy to the poor.

One of the worst features of child labor was the way the children moved about from job to job, remaining illiterate and untrained for any occupation. This was especially true of the bootblacks and newsboys who stumbled out of the Italian colony at 2:30 each morning to pick up the first edition of the morning paper, who sold each edition as it appeared, who filled the time between editions by shining shoes and pitching pennies. In the winter many of them went to night school, where they alternately harassed the teacher and simply dozed in the warmth, safe from the parental floggings at home. But this attendance was as voluntary as it was sterile, since the compulsory education law was woefully weak.

But how many child workers were there in Illinois? Nobody knew. The Federal census of 1890 reported 5,426 children in factories. But four years later, the state factory inspectors found more children than that in only 15 percent of the factories in the state. In the plants included in this sample, nearly one worker in ten was under sixteen years of age. Their wages ranged from $4 to 40 cents a week.

The children of working mothers often suffered as badly as children who themselves worked. Sewing-women during rush times, earning from 5 to 9 cents for doing the hand-finishing on a dozen pairs of trousers, worked at their paid job as much as possible and fed their families whatever canned goods could be gotten most quickly from the store. Mothers who went out to work often locked their children into a tenement room. One boy contracted a curved spine because day after day for three years he was tied to a leg of the kitchen table. At lunchtime an older brother would run in from a neighboring factory to untie him and share a lunch. The working brother then tied the smaller boy up again and ran back to work.

Near Hull-House a Bohemian mother sat sewing. At her

feet, hour after hour, sat her four-year-old daughter pulling out the basting threads.

Child labor was nothing new in America. From the earliest settlement, children on farms had labored twelve to fifteen hours a day, and, if they sometimes worked in sunshine and fresh air, they also worked in cruel heat, cruel cold, stifling dust. The earliest textile mills in New England hired children eight and nine years old. But there was a difference. Child workers of 1850 in the Massachusetts cotton mills became foremen before they were twenty-one; child workers of 1890 in the sweatshops of Chicago became tubercular or rachitic before they were thirty. It was the bleakness of the future, not merely the deprivation of the present, that fanned a revolt in the ranks of the Chicago workingmen.

CHAPTER 2

The Haymarket Bomb

Does clubbing a man reform him? Does brutal treatment
elevate his thoughts?

—John Peter Altgeld *

I

HONORÉ JOSEPH JAXON was a labor agitator in a Prince Albert
coat. Born in a buffalo camp on the northwestern plains of
the United States, he wandered into Canada and was educated
at the University of Toronto. His parentage was partly Indian,
and he felt keenly the subjugation of his people. When an
Indian rebellion started in Canada, Jaxon joined it. He was
captured. While his captors were awaiting transportation to
take him away to prison, they pegged him to the ground by
his wrists and ankles. Jaxon escaped to the United States and
toured the country giving lectures about the oppression of the
Indians. He was also concerned with other types of oppression.
When he turned up in Chicago in 1886, some six thousand
carpenters were on strike. They wanted the length of the
workday reduced from ten hours to eight. Jaxon began organizing and counseling them. Even when strikebreakers went
back to work, he advised patience. "Go to the strikebreakers,"
he said, "and ask them to quit for the brotherhood of man."

* *Our Penal Machinery and Its Victims,* 2nd ed. (Chicago, 1886), p. 41.

The strikers did so. Their appeal failed, and they went back to Jaxon for advice. "Now," he said, "try this persuasion," and he passed out clubs and wagon spokes.

This was language that workingmen in Chicago understood. Even before Jaxon arrived, created his brief stir, and left, they had known about violence. For at least fifteen years they had talked about clubbing, and had clubbed, and particularly they had been clubbed.

In October of 1871 the entire central district of Chicago was burned in the Great Fire. The loss included sixteen hundred stores and six hundred factories. Of a population of 300,000, a third were left homeless. In the next few weeks some 40,000 people left the city and established homes elsewhere. But five years later Chicago showed hardly a trace of the fire, and when the decade ended the population topped a half-million.

More miraculous still, this expansion took place during the worst industrial depression that the country suffered prior to 1929. After hard times hit suddenly in 1873, a spate of spontaneous strikes was set off by a series of wage reductions. But for every job there were two men, and the strikes were lost quickly. When a striking lumber shover committed suicide, a newspaper reported: "No cause, except despondency caused by poverty, was assigned." The unemployed paraded with banners: "Bread or Blood." What they got was a little bread and a lot of blood, and the blood lost was their own.

The climax came in late July, 1877, at the very middle of a Chicago summer when weather sets the tone for men, sinking them now in lethargy, driving them next to explosive terror. The air itself lay on men like a burden to be carried. The heat of their bodies was just beneath the skin, wanting desperately to burst through. The dust rising from the streets and the stench rising from the stockyards fused into a nauseous bath. It was the sort of time when the phlegmatic become short of temper and the excitable live at the brink of hysteria.

With men like tinder, the Michigan Central Railroad threatened to again cut the pay of switchmen. The switchmen did not wait for the event. They struck at once. The lumber shovers were on strike; so were the tailors on the North Side. Near the mammoth McCormick reaper works a thousand strikers stood howling at the "scabs" and fighting a pitched battle with the police. Hoodlums joined forces with the strikers. The police fought a mob on the Randolph Street Bridge. At the Burlington roundhouse a crowd destroyed two locomotives. A riot occurred at a viaduct near Halsted Street.

Businessmen were terrified. They shouldered rifles and patrolled the residential districts. The big merchants—Marshall Field and Levi Leiter, J. V. Farwell—loaned their delivery wagons and dray horses to move the police from one danger point to another. A prey to wild thoughts of the recent revolution in Paris, the business element at a mass meeting demanded five thousand more militiamen to suppress "the ragged commune wretches." And especially did they put up large sums of money to hire Allan Pinkerton and his private army of detectives and guards.

Pinkerton throughout his life liked to tell how he had been "a poor lad in Scotland, buffeted and badgered by boorish masters," and his career for some years after his arrival in Chicago in 1842 had shown a sympathy for the underdog. When he started Pinkerton's Detective Agency in 1850, its chief purpose was to help runaway slaves escape to Canada. During the Civil War he was assigned by Abraham Lincoln to organize the United States Secret Service. But after the war his agency turned increasingly to guarding industrial property, to protecting strikebreakers, to spying on trade unionists and radicals.

It was these radicals, said Pinkerton, who precipitated the rioting in Chicago in the 1877 strikes. He could narrow the responsibility even further, saying that the radicals' deeds were "largely caused by the rantings of a young American communist named Parsons." Albert R. Parsons could hardly have been more American. Born in Alabama, he joined the Confederate Army when he was only thirteen years old and served until the war ended. He went to Texas, and there he ran a newspaper. His editorial policy? Full rights for Negroes. He could not maintain a paper in Waco on that basis, and in 1873, the first year of the depression, he went to Chicago and became a typesetter on the daily *Times.* He became active in union affairs and, in spite of the language difference, won the confidence of the German members. He learned about socialism, and in March, 1876, he ran for alderman on the Social Democratic ticket. He was swamped.

His notoriety began the next year during the strikes. Even Allan Pinkerton conceded that he was an exciting orator, and Parsons found the chance to address thousands of strikers. Although he argued against violence and denied that he was responsible for the strikes, the newspapers branded him the "leader of the Commune." His chief offense was the issuance of circulars calling for the eight-hour day and a 20 percent wage increase. Finally the mayor, prodded by angry businessmen, told Parsons to quit addressing the strikers and go back to Texas, because the businessmen would "as leave hang you to a lamp-post as not."

Parsons refused, and the strikes and rioting continued until two companies of the United States Army arrived to restore order. By that time more than twenty men were dead, some of them strikers, some hoodlums; the strikers had shown that they could stop the trains from running; and the police had formed the habit of brutally breaking up any meeting of workingmen.

Scene: *Turner Hall, on West 12th Street*
Time: *July 26, 1877*

> A group of cabinet workers are sitting around. They are talking about wages and hours. Everything is orderly.
> Suddenly police enter the hall. They say nothing, and ask no questions about the purpose of the meeting.
> Instead they begin to club the workers with their billies and to fire their revolvers. One man is killed; several are injured.

When this episode became the subject of a court case, a Chicago judge ruled that the action of the police was a "criminal riot." But this did not deter the police from doing it again —time after time.

Such official brutality did more than batter bodies—it alienated spirits. The Lincoln ideal, even in its minimal statement, had held that all men were equal in the eyes of the law. But anybody could see that the police were gentle toward the privileged, ferocious toward the poor, the foreign-born, the wage-earner. The Chicago police, as much as the Chicago employers, acted in ways that made workingmen receptive to the radicalism of Albert Parsons, whose meetings attracted several sorts of men. Some, like Parsons himself, were native Americans who rejected the rags-to-riches theme as a tawdry and malicious hoax on most workingmen, a sop offered them in place of the comfort and status that rightfully belonged to every man. Others were foreign-born who had passionately clutched the Lincoln promise; many Germans had followed Father Abraham's flag at Gettysburg and Shiloh, only to see later the concrete fulfilment of that promise snatched away from them. Some immigrants had never responded to the Lincoln ideal at all; they had thought they were coming to an America where the streets were paved with gold, or they had turned socialist or anarchist in their European youth and had carried their radical bent with them to their new homeland. All of these groups felt that the old vision had failed them, and they flocked to Albert Parsons in search of a new Utopia to yearn for and to struggle for.

II

Following the 1877 strikes the socialist movement in Chicago surged forward. Its immediate program was moderate and constructive: a clean city, sanitary inspection, establishment of public baths, a balanced budget. On this platform a few aldermen and state legislators were elected, and a candidate for mayor got 12,000 votes. But disenchantment came in the spring elections of 1880, when a socialist named Frank A. Stauber won election as alderman only to be cheated out of his seat by the election judges. A year later, after lawsuits costing $2,000, Stauber was seated. But when the election judges, who had forged a tally sheet and stuffed a ballot box, were brought to trial, they were acquitted. Many socialists concluded that they could win nothing at the polls, and they turned to more extreme goals.

The new propaganda, ambiguous and self-contradictory as it was, was nevertheless clear in its demands for abolition of all government and abolition of the whole wage system. Led by Parsons, by August Spies, editor of the *Arbeiter Zeitung,* and by Samuel Fielden, onetime English weaver and then a teamster and Methodist lay preacher, the anarchists set about organizing branches of the International Working People's Association. Their adherents were few: a national convention in Chicago in 1881 drew only twenty-one delegates. But the Chicago anarchists, unlike their fellows in New York, who were mesmerized by Johann Most and his "propaganda of the deed," remained deeply devoted to the cause of trade unionism, and many of them were known as leaders of the labor movement.

Their chance came in 1884 when another depression hit. In that year in Illinois one man in four could not earn enough to support his family. The men who were lucky enough to have jobs were laid off one week out of four. If a man had to borrow money, he was charged as much as 25 percent a month interest. Chicago was so congested that rents on tenements soared; landlords could earn 40 percent a year on the value of their property. And Joseph Medill, an owner of the *Tribune,* went before a committee of the United States Senate and said: "The chief cause of the impecunious condition of millions of the wage classes is their own improvidence and misdirected efforts. Too many are trying to live without labor, . . . and too many squander their earnings on intoxicating drinks, cigars, and amusements."

The anarchists worked tirelessly to capture the discontented. Their first step was to withdraw the five local unions that they could control from the existing Trade and Labor Assembly and start the rival Central Labor Union. The anarchists held frequent outdoor meetings, and whereas formerly they had drawn crowds of only fifty or seventy-five, now audiences of a thousand or more came to the Lake Front on Sunday afternoon to listen to Parsons, Spies, and Fielden. In October, 1884, Parsons issued the first number of a weekly sheet called *The Alarm,* which bugled radical goals and violent methods. It was disquieting enough when Parsons wrote: "we require the abolition of this . . . wage system. We call upon all men to refuse to pay for anything." But it was much worse when he declared: "Down with pay and dynamite the man who claims it. . . ." Parsons' wife Lucy was quoted by the *Tribune* as having said: "Let every dirty, lousy tramp arm himself with a revolver or knife and lay in wait on the steps of the palaces of the rich and stab or shoot the owners as they come out." August Spies and the *Arbeiter Zeitung* swelled the chorus: "Each workingman ought to have been armed long ago. Daggers and revolvers are easily to be gotten. Hand grenades are cheaply . . . produced; explosives, too, can be obtained."

The daily newspapers were no more restrained. During a sailors' strike on the Great Lakes, the *Times* editorialized: "Hand-grenades should be thrown among those union sailors . . . as by such treatment they would be taught a valuable lesson, and other strikers could take warning from their fate." The *Tribune* proclaimed that a socialist proclamation was "as harmless as the barking of a mangy and obnoxious cur, who would be summarily dealt with should he venture to show his teeth." Mary A. Livermore, a lecturer popular with the women's clubs, said: "Tramps have no claim on human sympathy. . . . The hand of society must be against these vagrants; they must die off, and the sooner they are dead and buried the better for society."

Talk led to action. The national guard was enlarged. It was

reported that businessmen were forming private military bodies. Marshall Field went before the Commercial Club with the proposal that the members put up the money to build a military training station near their stores, offices, and homes; and the Club presented the Federal government with the site of Fort Sheridan, on the Lake thirty miles north of the city. A rival group in the Merchants' Club gave the land for a naval training station at Great Lakes. And the Central Labor Union, representing twelve thousand members within less than a year after its formation, recommended that all workers be armed to cope with police, Pinkertons, and militia.

Scene: *Exterior of the Newly Constructed Board of Trade Building*
Time: *Evening, April 28, 1885*

> While the city's financiers are holding an inaugural banquet for the building, Albert Parsons is addressing a crowd at the foot of La Salle Street. The audience carries red banners and black ones: black for starvation, red for the blood of humanity. Parsons denounces the "Board of Thieves," and proposes that the crowd march to the new building singing the Marseillaise. They do so, and Samuel Fielden shouts at the audience: "How long will you sit down to fifteen-cent meals when those fellows inside are sitting down to a banquet at twenty dollars a plate?" Police chase the marchers away from the building.

III

The mayor of Chicago was unperturbed. He was willing to let anybody say anything. Carter Harrison was a huge bearded Kentuckian who raced his big bay mare at a mad gallop through the streets of the city. The average voter cheered at the sight of him. He was one of the upper class, a man who had grown rich in real estate and who used part of his profits to buy silk underwear. The Protestant clergy disliked the cheerful openness with which he permitted saloons and gambling and brothels, but Harrison thought these institutions were as important as churches in ministering to the needs of man.

He was friendly to trade unions. When the street-car workers went on strike in the summer of 1885, the mayor smiled on their effort and said that nine citizens out of ten wanted the workers to win. When strikers were brought into court charged with rioting, the juries promptly freed them. But Carter Harrison's control of the police was far from perfect. Throughout the street-car strike, the agents of the law swung their clubs madly, at strikers, at bystanders, at businessmen. Inspector John "Black Jack" Bonfield won a special reputation for the zeal he showed in cracking heads.

In the face of this ferocity the unionists were armored by a vision. The sickly but professedly national Federation of Organized Trades and Labor Unions had proclaimed in 1884 that "eight hours shall constitute a legal day's labor from and after May 1, 1886, . . ." This program was taken up in several cities, and Chicago quickly became the center of the agitation. As 1886 opened, even the Chicago press was tolerant of the demand, especially so since its adherents were the conservatives in the Trades and Labor Assembly and not the radicals in the Central Labor Union.

Back in 1880 Albert Parsons had been a member of a national labor committee that canvassed Congressmen seeking support for the eight-hour day. But in the summer of 1885 he and the other Chicago anarchists smeared the demand as a compromise with the wage system that they were struggling to abolish. Then, seeing how many wage-earners were swarming to the movement, they came to view it as an opportunity rather than as an obstacle to their own program. Early in 1886 the anarchists joined the eight-hour crusade, and Parsons predicted that it "would break down the capitalist system and bring about such disorder and hardship that the Social Revolution would become a necessity."

Now the tone of the demand changed. The original proposal had seemed to assume that the reduction of hours from ten to eight would involve an equivalent reduction of pay. No, demanded the anarchists, cut hours but leave the daily pay the same. George Schilling, a leader of the Trades and Labor Assembly, replied that the anarchist demand was absurd, that Chicago manufacturers competing in a national market could not grant so great an increase in hourly pay unless Eastern manufacturers did the same. He cautioned against rash action and urged that strikes be avoided if possible.

During the spring the two factions contended for favor. A rally of the conservatives on April 17 drew seven thousand people into the Cavalry Armory and perhaps twice as many outside. Eight days later the Central Labor Union got thousands of workers from twenty-five unions to parade to the Lake front, where they were addressed by Parsons and Spies. The agitation excited many wage-earners who did not yet belong to any union at all. In Cook County the unions had perhaps 38,000 members, but by late April half that number had won the eight-hour day, another 25,000 had requested it without threatening to strike, and fully 62,000 were said by a business journal to be prepared to strike on May 1 if it was not granted. The menace was awesome: fully one person in eight in all Chicago was involved in the campaign, and support for it was nearly unanimous among the wage-earners.

The newspapers told the public who the villains were. "There are two dangerous ruffians at large in this city; two sneaking cowards who are trying to create trouble," wrote the Chicago *Mail* as the fateful day began. "One of them is named Parsons; the other is named Spies. . . . Mark them for today. Keep them in view. Hold them personally responsible for any trouble that occurs. Make an example of them if trouble does occur." The city was close to terror. All reserve police had been mobilized. Now, on May 1, to the fifty thousand men already on strike were added thirty thousand who sought the eight-hour day. Even worse, two thirds of them had embraced the anarchist demand of ten hours' pay for eight hours' work.

But the day passed without violence, and so did May 2, a Sunday. On Monday, August Spies went to the Black Road, near the McCormick reaper works, to address a meeting of lumber shovers who were on strike for shorter hours. Nearby was a picket line at the McCormick plant. More than a year earlier, in April, 1885, McCormick had been forced by a strike to grant a 15 percent wage increase. The company had bided its time, and in February, 1886, it had locked out its employees to break the union. In March the plant had reopened with nonunion workers, and daily since that time it had been the scene of abusive language and brawling.

As Spies was nearing the end of his rather mild speech, a bell rang at the McCormick plant. Some five hundred of the locked-out unionists ran to attack the nonunion workers. The police began to use their billies. More riot squads arrived. Policemen drew their revolvers and fired. When the riot ended, two unionists had been shot to death, and many other wounded.

Spies wrote a flaming account of the episode for the *Arbeiter Zeitung*. He also wrote leaflets, in German and in English, denouncing the police. The English text ended: "If you are men, . . . then you will rise in your might, Hercules, and destroy the hideous monster that seeks to destroy you. To arms, we call you, to arms!" That night delegates from the radical unions met at Grief's Hall and determined to hold a meeting the following evening, May 4, to protest against police brutality. As a site they chose the Haymarket, a widening of Randolph Street on the near West Side that would hold twenty thousand persons.

August Spies on Tuesday morning read the handbill calling the meeting. The last line read: "WORKINGMEN ARM YOURSELVES AND APPEAR IN FULL FORCE!" Spies declared that he would not speak at the meeting unless this line was deleted. They stopped the press and made the change.

That day workers throughout the city were in an ugly mood. At 9 A.M. a mob destroyed a drugstore from which the police telephoned messages to headquarters; the mob had concluded that the owner was a police spy. Another riot occurred at a saloon. In the afternoon a crowd at the McCormick plant fought another bloody engagement with the police.

Scene: *The Haymarket*
Time: *Evening, Tuesday, May 4, 1886*

At 7:30 August Spies and his brother Henry are on their way to the Haymarket. Although it is already time for the meeting to open, they do not hurry; it is customary for German speakers to appear last on any program. Spies stops at the home of a German friend and leaves there the revolver he usually carries.

It is nearly 8:30 when Spies arrives, but the meeting has not yet begun. A few knots of men are standing around. With an audience so disappointingly small, Spies convenes the meeting a half-block away in front of the Crane metal-products factory on Desplaines Street. He uses a truck wagon for a platform.

Spies: "Is Parsons here? Is Parsons here?"

A voice shouts that Parsons is speaking to another meeting nearby. Spies leaves to get him. In ten minutes Spies returns without Parsons, mounts the wagon, and says that Parsons and Fielden will arrive soon.

Spies begins his speech: "It seems to have been the opinion of the authorities that this meeting was called for the purpose of raising a little row and disturbance. This, however, was not the intention of the committee."

Spies, twenty minutes later: "The day is not far distant when we will resort to hanging these men."

Applause, voices: "Hang them now."

Spies: "McCormick is the man who created the row Monday, and he must be held responsible for the murder of our brothers."

Voices: "Hang him."

Spies: "Don't make any threats. They are of no avail. Whenever you get ready to do something, do it and don't make any threats beforehand."

A voice calls that Parsons and Fielden have arrived.

Spies introduces Parsons, whose wife Lucy and two small children stand near the wagon.

Parsons begins his speech: "Do you know that the military are under arms, and a Gatling gun is ready to mow you down? Is this Germany or Russia or Spain?"

Voice: "It looks like it."

Parsons: "It behooves you, as you love your wife and children, if you don't want to see them perish with hunger, killed or cut down like dogs in the street, Americans, in the interest of your liberty, to arm, to arm yourselves."

Applause, voices: "We will do it. We are ready now."

Parsons: "You are not." He mentions Jay Gould, the railroad speculator who has just smashed a strike on his roads in the Southwest.

Voice: "Hang him."

Parsons deprecates such proposals.

Close by, in the Desplaines Street police station, Mayor Harrison and the chief of police watch and listen. The reserves have been mobilized, the building is filled with police. The mayor goes out to mingle with the crowd. Repeatedly he strikes matches to relight his cigar. A friend urges him to quit, lest he attract violence against himself.

Mayor Harrison: "I want the people to know their mayor is here."

He thinks the audience is orderly. Parsons, in view of his reputation for blood and thunder, is quite calm; his forty-five-minute speech is about labor conditions around the world and proposes socialism as a remedy. A reporter for the *Tribune* also thinks the meeting is "peaceable and quiet." The crowd at its peak is only 3,000, instead of the 25,000 the promoters had hoped to draw.

The mayor goes back to the police station and says the meeting is "tame," that the reserves might as well go home. He and the chief of police go off to bed. The ranking officer at the station is now Inspector "Black Jack" Bonfield.

It is almost ten o'clock when Parsons introduces Fielden. The audience is only 1,200 or 1,300. Ten minutes later, rain begins to fall. Spectators look for shelter. Fielden says he will hold them only a few minutes; then the meeting will adjourn.

Scouts from the meeting run back to the police station and tell Bonfield what Fielden has said to the crowd: "You have nothing more to do with the law except to lay hands on it and throttle it until it makes its last kick. It turns your brothers out on the wayside and has degraded them until they have lost the last vestige of humanity, and they are mere things and animals. Keep your eye upon it, throttle it, kill it, stab it, do everything you can to wound it—to impede its progress."

At this absurd bluster, the inspector's temper flares. He calls out 176 of his men, forms them in ranks, and marches to the meeting.

Fielden is saying: "In conclusion . . ." He breaks off and stares. The crowd is amazed to see the long column of police.

Captain William Ward, from the front rank of the police: "In the name of the people of Illinois, I command this meeting immediately and peaceably to disperse."

Parsons, Spies, and Fielden start down from the wagon.

Fielden: "We are peaceable."

A lighted projectile flies through the dim light, its fuse spluttering in the rain. It lands near the front rank of police. With an enormous noise, it explodes. Scores of the police go down.

The two hundred spectators are white, numb, motionless.

The police re-form their ranks. Inspector Bonfield orders them to fire. They do fire in all directions.

The crowd panics. Men dash madly to right and left. The police chase them, using revolvers and clubs. Fielden falls, hit in the leg with a bullet. Henry Spies suffers a wound in the groin. Men fall on every hand. They limp into drugstores and saloons. They crawl on their hands and knees.

The adjacent doorways are jammed. Men trample each other. They leap over tables and chairs to use them as barricades. They crouch behind walls, behind counters, behind barrels.

Voice: "O God! I'm shot."

Voice: "Please take me home."

Voice: "Take me to the hospital."

A block away, a German socialist is shot down by the police. A big bell in the police station tolls out a riot alarm.

After two minutes, the shooting stops. All over the neighborhood, men have their wounds dressed on the public sidewalk.

IV

Seven police were fatally wounded; sixty-seven others had wounds, many from the bomb, but dozens from bullets. A high police official said that several of the police had been wounded by "each other's revolvers."

The police threw a dragnet over the working-class districts. "Make the raids and look up the law afterward," were the instructions from Julius S. Grinnell, the state's attorney. The police had the aid of the Pinkertons. A vigilante committee of prominent Chicagoans was formed, but its efforts were not needed, so vigorous were the police under the direction of Captain Michael J. Schaack. More than fifty radical hang-outs were raided. Schaack searched homes with little or no excuse, announced the discovery of "bombs" at a fantastic rate, found new conspiracies daily.

The Chicago newspapers were hysterical. The day after the bombing the *Inter-Ocean* had the headline: "NOW IT IS BLOOD!" The *Tribune* declared that unless the anarchists and communists were crushed, the residents of the city "must expect an era of anarchy and the loss of their property, if not of their lives." Large dailies outside Chicago were no more restrained; in New York the *Times* and the *Tribune* agreed on the assumption that the anarchists were guilty of the bombing. Part of the labor movement joined the condemnation; Grand Master Workman Terence V. Powderly of the Knights of Labor declared: "The anarchist idea is un-American, and has no business in this country."

The police did not spend much time wondering who had actually thrown the bomb. The anarchists were guilty and that settled it. The day after the bombing Spies, Fielden, and Michael Schwab of the *Arbeiter Zeitung* were arrested. Albert Parsons could not be found.

But State's Attorney Grinnell and City Attorney Fred S. Winston could not be so cavalier: they had to be ready to go before a jury and get a conviction that would not be reversed on appeal. How could they do this if the bomb thrower were not found? They called Melville S. Stone, whose *Daily News* had a bigger circulation than any other paper in the city, to the courthouse and put their worries to him. Stone later recalled: "I at once took the ground that the identity of the bomb thrower was of no consequence, and that, inasmuch as Spies and Parsons and Fielden had advocated over and over again the use of violence against the police and had urged the manufacture and throwing of bombs, their culpability was clear." And on that view of the law the anarchists were to be indicted and tried.

On May 27, a grand jury indicted ten men as accessories before the fact in the murder of Matthias Degan, a policeman killed by the bomb. Of those indicted, Parsons and Rudolph Schnaubelt had not been found. The others retained the two young lawyers for the Central Labor Union and also looked for an experienced attorney. Only one could be found who was willing to take the case—Captain William Perkins Black, whose success at corporation law did not prevent the press from assuming that he, like the other defense lawyers, was tainted with anarchism. Black at once applied for a change of venue on the ground that Judge John G. Rogers, who had presided over the grand jury, was biased. Black's hope was to get the case before Judge Murray F. Tuley, a liberal Democrat, but instead it was assigned to Judge Joseph E. Gary.

The news titillated young Ernest Poole, who lived in the same block with Judge Gary and saw him often walking along the street with his little dog. Rumor had it that the judge was getting letters threatening his death if he dared to hang the anarchists. To live near such a man was to live with imminent death. Ernest's mother was so distraught that she wanted the coachman to take him and his brother Ralph to school every day. The father exclaimed: "Rubbish!" But while going to school the next morning, Ernest looked back and saw his father following them.

After the school term ended, the Pooles moved to the country for the summer, and thus Ernest missed the excitement of the trial. On June 21, in spite of Black's requests for postponement, court opened. Seven prisoners were in the dock. Another appeared in mid-afternoon when Albert Parsons, who had left Chicago for Wisconsin immediately after the bombing, came to the courtroom and surrendered himself. Judge Gary denied motions for separate trials, and the tedious business of choosing a jury began. It was hard to find jurors who had not already made up their minds, so hard that after eight days the regular panel of veniremen was exhausted.

Perhaps a jury would never have been sworn at all had it not been for two men. One was Henry L. Ryce, who was appointed by Judge Gary as special bailiff to summon additional veniremen. Ryce had his own plan; as he put it privately: "I am managing this case and I know what I am about. Those fellows are going to be hanged as certain as death." Therefore, he said, he would summon men who were biased; the judge would refuse to excuse them for cause; the defense would have to challenge them peremptorily; and after the defense had used up its peremptory challenges it would have to accept as jurors the men that Ryce gave them.

This plan required the cooperation of Judge Gary, and he gave it. Albert Parsons, after two days of listening to the judge rule on the qualifications of jurors, passed a note to one of his lawyers: "In taking a change of venue from Judge Rogers to Lord Jeffries, did not the defendants jump from the frying pan into the fire?" They had indeed. The same sequence was reeled off repeatedly. First a venireman would say he was strongly prejudiced. The defense would challenge for cause. Judge Gary would deny the motion. Then he would wheedle or browbeat from the venireman a statement that he "believed" he could give a fair verdict on the evidence. The venireman would be admitted to the jury, and the defense would be forced to challenge peremptorily.

The judge overruled challenges for cause in such instances as these: a talesman who admitted prejudice against all anarch-

ists and who was a kinsman of one of the policemen killed
by the bomb; a talesman who was acquainted with the top police officials of Chicago and who was intimate with one of the
men who had been killed; a talesman who stated: "I hardly
think you could bring proof enough to change my opinion."
After twenty-one days, after 981 talesmen had been examined,
the jury was sworn. If Ryce and Gary did their work slowly,
they did it well. Of the twelve jurors, not one was an industrial
worker.

Judge Gary hardly acted like a veteran judge, and he surely
did not act like a man who was reported to read Shakespeare
aloud to his family every Sunday evening. Day after day he
had from three to five ladies sitting with him on the bench.
One day Judge Rogers' daughter sat there, and Judge Gary
showed her a puzzle while argument was in progress before
him. Even more damaging to the defendants was the latitude
that he gave the prosecution, both in its opening statements
and in the presentation of witnesses. As events unfolded,
Judge Rogers and his son-in-law Samuel P. McConnell, later a
judge in Chicago, agreed that "Gary was making new law and
ignoring every rule of law which was designed to assure a fair
trial for a defendant on trial for his life."

In presenting his theory of the case, State's Attorney Grinnell accused the anarchists of a giant conspiracy to destroy all
government by means of force. One of his milder remarks was
to say that the Confederate attack on Fort Sumter in 1861
"was nothing compared with this insidious, infamous plot to
ruin our laws and our country secretly and in this cowardly
way." All participants in this plot, he said, were equally guilty
of any murders committed as a result of the plot, whether the
actual murderer was ever found or not.

The state offered two witnesses to prove that the bomb had
been thrown by the missing defendant, Rudolph Schnaubelt.
But their stories were so clearly contradicted by other witnesses for the state that they earned small credence, and many
observers felt that Grinnell had deliberately offered perjured

testimony. It was not vital to Grinnell that these witnesses be believed, for he continued to emphasize that the defendants were guilty if they had been accessories to an unknown principal. To hammer home this thesis, he offered evidence of an alleged "Monday night conspiracy," formed on Monday, May 3, at the meeting at Grief's Hall which had planned the Haymarket meeting. The witnesses were Gottfried Waller, who had presided at the Grief's Hall session, and Bernard Schrade, who attended. The only defendants who had been present at it were George Engel and Adolph Fischer. Engel, according to the testimony, had put forward a plan that called for an armed uprising and the storming of police stations when the word *Ruhe* (peace) was printed in the *Arbeiter Zeitung*.

The story certainly hurt the defendants, but was it plausible? and was it pertinent? The Grief's Hall session was open to all comers—hardly the situation in which men form secret and treasonable plans. After the trial, Waller's sister and sister-in-law swore that he had been threatened with death by Captain Schaack if he did not testify to order. More important, the state did not show any connection between the Monday night conspiracy, assuming that one existed, and the throwing of the bomb on Tuesday night. Albert Parsons, for instance, had been in Cincinnati on Monday night. He did not even know that a meeting was scheduled for the Haymarket until he was drafted out of another gathering to speak. When he arrived at the Haymarket, he brought with him his wife and two small children, who stayed near him throughout the meeting.

The defendants were tried, not for a specific murder, but for their general views about society, and they could not overcome the prejudicial effect of the wild statements that most of them had made. Their words had been bad enough, and now the presence in the dock of Louis Lingg was fatal to them all. When a defendant contended, as Samuel Fielden did, that he had never used arms in his life, that he had only talked, that he had done nothing, the prosecution could point to Louis Lingg. Whereas the other defendants were grown men, Lingg was a twenty-two-year-old fledgling. The others had been born in the United States or had lived here many years; Lingg had not arrived from Germany until 1885. He did make dynamite bombs, and he had placed one in a saloon on May 4. Against this fact, it mattered little that he knew nothing of the Grief's Hall meeting and that he had not been within two miles of the Haymarket on Tuesday night.

At the other extreme was Oscar Neebe, a tinsmith by trade, who had built up a small but profitable yeast business. His connections with the other defendants were, to say the least, not intimate. He had organized trade unions in Chicago. He owned $2 worth of stock in the *Arbeiter Zeitung*, and he had been present in its office on May 5. He belonged to the International Working People's Association. When his home was searched (without a warrant), the police found a couple of guns and a red flag. "It seems hardly credible yet it is true," said a contemporary, "that all the testimony against Neebe would not justify a five-dollar fine."

But the closing statements by the prosecution demanded that no mercy be shown any of the defendants. Admitting that the bomb thrower was not in the dock, the state still urged that the defendants had advocated murder and that they were guilty as charged. Against this view, the final arguments of the defense contended: "If the principal [the bomb thrower] is not identified, then no one can be held as accessory." Judge Gary disposed of the matter in his instructions to the jury. If the evidence showed that the prisoners had agreed to overthrow the law by force and showed also that Matthias Degan had been killed "in pursuance of such conspiracy," the prisoners were guilty. It was not necessary to know the identity of the bomb thrower.

The jurors retired from the courtroom late on Thursday, August 19. Within an hour they had decided the fate of seven men. It took some two hours to agree what to do with Neebe. At 10 A.M. on Friday they read the verdict. All were guilty.

Neebe was sentenced to the penitentiary for fifteen years; the others, to death.

Outside the courthouse, the crowd of more than a thousand persons cheered. The newspapers showed unbridled enthusiasm, declaring that the verdict would smash anarchism in Chicago, and declaring further that it would warn radicals all over the world that they could not come to America and abuse the precious right of free speech. In the entire United States, not one important daily newspaper was critical of the way Judge Gary had conducted the trial.

But behind the public unanimity, there were private doubts. Many lawyers in Chicago thought that the evidence had failed to prove the defendants guilty of Degan's murder. They pointed especially to "the missing link in the chain of evidence —the link connecting the defendants with the actual murderer and the bomb-thrower."

Judge Gary denied a motion for a new trial, and court met on October 7 to impose sentence. First the prisoners claimed their right to make statements, and not one of them showed either fear or regret. Contending that he was being killed "for proclaiming the truth," Spies said: "Call your hangman!" Louis Lingg said: "I despise your order, your laws, your force-propped authority. Hang me for it!" Oscar Neebe made a request: "Hang me, too; for I think it is more honorable to die suddenly than to be killed by inches. I have a family and children; and if they know their father is dead, they will bury him. They can go to the grave and kneel down by the side of it; but they can't go to the penitentiary and see their father, who was convicted of a crime that he hasn't anything to do with." Then Judge Gary, having told the prisoners that they had received "a trial unexampled in the patience with which an outraged people have extended you every protection and privilege of the law which you have derided and defied," formally imposed the sentences.

V

Even during the trial a defense committee had existed, but its adherents were few and tainted with anarchism. Judge Gary's actions during the trial itself aroused resentment and disgust among men less subject to defamation, and they organized an Amnesty Association. The most effective organizer of the group was George Schilling, a wispy man with a small mustache, a conservative socialist who had been a longtime and vigorous opponent of the anarchists in the Chicago labor movement. The best propagandist was Henry Demarest Lloyd, a tireless writer and speaker, former editorial writer on the Chicago *Tribune,* a man who had insured his own financial security by marrying a daughter of one of the *Tribune's* owners. Moving in and through the amnesty movement was Clarence Darrow, who had just come to Chicago from his native northeastern Ohio and was out to make his mark. He spent his evenings alternately: some giving stump speeches in front of flophouses and brothels for the outrageously corrupt Democratic machine in the First Ward; others giving stump speeches in front of saloons and factories asking clemency for the Haymarket prisoners.

Progress was slow: even the trade unions were hesitant. The newspapers and the employers were using the Haymarket bombing to tar the entire labor movement, and its first reaction was to show that it too could denounce Parsons and Spies. But opinion began to shift during the trial, and by autumn many local unions and labor papers were asking for clemency or condemning the trial. When, in late November, a stay of execution was granted to allow an appeal to the state supreme court, the effect was twofold: the condemned men went on living, and the Amnesty Association was given several more months to work. By the time the supreme court heard the arguments in March, 1887, public contributions to the defense totaled $20,-000.

More than sixteen months after the bombing, on September

14, 1887, the state supreme court gave its decision. Not only did the court uphold Judge Gary's theory of conspiracy, it also ruled that he had conducted himself properly at every point in the trial. Although this decision was unanimous, its surprising result was to greatly increase the feeling in labor circles that the trial had been improper. The national executive board of the Knights of Labor had threatened to expel any affiliate that supported the clemency movement, but this did not deter district assemblies in New York and Chicago from doing so. In New York the appeal was also endorsed by the Central Labor Union of the American Federation of Labor. The campaign became international, with William Morris and the young George Bernard Shaw outstanding supporters in England, and many members of the Chamber of Deputies in France.

A further legal appeal to the Supreme Court of the United States proved vain, the Court ruling unanimously on November 2 that it had no jurisdiction because the case involved no Federal issues. Now the only hope of averting the hangings was the exercise of clemency by Governor Richard J. Oglesby of Illinois. The date set for the hangings was November 11, only nine days away. The Amnesty Association stopped talking about a pardon by the governor and asked only that he commute all sentences to life imprisonment. Scores of prominent Chicagoans supported the appeal: six active judges; Lyman Trumbull, Lincoln's old law partner and a former judge of the state supreme court; many leading lawyers; the president of the Chicago & Northwestern Railroad. When General Matthew M. Trumbull wrote a pamphlet about the case, Albert Parsons' wife was able to sell five thousand copies in a single day on the streets of Chicago. William Dean Howells, after trying fruitlessly to persuade the gentle Quaker, John Greenleaf Whittier, to publish an appeal for mercy in the newspapers, wrote himself to the New York *Tribune*.

On Sunday, November 6, the police claimed to have discovered four dynamite bombs in the cell of Louis Lingg. Word reached the Amnesty Association that the governor would probably not act unless the prisoners abjured their former views. Four of the men refused to do so, but Spies, Schwab, and Fielden declared in a statement that "we never advocated the use of force, except in self-defense." Almost at once Spies wrote to the governor withdrawing his request for clemency.

In fact Governor Oglesby wanted to intervene. He sent word to the business leaders of Chicago that he would commute the sentences if they requested it publicly. Lyman J. Gage, officer of the First National Bank, immediately called together fifty magnates, and he urged upon them that the inviolability of the law had been vindicated, and that execution of the men would only embitter the workingmen and upset labor relations for years to come. When Gage finished, Marshall Field got up. The great merchant was no talker; he said that State's Attorney Grinnell would speak for him. Grinnell merely repeated his speeches at the trial, demanding that the anarchists should pay for their misdeeds with their lives. That settled the matter. When the meeting broke up, several of those present went to Gage and said they agreed with him but that they could not risk offending Marshall Field.

The governor called a public hearing for November 9. But those who went to Springfield were men who had borne the weight of the amnesty movement from the beginning: Captain Black, Henry Lloyd, Samuel P. McConnell, George Schilling, Joseph R. Buchanan of the Knights of Labor, and from New York there was President Samuel Gompers of the AFL. Buchanan read aloud a letter from Albert Parsons stating that, since he was to be hanged because he had been present at the Haymarket meeting, the governor should know that Mrs. Parsons and their two children had also been present. The condemned man suggested that his own execution be delayed until his wife and children could also be indicted, tried, and convicted, so that they could be hanged when he was.

"My God, this is terrible!" exclaimed the governor.

Time dragged on, the hour of execution came closer, and still

Oglesby did not act. On November 10, just before nine o'clock in the morning, a muffled roar sounded through the county jail. Louis Lingg was found in his cell, the lower half of his face partly blown away. Having thus, at least to his crazy mind, thwarted the capitalist hangman, he lived for nearly six hours in this mutilated condition. Soon after the news of his death reached Springfield in mid-afternoon, the governor announced that he would issue a statement at seven o'clock in the evening. The hour came, and the statement was made. The governor announced that he was "precluded from considering the question of commutation of the sentences" of most of the men because they had declared that they would not accept a commutation. But Fielden and Schwab had asked for mercy, and while he was satisfied that they were guilty along with the others, he felt that their sentences could be reduced to life imprisonment, "in the interest of humanity, and without doing violence to public justice."

On November 11, in a city that had been turned into an armed camp in expectation of radical outbreaks, four men were hanged by the neck until they were dead. But the case would not die. Parsons, Spies, Engel, and Fischer became heroes. Fielden, Schwab, and Neebe were increasingly regarded as men unjustly in prison. Parsons' last words on the gallows had been: "Let the voice of the people be heard!" He got his wish at once. His funeral procession was viewed by at least a quarter of a million, one person out of every four in Chicago. The site of the graves in Waldheim Cemetery became almost a holy spot. Memorial meetings were held there annually.

The unflagging movement to get Schwab, Fielden, and Neebe released from jail was fed in many ways. In 1888 and 1889 there were charges of bribery against the Chicago police, and Chief of Police Ebersold, Inspector Bonfield, and Captain Schaack were all suspended from the force. The trade unions in Chicago built up their strength, and in 1889 the Illinois Federation of Labor dared for the first time to declare that the Haymarket defendants had not received a fair trial. A new era of free speech began in Chicago, and Lyman Gage presided every Sunday evening over public meetings at which all shades of opinion were expressed.

Each succeeding governor of Illinois was petitioned repeatedly to release the Haymarket prisoners from prison. But none did so. And then, in 1892, John Peter Altgeld was elected governor.

CHAPTER 3

The Pardon

If I decide they are innocent, I will pardon them if I never hold office another day!

> —John Peter Altgeld, talking
> with Samuel P. McConnell

I

ALTGELD WAS ACCUSTOMED to pain, to fighting against it, to defying it. In early manhood he nearly died of what was probably malaria, and for the rest of his life he had periodic attacks. Once, after he had become a successful real estate man and lawyer, he was at his home, helpless in bed, wrenched alternately by fevers and by chills. But he knew that his brief would soon be due in a law suit. He insisted that the lawyer associated with him in the case bring in the opponents' brief so that they could work out their reply.

While governor he gave many long speeches in his flat but forceful voice. If he was stricken by pain and exhaustion when in the middle of his speech, he would grip the arms of his chair and go on to the end.

Another man, in racking personal straits, came to him and asked to whom he could go for advice. Altgeld told him: "Ask no man! Go out into the night and look straight up to the stars. Take comfort and counsel of them."

61

He was a lonely man, with a face usually fixed and inexpressive. To some, he looked sinister because of the harelip that twisted his other features. He had a cowlick so bad that he wore his hair cropped; it was like fur. His beard was full but it too was cut close. He was medium-sized and stoop-shouldered. He walked awkwardly, more or less dragging himself along; it is possible that he had a spinal disease. Only on horseback was he graceful. He loved to ride, and he was a master at it.

Scene: *Yard of the Governor's Mansion, Springfield*
Time: *January, 1893*

Vachel Lindsay is standing in the yard. He is thirteen years old. His own home is so close that he can look out of its windows and see the official residence of the Governor.

Now he watches a mounted troop of the Illinois national guard swing into the driveway. They have come to escort the newly elected Governor.

Altgeld was very ill during the late stages of the election campaign. A rest at Hot Springs helped him, but he had a worse siege right after he returned from Hot Springs to Chicago. Now, as he comes down the steps to the black horse waiting for him, he is still a shaky invalid. Another man would choose to ride in a carriage.

The Governor mounts the black horse. It throws him and rolls on him. Men rush to help. He waves them away. With an appalling calm he mounts the horse again. The beast shies and nickers, perplexed that a man with wobbly knees can stay astride. Altgeld leads the procession that clatters up the street. He is indisputably the foremost citizen of the state. To Vachel Lindsay he is one of the greatest men who ever lived.

II

Altgeld's father and mother were peasant folk who emigrated to Ohio from southern Germany when he was three months old. Eking out a living by farming, the father could see no use in books. John gradually learned to read and write English, and he went to school for two summers and a winter. In 1864, when he was sixteen, he enlisted in the national guard and went off to the war. He did little fighting, but he did catch the "Chickahominy fever" that was to be his lifelong plague.

The war over, he spurned his father's objections and went to high school in Ohio for a while. At nineteen he was teaching school, applying his pay against the mortgage on his father's farm. In the spring of 1869, with $10 in his pocket, he struck out for the West, walking to Cincinnati, then moving on to St. Louis. Soon he was doing menial labor on the Katy railroad in Kansas and Arkansas. The fever hit, and he nearly died. He started back north toward Topeka. After walking one hundred miles bare-footed, the sickness coming and going, he came to Savannah, Missouri. There he worked as a farm hand; then he taught school. He made friends with the leading lawyer of the district, read law, and hung up his own shingle in 1871, just two years after he had wandered away from Ohio. In 1872 and 1873 he served as prosecuting attorney of Savannah.

His real start in politics came in 1874 when he ran for prosecuting attorney of the county. His opponent was a former mayor of Savannah. Altgeld already knew how to play the game. His associations with the substantial men of the district got him a reputation as a conservative, but the regular Democrats suspected that he was a radical because he consorted with the rebellious farmers organized into the Grange. He certainly knew how to give Granger speeches, all about how the laws were administered by men from those classes "who live off the farmers and who profit by the distress of the farmers." When the election came, Altgeld got 3 votes for every 2 received by his opponent. But Altgeld still was not satisfied. In the autumn of 1875 he sold his office furnishings for $100, sent his resignation to the governor, and left for Chicago.

Since the Great Fire four years earlier, Chicago had been booming. But it was slow work for a young lawyer without connections to build up a practice. Altgeld slept for some

time in his small office downtown. When clients or other lawyers brought him work, he tackled it with relentless industry.
But two years passed before he was earning enough to rent a
bedroom in a middle-class German neighborhood. That summer he made a trip east to fashionable Newport, and on his
way back to Chicago he stopped in Ohio to visit his parents.
Meeting there a friend of his early manhood, Emma Ford,
Altgeld added to his financial pressures by marrying her.

And again he fought his way ahead. By 1879 he had saved
$500. He put it into real estate and made a profit. Within
three years he had organized a group to buy seventy-five acres
in fashionable Lake View, where the Altgelds now lived. Improving the site as a residential subdivision, he sold off the
lots. It was a $200,000 deal. He became even bolder, bold
enough to buy unimproved lots in the business section of Chicago and to build a seven-story building in the wholesale center. In a single year he put up five blocks of buildings at a cost
of more than $500,000. The city grew, and Altgeld got his
share, and more. But he was no mere speculator in vacant lots
or existing properties; he was a builder.

As he earned, he spent. He and Mrs. Altgeld lived quietly
and graciously in their solid, gray-stone home. Mrs. Altgeld,
who had studied music at Oberlin College, was also a painter
and a writer of short stories. She published a novel. A handsome woman who dressed expensively and with taste, she became a member of the Chicago Woman's Club, while Altgeld
joined the Germania Club, the Sunset Club, and the North
Shore Club. They often rode horseback together.

Altgeld found other ways to spend his money. In 1884, although his district was strongly Republican, he ran for Congress on the Democratic ticket. Not only accepting, but
courting, support from all quarters, he pulled together a combination that any politician could boast about. One of his main
backers was the attorney in Chicago for the Vanderbilt railroads, William C. Goudy, who had also given him valuable tips
about real estate. But another was Joseph S. Martin, gambler

and ward boss. With this backing Altgeld won 45 percent of the votes in his district, even though Grover Cleveland was licked for reelection to the presidency and Mayor Harrison failed to get into the governor's mansion.

About this time Altgeld also wrote a little book, *Our Penal Machinery and Its Victims*, in which he disputed the assumption of the law that everybody had the power to decide for himself whether he would live within the law. "Only recently," Altgeld wrote, "have we begun to recognize the fact that every man is to a great extent what his heredity and environment have made him, and that the law of cause and effect applies here as well as in nature." On the basis of statistics he estimated that every year 100,000 persons were jailed for the first time. But jailing did not reform these first offenders; it was more likely to make habitual criminals of them. "The human mind is so constituted that it must be led towards the good, and can be *driven* only in one direction, and that is toward ruin." Nor did the present penal system serve to reduce the amount of crime, because "the crafty criminal—especially if he be rich—is gently dealt with." Since it was clear that the penal machinery did not protect society, society had no moral right to do these destructive acts.

Besides exposing the general tendency of the criminal law, Altgeld urged specific reforms. In Chicago nearly half of the women sent to the house of correction in a year had committed the same offense—they had failed to pay a fine imposed upon them. But jailing them aggravated their financial troubles and thus encouraged them to transgress again. Fines, Altgeld argued, should not be imposed except in rare instances where reformation of the criminal was no object.

Equally bad was the practice of paying officers of the law in the form of fees, so much for every dollar in fines they imposed, so much for every criminal they caught. The result was to give these men a direct interest in increasing the amount of crime.

Likewise the delays of the law were oppressive. After a man

was arrested, he might have to wait for months for the grand jury to indict him; if he was indicted, more months might pass before he was tried. If the man was too poor to post bail, he was forced to remain in jail during this entire period, even though the ultimate outcome might be to acquit him altogether. The only just solution would be to abolish the grand jury, and to bring anybody arrested to trial promptly.

Mistreatment continued after a man had been convicted. The law should merely set a maximum and minimum term of imprisonment for each crime and leave indeterminate the exact time an individual served so that this period would be influenced by his behavior in prison. Deserving prisoners should be free during working hours to pursue ordinary occupations outside the prison walls. They should be paid the market wage for their labor and should be charged a reasonable daily rate for their room and board in prison. The surplus should be deposited to their accounts and given to them upon discharge, by which time they would also have learned trades to pursue as civilians.

If *Our Penal Machinery* showed a strange interest for a lawyer occupied mainly with real estate promotions, Altgeld's aims in writing it were not wholly disinterested. More than ten thousand copies were printed, and he bought most of them himself and sent them free to influential men throughout the Midwest. One went to George Schilling, then a cooper at Libby, McNeill & Libby, who was so impressed by the tract that he determined to meet Altgeld. Another went to a police magistrate in Ashtabula, Ohio, who put it into the hands of a young lawyer there named Clarence Darrow, a shambling giant with lank hair falling over his eyes.

Darrow was born in 1857 in the tiny village of Kinsman in northeastern Ohio. His father Amirus had studied at the Meadville Theological Seminary, but a year after graduation he had quit the ministry, the church, and all traffic with worldly and other-worldly creeds. A bookish free-thinker, he cared less for practicalities than for the big questions of human

existence (the questions the Bible poses, and that Meadville
Theological had not answered). Clarence grew up in this at-
mosphere of nineteenth-century rationalism, and it made him a
lifelong dissenter and seeker. After a desultory education he
fixed on the law as a trade that would let him eat without
working. Admitted to the bar in 1878, he practiced for nine
years in towns around northeastern Ohio. But he remained his
father's son, and the doctrines in Altgeld's book came to him
as a "revelation." Within a year he moved to Chicago, where
his ability and guile (and Altgeld's aid) sent him soaring to the
top of the legal profession.

Thus distribution of the book paid off for Altgeld: it brought
him two invaluable lieutenants in his drive for public office.
And his political ambitions were now serious. In 1885, neither
Democrats nor Republicans could muster a majority of the
Illinois Assembly in the balloting to elect a man to the United
States Senate. Altgeld rushed to Springfield and spoke to some
friends. On the 109th ballot, he got two votes. It was simply
an effort to put his name before the public—and before the
professional politicians. He worked hard to keep it there, going
to Detroit to address the National Prison Reform Association,
writing for a Chicago paper an article which advocated the
arbitration of labor disputes. He was eager to seem a cham-
pion of the public interest.

And so he was—up to a point, the point at which the public
interest clashed with his own aspirations. This became clear
during the agitation to win clemency for the Haymarket prisoners. Altgeld would not say a word about the case publicly.
He knew what he was doing, and he did it with his eyes open.
One day he met George Schilling on the street, and Schilling
said he hoped the Supreme Court would grant the Haymarket
prisoners a retrial. "You are wrong," said Altgeld. "The Supreme Court will uphold the convictions. There is not a man
on the court brave enough to go against the newspapers and
the public hatred that has been stirred up." Schilling looked
at Altgeld's face and thought it was "the saddest I have ever

seen on any man." No wonder: if the judges would not stand up against the hatred, neither would Altgeld. A man is often sad if he can look squarely at his own deeds and call them by the right names.

While Altgeld would not speak out about the Haymarket trial, he was willing to benefit from the opportunities it created. In 1886 the labor movement of Chicago, finding itself stigmatized for the bombing, fought back by organizing the United Labor party, in which Schilling was influential. When Altgeld wanted to run for Congress again, the unionist suggested he would have a better chance of election to the county superior court. Altgeld ran for judge as a Democrat—with the endorsement of the new party. He won, thus becoming a colleague of Judge Gary. The United Labor party elected eight men to the state legislature, and five of the six judges it had endorsed were elected.

"What ought to be done now," said Darrow, "is to take a man like Judge Altgeld, first elect him mayor of Chicago, then governor of Illinois." Altgeld was more than willing. Certainly he did nothing as judge to damage his availability. He was scrupulously—even ruthlessly—impartial. When railroads, as was the custom, sent him passes for himself and his wife, he returned them. His treatment of William C. Goudy, the railroad lawyer, was so cool that their friendship ended. But for every time he ruled against a corporation, he ruled for one. He wanted all to know that his personal views would never influence his official acts. As between capital and labor, he kept an even hand. Although he ridiculed the wearing of judicial robes, he was hard-faced in his judiciousness. He demanded that everybody in his courtroom stand when he entered and would brook no interruptions when he was speaking.

And he continued with his private real estate ventures, one of which led to his first clash with Judge Gary. The dispute, important enough when it happened, was even more so after Altgeld became governor, because the newspapers revived it in an effort to prove that Altgeld was motivated by spite against his erstwhile colleague on the bench.

In 1887 Altgeld brought suit against Chicago, claiming that a grade change carried through by the city had damaged one of his buildings. The Republican mayor intervened in the trial by asserting that Altgeld was improperly using his official position. Altgeld won anyway, and the city took the case to the appellate court, of which Gary was now a member. When that bench not only reversed the decision but also patronized Altgeld by saying that his actions had been "free from any just grounds of censure," he was furious, and in his fury he wrote to the court, "as I do not want your praise I ask you to strike it out." He was a hot-headed man, with a huge capacity for bitterness.

He got his revenge. When the mayor ran for reelection in 1889, Altgeld secretly organized an "anti-machine" ticket, which he financed liberally, and secured the election of a Democrat. Then Altgeld exacted his reward by getting the new mayor to name Clarence Darrow as corporation counsel of Chicago, top legal adviser to the city on civil affairs.

A politician needs powerful friends and he needs money, and Altgeld was getting both. His business operations reached as far as Newark, Ohio, where he got the first franchise for a street railway. In 1888 he built a mile of track with four cars drawn by mules. Then the track was lengthened and converted to electricity. By 1890, the property of John Peter Altgeld was valued at a half-million dollars, and he undertook his biggest project. Taking a 99-year lease on a lot in the most expensive part of downtown Chicago, he set up a one-man corporation and began erecting the Unity Building, sixteen floors of offices. But he slipped. The project was too ambitious for his personal wealth. An error in construction had to be corrected at an unforeseen cost of $100,000. Unable to finish the building, he sold or mortgaged his other property. Still short, he went to the Chicago National Bank to underwrite a bond issue, and they drove a hard bargain. Still short, he raised the balance needed on short-term paper. Construction went forward.

Involved now in three full-time careers—on the bench, in business, and in politics—he resigned as judge. He did it, characteristically, by saying publicly that the job was not worth having anyway. Men in public office, he said, were "a cowardly hanging-on class, always careful to see how the wind blows before daring either to have or express an opinion. . . ." Judges were among the worst. When a man became a judge, he was removed from the fierce struggles of life; he relaxed and stopped growing: "he ceases to create, to shape and to originate. It is his business to discover and apply what others have said." The job of a judge, he concluded, was to draw "learned distinctions between tweedle-dee and tweedle-dum."

But he was eager to rejoin this "cowardly hanging-on class." In 1891 the legislature was again deadlocked in its efforts to elect a United States Senator. The 101 Democrats were standing by John M. Palmer, attorney for the Illinois Central Railroad. The balance of power lay with three Independents. Altgeld and Darrow left Chicago for Springfield. Darrow tried to persuade one of the Independents to vote for Altgeld in the hope that the entire Democratic bloc could be swung by the prospect of victory for a Democrat. Altgeld hired a notorious lobbyist to work in his behalf. The plot failed, and Palmer ultimately won. Altgeld left Springfield without participating in the Democratic celebration. He had tried again.

For six years he had been reaching diligently, systematically. All his actions had been consistent with the attitude he revealed to George Schilling. "You know," he told Schilling, "I have some of the same ideas you have. But if I talked now as radical as I feel, I could not be where I am. I want to do something, not just make a speech . . . I want power, to get hold of the handle that controls things. When I do I will give it a twist."

He was not entirely silent about what ideas would guide his hand. In the modern age, he wrote, the tendency is toward consolidation. The great are devouring the small and becoming greater. Factories, railroads, stores, companies of every sort, all are combining. Companies are fewer and bigger. The law cannot check this development. The only way to keep "an equilibrium in our institutions" is to build up "counter-balancing forces" against the giant corporations. Of these, the trade unions are among the most important. Workingmen can accomplish nothing as individuals. Their future welfare depends on organization. If they organize properly, they can win the eight-hour day, at least in trades such as construction, which produce for a local market and are free from outside competition.

Such advocacy of trade unions and the eight-hour day was extremely bold for an ambitious man, but Altgeld would say nothing directly about clemency for the Haymarket prisoners. The closest he came was in November, 1891, when a squad of police broke into a meeting of working people at Turner Hall, ascertained that the American flag was not on the stage, and commanded the meeting to disperse. Altgeld denounced this action in a letter to the chief of police. Emphasizing that the meeting had been peaceful, he wrote, "It is an axiom of the law that mere talk, no matter how abusive, does not constitute a crime. . . . The law takes notice only of acts, of deeds, and not of talk." He went on to remind the chief that similar conduct by the police in 1886 had prompted "some wretch" to throw a bomb "at a squad of police who were in the act of dispersing another peaceable meeting. . . . If the course which your force has started to pursue shall long continue, can you, in all reason, expect any other result to follow than bloodshed?"

So carefully did Altgeld build his fences that by December, 1891, the Chicago *News* conceded that he could have the gubernatorial nomination if he wanted it. The gambler Joseph Martin, the labor leader George Schilling, the railroad lawyer Clarence Darrow, and the writer Henry Demarest Lloyd, were all working tirelessly for Altgeld. But the decisive recruit to his cause was "King" Mike McDonald, saloon-keeper and the strongest Democratic boss in Chicago.

Altgeld looked like a good answer to McDonald's problems. Prior to 1891 there had been no official ballots in Illinois elections; any private group could print its own ballots. The system was ideal for electoral fraud, but in 1891, to the disgust of many ward bosses in Chicago, it was abandoned in favor of the Australian ballot. The reform did not prevent crooked votes, but it did make them more difficult and thus made it more desirable to have a candidate who could win votes honestly. Political leaders then as now were also concerned with raising campaign funds, and Altgeld was wealthy enough to fill a large part of the Democratic war chest himself. Best of all, Altgeld was a hard-headed man who would remember his friends after he got into office.

In March, 1892, the Democratic convention of Cook County almost unanimously instructed its delegates to the state convention to support Altgeld. Six weeks later at Springfield, the machine got its man the nomination on the first ballot. Altgeld did his part; to raise cash for the campaign, he sold his street railway in Newark, Ohio, for $100,000. But his lavish political spending was not matched by any change in his style of life. When a state senator took Brand Whitlock, a young reporter in Chicago, to meet "the next governor of Illinois," they went to the top floor of a narrow building downtown. In a crowded and dingy office, sitting by a queer little desk, they found Altgeld.

He dominated the campaign from first to last. The opposition called him a "millionaire fraud" and accused him of "socialist tendencies." He replied that the charges were aimed at the rural districts, and that rural voters would "know that it is absurd to talk about a man being a socialist or anarchist who has spent his life enforcing the majesty of the law and who has built some of the finest building blocks in Chicago." But his common method was to attack, attack, attack.

Republicans in Congress had tried to pass a Force Bill, aimed mainly at ensuring that Negroes in the South could vote in Federal elections. Altgeld, appealing to the state-rights sentiment and the anti-Negro feeling that were both strong in Illinois, said the bill was an effort to establish a despotism, to "enable a President to absolutely control any election in any State of the Union. . . ."

Denouncing the McKinley Tariff of 1890, he said that it had raised tariff rates by 40 percent. The whole effect of the tariff was to victimize the farmer and the workingman for the benefit of the rich. While the manufacturer was protected from foreign competition, the laborer had to bargain for his wage in a market swamped with pauper labor from other lands. The farmer suffered because exporters abroad, finding that the tariff kept them from selling their goods in this country, naturally stopped coming here to buy farm products. The Republican party had followed the consistent policy of enriching the few at the expense of the many. It had given huge subsidies to railroads and to sugar planters. It had turned over the public domain to speculators.

He played on every theme that might win some votes. He found a way to praise the immigrants in Illinois as the backbone of the state, the men who had won the Civil War, and simultaneously to tell the immigrants already in the United States that they should be shielded from the competition of more immigrants. He said that the state of Illinois was greater than Greece or Rome. In the areas thick with German immigrants, he spoke German. In all areas he was the humble, friendly man, a chip from the block of Abe Lincoln.

But his political genius and his unprincipled opportunism showed in the way he seized on the school issue. The legislature in 1888 had passed the Edwards Law, with both parties supporting the measure. But in operation the law had proved offensive to religious groups that maintained parochial schools —Catholic and, especially, Lutheran—because it provided for state inspection of all schools and also that all elementary subjects be taught in the English language. Before the campaign ended, Altgeld had persuaded thousands of voters that the Republicans were responsible for the law, and that their purpose had been to destroy freedom of religion.

The success of this tactic is clear. In Chicago there were twenty wards where naturalized voters outnumbered the native Americans. Of those, nineteen voted Democratic. Of the fourteen wards where native Americans predominated, the Republicans won eight. The Democratic majorities in Chicago brought victory in the state. Illinois had its first Democratic governor in thirty-six years—and its first foreign-born governor. Also, it had its first governor who lived in Chicago. And when Altgeld became governor, Grover Cleveland returned to the White House that he had left four years earlier.

III

Although Altgeld had not made any campaign promises to free the Haymarket prisoners, his election brought new hope to the Amnesty Association and stimulated it to increased effort. But Altgeld was very ill after the campaign ended, so ill that his doctors forbade him to go to Springfield for his inauguration on January 10. He went anyway. During the ceremony the air in the overheated Capitol was stifling, but Altgeld did not remove his overcoat. At the reception afterward he nearly fainted and was forced to leave. After ten days in bed he was ordered by his doctors to go south for a rest. This time he followed orders.

Meanwhile, his liberal supporters chafed, and not merely those who wanted action about the Haymarket case. The corruption of politics in Illinois had come to seem excessive to almost everybody who did not benefit from it, and Altgeld himself had given speeches about it in which he denounced government by committee and advocated one-man responsibility. "Put one man in a position of responsibility," Altgeld had said, "and he will make an effort to appear honest. Join nineteen men with him, and then frequently fourteen of them

—enough to pass a measure over a veto—will brazenly divide up a corruption fund and laugh about it."

But now that he was the one man with the responsibility he refused to accept it. His appointments followed the old custom of turning out your enemies and rewarding your friends, and Altgeld usually let the Democratic machine suggest who his friends were. When the reformers in his camp objected to any of the men being considered, Altgeld demanded that the dissident give specific evidence that the man had done wrong. He ousted a good man as head of the state insane asylum at Kankakee and replaced him with another good man, but soon he was trying to oust the second man also because the machine chieftains could not get along with him. Such conduct on Altgeld's part was hardly offset by his selection of some liberals: a progressive penal authority as warden of the Pontiac reformatory; Florence Kelley, who came recommended by Henry Lloyd and by Jane Addams, as chief factory inspector for the state; George Schilling as secretary of the state board of labor statistics.

He was not very active in guiding or prodding the legislature, and it did little. The Edwards Act regulating schools was repealed. A law was passed to eliminate sweatshops, restrict child labor in factories, and prevent women from working more than eight hours a day, but Altgeld refused any credit for it. His two special messages to the legislature dealt with minor matters, and neither led to any action. The most important advance of the whole session was to increase appropriations for the University of Illinois.

During those months, that was Altgeld's main impact on life in Springfield, and few felt it, and the others didn't care. Brand Whitlock, who had come down from Chicago to work in the office of the secretary of state while finishing his law studies, went often to the Governor's mansion for lunch or for an evening playing cards, and the talk was usually of books. They discussed George Meredith and Thomas Hardy, and conducted themselves like civilized gentlemen.

Altgeld did show his face occasionally. In June a Negro was lynched at Decatur, and he gained a national press with a statement denouncing "this cowardly and diabolical act as not only murder under our laws, but as a disgrace to our civilization and a blot upon the fair name of our State." A week later during a quarry strike at Lemont, a riot occurred in which armed scabs killed two strikers and wounded many others. The sheriffs of three counties wired the Governor that they could not prevent violence, and he sent in the state militia. But he also went himself to learn the situation. Finding but a few deputy sheriffs in the strike zone, he criticized the local authorities for not straining to keep order. He also talked with the strikers, told them the militia would be impartial, and blamed the contractor and the scabs for the shooting.

The return of warm weather seemed to have brought the Governor back to life. But in fact he had been alive all winter —trying to come to terms with the facts and his God about the Haymarket case.

Clarence Darrow had told Altgeld that release of the Haymarket prisoners should be his first act as governor. Altgeld said no, that many other things had to be done first, but that after he had time to study the case he would act. Within ten days after the inauguration he asked the sheriff of Cook County to send him the files about Haymarket, and he also got the transcript from the state supreme court at Ottawa. But he did nothing beyond talking to George Schilling, now part of the administration in Springfield. Altgeld speculated about freeing only Neebe and reducing the sentences of Fielden and Schwab from life imprisonment to a fixed term that would expire sometime in the future. "But he doubted," Schilling recalled later, "whether any man could continue to live in Illinois and pardon all three."

Darrow could not see it that way. He thought that Governor Oglesby's earlier commutation of the sentences of Fielden and Schwab from execution to life imprisonment, and especially the many petitions for mercy from well known men, would protect Altgeld from censure. Darrow did not miss a chance to urge the pardon on the Governor, but always Altgeld evaded him. Darrow began to be rent by doubts. Had he been mistaken in Altgeld? Was the man lacking in courage? Had he no feelings for justice? Darrow could bear it no longer, and he went to Altgeld—the massive lawyer towering over the slight Governor—and told him that his friends could see no excuse for delays. It should be done at once.

Altgeld spoke precisely: "Go tell your friends that when I am ready I will act. I don't know how I will act, but I will do what I think is right."

Darrow showed his irritation and disappointment, and Altgeld spoke again.

"We have been friends for a long time. You seem impatient; of course, I know how you feel; I don't want to offend you or lose your friendship, but this responsibility is mine, and I shall shoulder it. I have not yet examined the record. I have no opinion about it. It is a big job. When I do examine it, I will do what I believe to be right, no matter what that is. But don't deceive yourself: If I conclude to pardon those men it will not meet with the approval that you expect; let me tell you that from that day I will be a dead man politically."

Darrow returned to his friends and reported that it was hopeless to discuss the case with Altgeld again. There was nothing to do but wait.

Samuel McConnell agreed with Altgeld. He too took the matter up with the Governor, telling him: "I am afraid that it will end your political career, but still I cannot help but urge you to pardon all three of the men, and I hope you will do so."

Altgeld, irked at the suggestion that his political ambitions might stay his hand (as any man is irked at the recognition by others of facts that damage his self-image), flared up: "By God! If I decide they are innocent, I will pardon them if I never hold office another day!"

All of us are victims of self-deception, and Altgeld was trying to persuade himself that he could come to an honest decision on the Haymarket case without regard for the consequences. He was working desperately to fit himself into that stance, but it was a struggle for him. So far he could only talk it; he could not yet live it. To another man who mentioned the political considerations to him, he said: "As for our party, that must stand or fall by its principles and its policy. As for myself, no man has the right to allow his ambition to stand in the way of the performance of a simple act of justice."

Brave words, but no deeds. The ways of righteousness are strewn with misery of spirit.

In March the AFL central council of Chicago issued an open letter asking clemency for the Haymarket prisoners. Significantly, it made no claim that they had been unjustly convicted, saying rather that they should be forgiven because they had "suffered so long for their fanaticism and excessive zeal." Word also reached the Governor that the Amnesty Association was getting signatures on a petition that asked only for mercy.

Altgeld asked a state senator from Chicago, also a labor leader, to come to Springfield to see him. Schilling was at their meeting, for he suspected what was up. Altgeld asked that the petition not be presented; he needed no petitions. He then asked if Schilling could get affidavits about the case; he was especially interested in a newspaper story of 1889. The Chicago *News* had quoted Frederick Ebersold, chief of police at the time of the bombing, as saying that Captain Michael Schaack had wanted to use police agents to organize anarchist clubs so that he could have the glory of breaking them up. If affidavits were wanted, said Schilling, he could get a stack "this high!"

Judge Gary in April made his first extended defense of his conduct of the trial. He began an article in the *Century* magazine by setting down his purposes in writing it: To show that the anarchists were convicted, "not for opinions, but for horrible deeds"; and to show that the force really moving the anarchists was "envy and hatred of all people whose condition in life was better than their own."

At the first of these purposes, he failed. Most of his article was made up of lurid quotations from Parsons and Spies. And the judge conceded that the conviction had been gotten on the ground that the defendants had "advised large classes of people" to commit murder, and that pursuant to that advice "somebody not known" had thrown the Haymarket bomb. As to the second purpose Judge Gary did better: certainly the rodomontade he quoted showed ample envy and hatred.

But it was a querulous piece, a prosecutor's brief rather than a jurist's reflections. Gary quoted statements by defense counsel William P. Black and Mrs. Black so that he could scorn them as maudlin sympathy for anarchy. His hostility to trade unions and strikes showed at many points. When he came to factual matters, he was grossly careless, writing of the riot at the McCormick plant on May 3, 1886, that "probably" none of the strikers was killed when in fact two were killed; writing that the Haymarket crowd was listening approvingly to arguments for bloodshed, but not mentioning Mayor Harrison's testimony that the crowd was orderly.

Altgeld, to the despair of many liberals, made no comment on Judge Gary's article. But he was moving now, quietly, or his agents were. Schilling brought in a pile of affidavits on police violence against workingmen, and especially about the headcracking by Inspector Bonfield during the street-car strike of 1885. Altgeld then sent Schilling to Lyman Trumbull, former United States Senator and Lincoln's friend, who was practicing law in Chicago, to ask him to appeal to Altgeld for clemency for the Haymarket men.

The Governor was looking for ways to fend off the criticism he expected.

Scene: *The Governor's Office*
Time: *Probably May, 1893*

> Schilling says that Lyman Trumbull has refused. The refusal is astonishing.
> Altgeld: "How do you explain Trumbull's action?"

Schilling: "I can't explain it. I can only surmise."

Altgeld: "Surmise then."

Schilling: "Listen, here is a man who has spent many years in the public service with clean hands, and therefore has no wealth. He is past eighty, without a competency and still obliged to work for his daily bread. He has perhaps a few clients. Among them are large corporations. . . . Perhaps he fears that if he mixed up in this matter, these corporations would withdraw even this opportunity for him to draw his bread."

He hesitates, and goes on: "Governor, if my surmises are true, the corporations have even this great man hamstrung, so that out of fear he does not do what he would like to do. . . . If you expect any aid in this matter from prominent citizens, you will be disappointed. Governor, unless you are willing to do this all alone—without regard to consequences, and thereby serve notice that there is at least one man in public life the corporations have not cowed—the situation is hopeless. Then we might as well drop it!"

Altgeld paces the floor. He stops to stare at a picture of Lincoln. He walks to his desk, sits down, leans forward.

"Schilling," he says, "we don't need them! We don't need them!"

But he wished that he had them. He was reading the records, and writing, writing. At last one day in the spring Samuel McConnell was again in Springfield and called at Altgeld's office. He was invited to lunch. After the meal at the Governor's mansion, Altgeld beckoned his guest into the library. He said that he had resolved to pardon the three men. He had studied the evidence, and he had written a message explaining his pardon. He wanted McConnell's advice about it. McConnell, listening to the harsh voice read aloud the lengthy document, was elated and distressed by turns. Altgeld finished reading and waited.

McConnell praised the dissection of the trial record, but added that the message was too bitter in its comments on Judge Gary's actions. The tone was wrong; it was too personal.

Altgeld was not impressed and asked McConnell to amplify. The latter said the message held too much Altgeld and not enough Governor.

But Altgeld, as McConnell would learn later, did not change a word. Clearly he did not want McConnell's advice; probably he had not even heard McConnell's words. Perhaps what he wanted was to commit himself to someone else so that he could not turn back, so that he could not merely file the message in a drawer or burn it.

On Sunday, June 25, eight thousand gathered at Waldheim Cemetery in Chicago to dedicate a monument to the Haymarket martyrs. The monument portrayed a workingman dying while a heroic bronze figure of Justice put a laurel wreath on his head.

The next morning, very early, Brand Whitlock was summoned to the Governor's office. Altgeld's secretary told him to immediately make out pardons for the three Haymarket prisoners. "And do it yourself, and don't say anything about it to anybody."

Whitlock was stunned. In a daze he went to the office of the secretary of state where he worked, and got out three large sheets of imitation parchment. In the still deserted office he made out the pardons for Oscar Neebe, Samuel Fielden, and Michael Schwab. Impressing them with the Great Seal of State, he took them to Altgeld.

The Governor was having trouble with the secretary of state, Buck Hinrichsen. Altgeld told him, "I am going to pardon Fielden, Schwab, and Neebe this morning. I thought you might like to sign the papers in person rather than have your signature affixed by your chief clerk."

Hinrichsen thought that, since he was chairman of the Democratic state committee and this act was sure to affect the party's fortunes, Altgeld had broken the news "rather carelessly." Altgeld looked at him curiously. Hinrichsen asked, "Do you think it policy to pardon them?" Without waiting for an answer he added that he did not think it was.

Altgeld hammered his desk with his clenched hand and exclaimed: "It is right." The pardons were signed.

Also present in Altgeld's office was Edward S. Dreyer, a Chicago banker who had been foreman of the grand jury that returned the Haymarket indictments. Dreyer had later suffered deeply over his role in the case, and none had worked harder to secure clemency for the survivors. The plan now was that he would take the Alton train to the Joliet prison, deliver the pardons to the three men, and go with them to Chicago that same night.

Altgeld handed the pardons to Dreyer. The banker took them, and said, "Governor, I hardly—" and broke down and wept. Altgeld gestured impatiently. He was looking out the window at the elm trees. He took out his watch and said that Dreyer must go or he would miss his train.

On the table was a high pile of proofs of the message in which the Governor explained his reasons for the pardons. The proofs were released to the newspapers that same day.

IV

The message opened with a brief account of events on May 4, 1886, when the bomb was thrown. It then declared that two general grounds for clemency in the case had been urged. First, the majority of the appeals assumed that the prisoners were guilty, but held that they had been punished enough. Altgeld flatly rejected this. "Government must defend itself; life and property must be protected, and law and order must be maintained; murder must be punished, and if the defendants are guilty of murder, either committed by their own hands or by some one else acting on their advice, then if they have had a fair trial, there should be in this case no executive interference. The soil of America is not adapted to the growth of anarchy. While our institutions are not free from injustice, they are still the best that have yet been devised, and therefore must be maintained."

But other appeals argued that the prisoners had not been fairly tried: (1) the jury was packed; (2) the jurors were biased and therefore incompetent; (3) the evidence had not proved guilt; (4) the state's attorney had admitted that there was no case against Neebe; (5) Judge Gary was prejudiced. Altgeld examined these charges in detail.

He dealt first with Henry L. Ryce, the special bailiff who had summoned the special veniremen at the trial. Ryce had said in the presence of Otis S. Favor, Chicago businessman, that he intended to pack the jury. The police prevailed on Favor not to make an affidavit about this conversation. But the defense heard of it, and told Judge Gary that Favor was willing to come into court and be examined about it. Gary refused to do anything without an affidavit. Finally, on November 7, 1887, four days before the hanging, Favor made the affidavit. It had no effect. The men were hanged. Altgeld felt the record of the case proved that Favor's statement was true. Of the 981 veniremen examined for service on the jury, most were employers or men who had been pointed out to Ryce by their employers. And Ryce had in fact forced the defense to exhaust their peremptory challenges. Altgeld quoted at length from the examinations of fourteen veniremen, all of whom had admitted their prejudice against the defendants—and in every instance Judge Gary had overruled the defense challenges for cause.

The rule governing the competency of jurors had been laid down by the Illinois supreme court, after its Haymarket decision, in the Cronin case: "where it is once clearly shown that there exists in the mind of the juror, at the time he is called to the jury box, a fixed and positive opinion as to the merits of the case, or as to the guilt or innocence of the defendant he is called to try, his statement that, notwithstanding such opinion, he can render a fair and impartial verdict according to the law and evidence, has little, if any, tendency to establish his impartiality."

To show that this rule had not been followed in the Haymarket trial, Altgeld quoted from the examination of four veniremen actually accepted on the jury. One had said: "I have formed and expressed an opinion as to the guilt or innocence of the defendants. . . ." Another: "I have an opinion in my own mind that the defendants encouraged the throwing of that bomb."

Turning to the allegation that the evidence had not proved guilt, Altgeld ridiculed the main rule of law laid down by Judge Gary. "It was necessary . . . to prove, and that beyond a reasonable doubt," Altgeld wrote, "that the person committing the violent deed had at least heard or read the advice given to the masses, for until he either heard or read it he did not receive it, and if he did not receive it, he did not commit the violent act in pursuance of that advice. . . . In fact, until the State proves from whose hands the bomb came, it is impossible to show any connection between the man who threw it and these defendants."

Altgeld then used the affidavits collected by Schilling about police brutality against workingmen from 1877 to 1886. He concluded, "the occurrences that preceded the Haymarket tragedy indicate that the bomb was thrown by someone who instead of acting on the advice of anyone, was simply seeking personal revenge for having been clubbed, and that Captain Bonfield is the man who is really responsible for the death of the police officers."

Altgeld further pointed out that the police had introduced perjured testimony at the trial about the alleged Monday Night Conspiracy, that they had obtained this testimony by alternately threatening and bribing prisoners in their custody, and that Captain Schaack had planned to cook up fictitious conspiracies merely to keep himself in the public eye.

He analyzed the evidence against Schwab, Fielden, and Neebe, individually, and concluded that it all failed of proof. He then cited statements by Mayor Harrison and Fred S. Winston, corporation counsel of Chicago, about a conversation with State's Attorney Grinnell during the trial, after the state had closed its case. Grinnell had said that there was not enough evidence to convict Neebe. Harrison had urged him then to dismiss the case against Neebe. Grinnell had refused to do so because he thought such an act might harm his case against the other defendants.

Altgeld came to the last charge: the bias of the judge. He wrote a summary of allegations against Judge Gary: "that the judge conducted the trial with malicious ferocity"; "that every ruling throughout the long trial on any contested point, was in favor of the State; and further, that page after page of the record contains insinuating remarks of the judge, made in the hearing of the jury, and with the evident intent of bringing this jury to his way of thinking. . . ." Now Altgeld twisted the knife: "These charges are of a personal character, and while they seem to be substantiated by the record of the trial and the papers before me . . . I do not care to discuss this feature of the case any further, because it is not necessary." He granted the pardon.

The message was released to the press on June 26. The next morning as Brand Whitlock was walking to work in Springfield, he met Altgeld. The Governor was on horseback. He bowed to Whitlock and pulled up at the curb a moment.

"Well," said Whitlock, "the storm will break now."

The Governor smiled wanly. "Oh, yes, I was prepared for that. It was merely doing right."

The storm broke. It broke with appalling fury, to beat at Altgeld's head for the rest of his life. The newspapers paid no attention to the factual content of Altgeld's message. Quite the contrary: they tried desperately to divert attention from the factual content of his message. Their tactic was a barrage of slander.

The Chicago *Tribune* said: "Fielden's simple creed of 'Kill the law; stab the law; throttle the law' is expanded by the Governor." The Washington *Post* called Altgeld "an alien himself" who had "little or no stake in the problem of American social evolution." The New York *Times* held that he "would have developed into an out-and-out Anarchist if his lucky real estate speculations had not turned the course of his natural tendencies." The Toledo *Blade* declared: "Governor Altgeld has encouraged anarchy, rapine and the overthrow of civilization." And so it went, day after day, from coast to coast, in huge headlines, in long dispatches, in editorials and news stories.

To the conservatives of the country, the Governor's message was so monstrous that it was almost unthinkable. They were frightened, genuinely fearful of trade unions and radicals. They were determined to suppress these groups. The clean and convenient and effective way to do so was to use the police and the courts against them. Now Altgeld had exposed the system. He had shown that workingmen had been framed for murder to shut them up. He had shown that courts can become tools of injustice when a community suffers intense social conflicts, that the men who hold power will use the government to suppress those outsiders who dare to reach for power. He had shown how reputable men had perverted the instruments of the law into a judicial murder of four men. And he had shown this with a body of evidence so overpowering that it could not be refuted; it could only be ignored. So they ignored it, while they competed at inventing new epithets for Altgeld.

Even some of his friends deserted him. Mayor Harrison's Chicago *Times*, one of the few papers to approve the pardon, deplored his attack on Judge Gary. So did Jane Addams and Darrow. Others felt that he should have centered his criticism on the state supreme court so that seven judges could have shared it rather than one carry it alone. But the main fact was clear: most of those who had petitioned for amnesty had done so on the ground of mercy alone, and they were unable to bear the exposure by the Governor of the prejudice that had operated in the trial.

Why then had he made this merciless exposure? For one thing, he was outraged at the corruption of democratic processes that he had found when he brought himself to read the trial record. But his sense of outrage for months warred with his ambitions. He never believed that a pardon would be popular, or accepted, or escape abuse—even if it were grounded on mercy alone. He knew terrible anguish before he could bring himself to act at all. The only way he could finally do so was to unleash his personal feelings. He believed the methods used to convict Albert Parsons were a greater menace to the republic than anything Parsons had done. And he said so. Altgeld, the poor boy grown rich and famous, the embodiment of the Lincoln ideal, had reasserted that legend as a guidepost for conduct.

While the attack on Altgeld was near its crest, his mother died, and he went east to Ohio. To the old folks in his home town he said: "Those fellows did not have a fair trial, and I did only what I thought was right."

But he was shaken by the criticism. A few weeks after the Haymarket pardons, Brand Whitlock went to him with another case. A young man in prison was dying of tuberculosis; his mother hoped to have him released so that he could die at home.

Altgeld refused even to look at the papers. "No, no, I will not pardon any more," he said. "The people are opposed to it; they do not believe in mercy; they love revenge; they want the prisoners punished to the bitterest extremity."

But a few days later Altgeld said to Whitlock, "Oh, by the way: that pardon case you spoke of the other morning—I was somewhat hasty I fear, and out of humor. If you'll get the papers, I'll see what can be done."

As Whitlock was carrying the documents to the Governor's office, he was shown a telegram saying that the prisoner had died.

Some of Altgeld's friends later said that he never deigned to reply to the charges against him, but he did reply, repeatedly. When a reporter asked what associations he had with anarchists, he said: "I have in Chicago designed and built six of the finest business blocks of their kind in this city, one of them being among the finest on earth. Did you ever hear of an anarchist *building* a city?"

To the charge that he had issued the pardon to advance his political ambitions, he said: "On the one side, there was nothing—the anarchists were a lot of friendless devils without sympathy from the vast majority. Every man's hand was against them. On the other hand I knew that in every civilized land, and especially in the United States, the press would ring loud and bitter against me for what I did."

To the charge that he had been moved by personal animus against Judge Gary, he said: "It is simply nonsense. I have got something else to do, and am not wasting my time in that way. I denounced, not Gary the man, but Garyism, and in doing this I simply quoted from the record made by Gary."

Four months after the Haymarket pardons, the Republican Judge Gary stood for re-election. He was overwhelmingly supported, not only by the newspapers, but by such prominent Democrats as Marshall Field and the real estate magnet Potter Palmer, and even by Democratic judges. He won, in a landslide Republican victory. The Chicago *Tribune* chortled that Governor Altgeld had been expelled "into the outermost political darkness. . . ."

CHAPTER 4

The Gray Wolves and Their Flock

If you want to get anything out of council, the quickest way
is to pay for it—not to the city, but to the aldermen.
—C. C. Thompson, of the Chicago Chamber of
Commerce, 1882

I

GOVERNOR ALTGELD can hardly have been indifferent to the
tides of abuse that swept over him. Likewise he can hardly
have been surprised by them. He had looked at the prospect
of them, in advance, squarely, and he had acted in awareness
of them. He not only faced the sterner truths himself; he also
tried to get others to face them.

Just three weeks before he pardoned the Haymarket men
he went to Champaign to give the commencement address at
the University of Illinois. Instead of giving the usual gelded
homily, he talked candidly of his picture of modern life and its
demands. He began by speaking to the still rare women graduates. The world, he said, respects only those whom it is compelled to respect. For countless ages the voice of women had
been a "long wail of misery" because they were absolutely
dependent on men for their livelihood. A woman had either
"to eat the bread of charity, sell herself in the market place,
or lie down by the wayside to die." Now other chances were

open. But they were only chances, not guarantees. The woman who would command homage must struggle to be independent.

He urged the graduates to be ambitious, which would teach them "the three great virtues": labor, aggressiveness, and perseverance. But they must have the right ambitions. They must not be like most men in public office: "moral cowards, following the music wagon of their time, and holding the penny of immediate advantage so close to their eyes as to shut out the sunlight of eternal principles." They must not become men and women whose vision "is limited to the weather vane on public buildings."

They would have to live their lives and make their way in a highly imperfect world, he continued. The institutions of a country are never better than the people, and often they lag a century behind the people. In the United States the law courts were better than they had ever been, but they still were no even-handed dispenser of justice. "The men who administer the laws are human, with all the failings of humanity. They take their biases, their prejudices, with them onto the bench. Upon the whole, they try to do the best they can; but the wrongs done in the courts of justice themselves are so great that they cry to heaven." Similarly, he said, legislatures were seldom concerned with the best interests of mankind. They were arenas where selfish interests fought for advantages, and the level of the outcome was the point at which these selfish interests checked or compromised each other. But it was vain to suppose that these faulty institutions could be abolished, since no better substitutes existed; the only course was to strive to improve what existed. The chief way to do this was to publicize evils (as, he doubtless thought, he had done in his pardon message so recently written). "Wherever there is a wrong, point it out to all the world, and you can trust the people to right it."

The graduates should not imagine that they had achieved very much simply by finishing college, Altgeld warned. An education "is only a training to begin work. . . . Education means training, not memorizing or stuffing. The mind must be a workshop, not a storehouse. It has at times seemed to me that many young men coming from the great universities had had their minds transformed into garrets, in which you could find many antique and interesting things but nothing that was needed in a modern workshop."

Three years after Altgeld gave this speech, John Dewey was to found the Elementary School at the University of Chicago and begin trying to work out a type of schooling that would provide the education suited to "a modern workshop." But that was the future, and for Altgeld, in the summer of 1893, the problems of the present were compelling. The newspapers were hammering at him daily, and just offstage lurked the depression that was sweeping the rest of the country. The extra business brought to Chicago that summer by the Exposition staved off economic collapse. By autumn, bank clearings in New York had dropped 22 percent, but in Chicago only 7.7 percent. But Altgeld knew the respite was temporary. Speaking on Labor Day to the workingmen of Chicago, he told them that the depression, which had grown out of a financial crisis, would probably seize them too. They faced "a long dark day" of "suffering and distress." Altgeld refused to promise that the state would step in to alleviate the situation by a public-works program or in any other way. The coming deprivation, he told his audience, could not be escaped, and he counseled them "to face it squarely and bear it with that heroism and fortitude with which an American citizen should face and bear calamity."

Even if a better economic system could be imagined, he continued, "we are forced to cling to the old system for the present, and probably for a long time to come, until the foundations can be laid for a better one by intelligent progress." The depression showed that, while the interests of employer and worker might conflict in regard to wage rates, their interests were identical in all other respects; neither could prosper unless the other did. But workingmen must recognize that the modern age was an age of combination, of concentrated force, when a worker who tried to stand singlehanded against a giant corporation would be crushed. The only course, he concluded, was for the wage-earners to combine in defense of their interests.

For the moment Chicago was protected by the dam of the Exposition, but behind the dam the waters grew ever higher, and on October 30 the Exposition closed and poverty poured over the city in a deluge. The thousands of casual laborers drawn to Chicago by the Fair were now thrown onto the labor market. Businesses, having lost their out-of-town customers, retrenched or closed down. Restaurants became empty storefronts. Hotels went out of business. The department stores suffered a severe loss of trade. The swirling mob of unemployed grew and grew, until Mayor Harrison estimated their number at 200,000. Men, women, and children trudged to the garbage dumps in search of food. By December the floors and stairways of the City Hall were littered nightly with sleeping men. Every police station in the city was sheltering from sixty to one hundred destitute people. Students at the University of Chicago watched one day while an itinerant army straggled northward toward the city seeking food and shelter.

But the state government had no program. The city's relief work was woefully inadequate, even though the mayor predicted that the destitute would riot unless they found succor. In this desperate situation, a hand reached out to help the poor. It was the hand of the saloonkeepers, who were also the political bosses. Politics in those days, as Brand Whitlock wrote sadly, "were almost wholly personal."

A newspaper estimated that the Chicago saloonkeepers were giving free lunches to sixty thousand men a day. None was more lavish than Michael "Hinky Dink" Kenna, alderman in the First Ward, who fed eight thousand destitute men in a single week in his saloon. Once a vagrant helped himself to the food too freely, and a bartender demanded a nickel from him. "Hinky Dink" fired the bartender. Nobody forgets that sort of friend when election day comes, and the First Ward regularly returned Democratic majorities of 80 percent (unless, of course, "Hinky Dink" had his own reasons for supporting the Republican candidate. That happened, too).

The other alderman from the First Ward was "Bathhouse" John Coughlin, a man of stylish dress. For his maiden appearance on the floor of the city council in 1892, he wore a delicate gray suit, darkish green waistcoat checked with white (his racing colors), and a brown silk shirt. His mustache was flawlessly waxed. At the uproarious balls of the First Ward, "Bathhouse" John delighted the reveling throngs of gamblers, thugs, pimps, and prostitutes by singing a melodious ballad of his own composition called "Dear Midnight of Love."

The official spokesman in the city council for Mayor Harrison was "Little Mike" Ryan, who was noted for kiting every appropriation measure so that it would include a generous rake-off for himself. So consternation resulted one day when "Little Mike" rose in the council and spoke against a proposal to buy six gondolas for the lagoon in Lincoln Park. He demanded strict economy. "Why waste the taxpayers' money buying six gondolas?" he demanded. "Git a pair of 'em and let nature take its course."

The aldermen were all independent entrepreneurs. They paid no heed to party discipline or to anything else. It was strictly each man for himself. The peak of ethics among them was embodied in Johnny Powers, who tried to keep the others in line so that they would not sell their votes simultaneously to competing interests. In the Nineteenth Ward, Powers outstripped even Hull-House as a benefactor of the poor. His invariable attendance at funerals earned him the name of "The Chief Mourner." In the city council he shared his colleagues' attention to the main chance, but he showed more ingenuity. It was Powers who cooked up several innovations in the granting of franchises by the city council to utility companies. He pointed out that a street-car company could be required to get a separate franchise for each block of street its lines occupied. A franchise could be granted only for one type of conveyance, so that if a street-car line shifted from horsecars to cable cars it would have to get a new franchise. On a single street the ground level could be granted to a trolley line, the air above it to an elevated, and the right to tunnel beneath it to a gas or electric company.

Every franchise cost hard cash, which was often paid to the aldermen as a fee for "legal services" that had never been rendered. From 1860 to 1890, 25 percent of the streets in the First Ward had been granted to railroads by ordinances; sixty companies had gotten possession of 175 public streets. The price for these favors might be as low as $100 per alderman, but in one instance, reported the Chicago *Record*, four aldermen had gotten $25,000 each for their activities in behalf of a franchise, and its other supporters had gotten $8,000 each.

The situation was summed up in a popular skit performed by the vaudeville team of Harrigan and Hart. The skit showed the city officials at the Mulligan home, sleeping after a plethora of amusement. "Will I wake them?" Mrs. Mulligan asked her husband.

"Leave them be," he answered. "While they sleep the city's safe."

Of such stuff were the gray wolves made. Greedy but generous, unscrupulous but sentimental, they gave away a dollar for every two they stole.

II

To understand why egregious boodlers controlled the city council of Chicago, we must look, paradoxically, at the phenomenal growth of the city and at the forms in which that growth occurred. The census figures in themselves are hard to believe:

Year	Population	Absolute growth in decade	Percentage growth in decade
1840	4,470	. . . . .	. . .
1850	29,963	25,493	570
1860	109,260	79,297	264
1870	298,977	189,717	174
1880	503,185	204,208	68
1890	1,099,850	596,665	118
1900	1,698,575	598,725	55
1910	2,185,283	486,718	28

Population densities in Chicago did not follow any pattern at all. The city was originally surrounded by a host of smaller cities, each with its own business district, its own factories. Each of these smaller cities grew to its legal boundaries, and Chicago grew out to meet them and ultimately to engulf them, first physically and then legally. About 1890 one previously independent town after another was legally incorporated into Chicago. The result was a city of patches, enormous vacant areas within a mile of an impossibly congested slum.

Industry grew even more rapidly than population. In the decade from 1880 to 1890, the number of factories almost trebled. The capital invested in them increased more than 300 percent. The number of workers more than doubled, the total wages paid to them more than trebled. Cost of materials and value of product each rose more than 100 percent. In 1890 Chicago beat its old record for construction: it put up 11,640 new structures, costing $48 million.

The population growth and the industrial growth fed each other. As the growth of industry created a demand for additional workers, so the growth of population expanded the market for the output of the factories. Together they soared upward, and in doing so they created heart-rending problems— and succulent opportunities. For what is a problem to some is always an opportunity to others. This was the truth that the venal politicians grasped and acted upon.

The population growth of Chicago was fed by three main

streams: natural increase, migration to the city from rural areas of the Midwest, and immigration from Europe. It was the last of the three that captured the eye of the ward bosses. In the late nineteenth century the immigrants were not mainly industrial workers from the British Isles or Germany; they were, rather, peasants from Italy or Poland or the Balkans. They were peasants when they boarded ship in Europe, and they were still peasants when they arrived in Chicago. Unable to speak English, having no acquaintance with the skills that might advance them in their new locale, lacking the habits demanded by a giant corporation, they were hopelessly unfitted for an urban industrial society. They needed aid and protection, but the governments of city and state gave them little. Lacking protection, they needed alms. These the ward bosses cheerfully provided, for a price.

Chicago was a mosaic of foreign-language cities. The people of each nationality clustered together, speaking their own language, drinking in their own saloons, worshiping in their own churches, the sweater or the padrone usually preying on those from his own homeland. In 1890, persons of German birth or German parentage outnumbered "Americans" by nearly 100,-000. There were 215,000 Irish, 90,000 Scandinavians. Only two cities in Germany had more Germans; two cities in Sweden, more Swedes; two cities in Norway, more Norwegians. But these groups, while foreign-born, had immigrated early and had risen on the economic ladder. The lower rungs were filled by Bohemians, Italians, Russian and Polish Jews, and Negroes.

Most of the sixty thousand Bohemians lived in one solid area on the South Side. Although they worked as lumber shovers for $1.25 a day, they tended to be thrifty to the point of avarice. They grubbed together a little money, bought a house on mortgage, paid for it, added a story and rented it, saved more. When they could manage it, they pushed the frame house back from the street onto what had been a rear garden, and built a substantial stone or brick structure facing the street.

Now the landlord moved into the best rooms of his new property, covered the floors with Brussels carpet, acquired upholstered furniture and a piano. That is what the fortunate, the able, the strong, did. For others, the story was different.

One Bohemian had been a goldsmith in the old country. In America for twenty years he shoveled coal in the furnace room of a huge factory. Periodically he would become gloomy. His wife easily detected the onset of misery; if she could get him a bit of metal and persuade him to work on it, the spell would pass. But often there was no money for this therapy, and the man would turn to drink—with what, God only knew. Once in a drunken fit he nearly choked his daughter to death. Finally he committed suicide while suffering from delirium tremens.

So too had many of the twenty-five thousand Italians brought their native ways with them. As they had kept their livestock in their homes in Italy, so did they in Chicago, in spite of the health regulations against it. As they had lived in crowded conditions in Italy, so did they in Chicago, where necessity reinforced habit. It was common to find more than one family living in a single room. A survey of one ward on the West Side showed the extremes that existed. Of structures intended to house a single family, one had twelve families, two had ten, eight had nine, five had eight, and so on; 491 single-family homes actually housed three families each. Nearly all the Italian men had been peasants in the old country, but they began their careers in America working on railroad construction gangs, or wielding shovels at excavations, or sweeping the streets.

The two ghettoes, holding, together, some thirty thousand Jews, were both on the West Side. In most ways they were like the Bohemian or Italian neighborhoods, but they held fewer saloons and more adherents of such radical faiths as socialism and anarchism. Here as elsewhere were the one-story frame shacks, the massive and ill-lighted brick tenements, the deadly rear tenements. Here as elsewhere the only water sup-

ply was often a faucet in the back yard, fire escapes were unknown, and fastened to the narrow pavement in front of each
house was a wooden box, filled to overflowing with ashes and
garbage.

At the very bottom of the social scale were the Negroes, doing chiefly menial and domestic work and fearing that newly
arrived immigrants would take even those jobs from them.
Occasionally a strike would give Negroes a chance at more
skilled work, as happened during the stockyards strike of 1894
and the teamsters' strike of 1905. During a steel strike in 1901
and a stockyards strike in 1904 the employers recruited Negro
strikebreakers all over the South: in the former instance, the
Negroes refused to work as soon as they found out there was
a strike going on; in the latter, the packing firms discharged
most of them when the strike ended and sent them back south
on special trains.

The struggle for life was bitter, and only the politicians
seemed willing to help. When an Italian wanted a job sweeping streets, the ward boss fixed him up. When a Bohemian
family needed more flowers for a funeral, the ward boss sent
them. When a Jewish garment worker collapsed with tuberculosis, the ward boss sent a basket of kosher food to his family.
If a first-generation son got in trouble with the police, the
ward boss used his influence.

The precinct workers, more than any others, caused W. T.
Stead to hope for "the redemption of Chicago." In talking to
them, this visiting English editor and reformer discerned "the
principle of human service," and he declared that the usefulness of their deeds was not negated by their purpose of controlling votes. The ward bosses stole, but they did it openly and
good-naturedly, and they also listened, and smiled, and didn't
make a supplicant fill out forms or answer embarrassing questions, and they knew how to help a man who was down.

The immigrant politician was also a man who had succeeded
in America while most of his countrymen had failed. They
looked up to him and shared in his prestige. In the old country

they had conceived of politics in terms of personal loyalty and urgent needs, not in terms of abstract principles. They would support the boss, and he would take care of them. Most of all, he would help them and their families to survive.

To do that, he needed three resources: political influence, control of jobs, and cash. He got the first simply by his ability to win voters. The second came to him in two ways. The ward bosses together controlled the nominating conventions of both major parties. When their candidates won, it was the bosses who dispensed the jobs on the payrolls of city and country and state. Also the ward bosses gave out franchises to the public utilities and favors to other big corporations; in return, the private firms hired men suggested by the bosses.

At first, the bosses raised their campaign funds and their charity chests by selling protection to shady enterprises; they could see to it that gambling houses and brothels were not disturbed, that saloons did not need to observe the closing hours. Thus Mike McDonald got contributions from two thousand gamblers in Chicago. But as the growth of the city increased the value to ordinary business of government favors, the politicians learned that legitimate enterprises were more succulent victims than the entrepreneurs of vice. If the boss got most of his votes from depressed immigrants, he got most of his funds from respectable businessmen. His power depended on both groups, and both benefited from his power.

III

Many businessmen thought only in terms of dollars and cents. Yerkes saved money when he paid the aldermen $250,000 for a crooked franchise instead of paying the city $1,000,000 for an honest one. A man came out ahead if he paid off the tax assessor instead of paying his proper taxes. Railroad crossings in Chicago were at the same level as the public streets—a condition that resulted in numerous deaths and accidents; but it was cheaper to bribe city and state officials than to see safety laws passed that would force railroads to build costly bridges and viaducts.

It seemed that some businessmen would stop at nothing. The city of Chicago had long owned the water works, which was operated efficiently and profitably. Officials of two packing companies in the stockyards were arrested for bribing the meter reader. Officers of other firms were not content with that: they tapped the city's water mains and stole millions of gallons of water that did not pass through the meter.

Even more scandalous was the tunnel of the Illinois Telephone & Telegraph Company. This firm got a franchise authorizing it to bore a tunnel for wires under the streets of Chicago. After the ordinance left the city clerk's desk in the council chamber, but before it reached his office for its legal reception, somebody altered it. The company did its digging in accord with the revised terms. Finally it became apparent that an incredible amount of dirt was coming out of that thin little tunnel for electric wires. The facts emerged. The company had dug a well behind a saloon owned by one of the gray wolves. From that beginning, it had dug tunnels in all directions: more than 12 feet wide, 14 feet high, miles long. A railroad was installed in the tunnel, connecting the downtown stores with freight terminals and warehouses. The installation would be cheap and convenient at all times; and especially convenient to the department stores in case of a strike by the troublesome teamsters' unions.

Of course there was an investigation of the forgery. Some of the gray wolves were indicted, and tried, and went free to celebrate with a good lunch at Vogelsang's restaurant.

Such politicians and such businessmen cared only for results, nothing for methods. "This town of ours," wrote the Chicago novelist Henry Blake Fuller, "labors under one peculiar disadvantage; it is the only great city in the world to which all its citizens have come for the avowed purpose of making money." Doubtless Fuller exaggerated the differences between Chicago and other cities of the time, and he erred in saying that Chicago's citizens were unanimous in their single-minded pursuit of wealth; but certainly its most powerful residents agreed on that objective. When Cyrus McCormick, the reaper king, lay on his death bed in 1884, a physician suggested to him, "Now you have done your work."

"Yes," McCormick whispered, "work. Work."

But this was not the craftsman's doctrine of work, which finds pleasure in the motions of production and in the final result of a useful and lovely object. This was the businessman's doctrine, which defined as "work" only those activities that yield a net balance at the bank. It was this that disgusted Henry Fuller and other esthetes and humanitarians.

True, many of the giant capitalists were immensely constructive in rationalizing sections of the economy, in pioneering the methods of large-scale organization that would coordinate the work of thousands of men, in improving technology; such men were Marshall Field in dry-goods merchandising, Gustavus F. Swift and Philip Danforth Armour in meat packing, Richard T. Crane in metal products, even Samuel Insull in the Chicago Edison Company. True, too, some of them, in discussing their own motives, might have been talking about their delight in solving these problems of organization. Thus Philip Armour could say: "I do not love the money. What I do love is the getting of it. . . . What other interest can you suggest to me? I do not read. I do not take any part in politics. What can I do?" There it was. Solving organizational problems was fun only if it led to "the getting of it." Besides, Armour was hardly comforting to such men as Henry Fuller when he said so bluntly, "I do not read." And if Armour took no part in politics, his company did.

The very expansion of Chicago created fabulous opportunities. This was true from the beginning; men who bought lots for $100 in 1833 sold them for $60,000 two decades later. But if the opportunities were there, so were other men who were eager to snatch them away. The business world of Chicago was a world of alert, monomaniacal, hard-driving men, and of young men. In England, wrote the New York author and journalist Julian Ralph, it was believed that nobody could be trusted to run a company "until he has lost half his hair and all his teeth," but the men who built the giant firms of Chicago were often less than thirty years old when they hit the top.

Everything happened fast. In New York the horse-drawn street cars made six miles an hour; in Chicago the cable cars made nine to thirteen. In the business district, said Ralph, it seemed that "the men would run over the horses if the drivers were not careful." A stranger who asked directions of a native often had to trot alongside him to get an answer; nobody could afford to pause a moment for so trivial a reason. When Rudyard Kipling visited Chicago, he was advised to see that palatial hotel, the Palmer House. A "gilded and mirrored rabbit-warren" was his opinion of it, "crammed with people talking about money and spitting about everywhere. Other barbarians charged in and out of this inferno with letters and telegrams in their hands, and yet others shouted at each other." An Italian poet and playwright was astounded at the speed and efficiency: "The day of my arrival, I saw rubbish—still smoking—from a house burned the night before. The day of my departure (and I stayed but a single week), I saw on this same site, the iron framework of a new building, already erected to the height of a third story and already the scaffolding of each story completed."

The men who succeeded in this seemingly frantic society were far from being frantic: rather were they decisive, industrious, and shrewd. Marshall Field, the richest man west of New York, started a wholesale-retail firm in 1864 in partnership with Potter Palmer and Levi Leiter. Palmer withdrew to go into real estate and the hotel business, and the other two rented a sumptuous new store from him. Their policies were simple: Buy for cash and sell for cash. Keep money in the bank. Get merchandise that is a little better than what people want and get it cheaper than your competitors do. Field and Leiter started their own factories all over the country. They contracted with other factories for their entire output and thus drove the price down. They set up agencies in Paris and other cities abroad to meet the demand for better taste. By 1881 their department store had sales of $25 million. Their net profit was 10 percent of sales. Field took probably $1,600,000 as his personal income for that year.

But Field was finding Leiter hard to get along with. Field set a very low price on a half interest and gave his partner the choice of buying the firm or selling out. Leiter wanted to buy. But he found that he could not keep the key men in the organization, as Field had known when he set the low price. So Leiter sold, at Field's figure, and thereafter Field never took a partner except on his own terms. Marshall Field became immensely wealthy out of the company, but nobody else did.

Having given nearly his whole life to business, Field finally began to look for other fascinations. At the peak of his career he wistfully asked a reporter: "How do you like newspaper work? It must be interesting to one who wants to study life. Do you find life interesting?" Field turned to golf. But he found it frustrating. One day when he was playing with the famous columnist Finley Peter Dunne, creator of that incisive humorist "Mr. Dooley," Field said that he had "lost his drive."

"Why don't you try putting a dollar on the ball?" Dunne asked.

"What good would that do?" Field said.

Dunne told him: "Well, all Chicago believes that you can make a dollar go farther than anyone in the world."

Another man who dared speak frankly to Field was Peter Funk, an elderly salesman at the store. The day he heard that Mrs. Field had gone to live in the south of France, an invalid for life, Funk looked through the half-open door of Field's office and said to him: "Marshall, you have no home, no family, no happiness—nothing but money."

Field did not answer.

He did not talk much. He acted. When the railroad strike of 1877 turned into a general strike in Chicago, police were carried in the drays of Marshall Field and Company to put down the "riots." It was Field, more than any other single man, who stood behind the hanging of the Haymarket prisoners. But perhaps Field, too, would have said, like Philip Armour, that he did not "take any part in politics."

Armour was another who claimed to be a taciturn man. "Most men talk too much," he contended. "Most of my success has been due to keeping my mouth shut." It was due to other causes also. Before the Civil War, Armour was in California, panning gold. He spent the war years in Milwaukee, profiteering in pork. In 1875 he moved to Chicago. Four years later he and a group of associates began systematic manipulations of the market for pork, buying when the price was low, driving the price up, selling their holdings, plunging again when the price was low. In a year they cleared $6 million. Armour expanded his activities in meat packing and grain shipping. His agents were all over the West, buying livestock; the live animals were hauled in his freight cars; the dressed meat moved in his refrigerator cars, the grain was shipped in his fleet of Lake steamers and stored in his grain elevators. He continued to make huge sums speculating in wheat and meat.

Some Chicago businessmen objected to these manipulations of the price of foodstuffs. The president of a steel company complained that they were directly responsible for the restlessness of workingmen, who were forced to resist wage cuts in hard times because the cost of living remained high. Armour never heeded such criticisms. He went his own way. When the wholesalers of meat were not aggressive enough in pushing his products, he set up forty branch offices to sell directly to retailers. By 1892 the Armour packing houses in Chicago, Omaha, and Kansas City employed twenty thousand men. The company did a business of $100 million a year on a net worth of $11 million. Its profits for the year were 16.8 percent of net worth. Armour saw no reason to apologize for his activities. "Through the wages I disburse and the provisions I supply," he boasted, "I give more people food than any man living."

He had only scorn for abstract theorizing. "If there were fewer theorists in the world," he contended, "there'd be more success. Facts can be discounted at any bank, but a theory is rarely worth par. Stick to facts!" Every situation is individual and calls for its own response. You cannot cope with reality if you are burdened down with all sorts of general precepts. The big thing is to do whatever is required by the situation, however difficult it might be, and to do it immediately.

Once Armour made heavy commitments to deliver wheat in the future. Delivery was to be made in May at grain elevators in Chicago. Another gang of speculators, knowing of this, bought enough wheat to fill all of the grain elevators in the city, and they left it there, thinking that Armour would have to buy them out at their price in order to fulfill his contract. He discovered the plot twenty-eight days before he had to make delivery. In twenty-seven days he built in Chicago the largest grain elevator constructed up to that time. He carried out the contract, and in doing so he got into another lucrative business: his elevator was more modern and better situated than any other.

In 1897 Levi Leiter gave his son Joseph Leiter a million dollars to take a trip. Instead, the son used the money to try to corner the wheat market. By the early spring of 1898 he owned 18 million bushels in hand and had bought another 22 million for future delivery. Of those 22 million, 9 million had been bought from Philip Armour. The contract called for delivery in Chicago. But as the date for delivery approached, Armour's grain elevators in Chicago did not hold any wheat. It seemed that nobody in Chicago owned any wheat except Leiter. Armour was a realist. He had been beaten before. He knew the Lakes were still frozen so that spring wheat could not be brought from Minnesota. He went to Leiter and offered to buy the wheat he needed to fulfill their earlier contract. The deal would have netted Leiter $4 million, but the young man was flushed with victory, and he could not understand the danger of getting Armour with his back to the wall. He refused.

Armour sent a fleet of ice-breaking tugs to Duluth. They opened a channel for Armour's grain freighters. He delivered the 9 million bushels to Leiter. He then dumped on the market an additional 9 million bushels. The price of wheat broke badly. Leiter's corner on wheat had ended. His paper profits of $10 million disappeared. He had been buying those wheat futures on credit. Now he could not pay. When the air cleared, Leiter's creditors had claims totaling $20 million. That was what Philip Armour did to a man who didn't know how to be reasonable.

The other great meat packer, Gustavus F. Swift, was the same breed. Not only was he taciturn; few men ever saw him. But he too was direct and emphatic. During the panic of 1893, word reached him that the ticker at the Chicago Board of Trade had stated that Swift and Company had gone bankrupt. Swift went at once to the Board. A bearded six-footer, he went straight onto the tumultuous floor where all was pandemonium. Swift went to a table and hammered on it with his fist, and shouted, "Attention! Attention!"

Delirious traders paused, were silent. "It is reported that Swift and Company has failed," said the voice. "Swift and Company has not failed. Swift and Company cannot fail."

He walked out.

Like Field and Armour, he was a man of affairs, a practical man. His business was his life. He cared nothing for the reputed culture of New York. "I do not go in for luxuries myself," he said. He made money, and put it back into his company, and made more money by thrift, industry, an unremitting attention to day-by-day opportunities. Philip Armour said: "Always keep at it. Don't let up. Let liquor alone, pay your bills, marry a good wife and pound away at whatever you want—and sooner or later you'll make good." Gustavus Swift warned: "No young man is rich enough to smoke 25-cent cigars."

Charles Tyson Yerkes was in some respects another sort. The others were born into modest circumstances; Yerkes' father was a bank president in Philadelphia. The others had no real interests or knowledge except business; Yerkes grew up a cultured and diversified human being, one of the few millionaire art collectors of that era who had taste of his own to verify the advice of the dealers. Where the others dealt in politics sporadically, often indirectly, and through the medium of agents, Yerkes was in politics incessantly, head on, and personally. Where the others (Armour's speculations to the contrary notwithstanding) spent most of their energy in building up personally owned companies to produce and distribute goods, Yerkes always focused on making money out of juggling the stock in his bewildering network of corporations.

He began as a stockbroker and private banker in Philadelphia, early becoming known as a genius at marketing municipal bonds. But when the Chicago fire of 1871 brought panic on the Philadelphia stock exchange, Yerkes was called on to deliver at once funds he had gotten as agent in the sale of the city's bonds. He had the money tied up in other securities which could not be liquidated immediately; he could not pay. Technically guilty of embezzlement, he served seven months in prison.

He began again and quickly recovered much of his wealth. But he left his wife and six children to marry a famous local beauty, and high society froze him out. He went to Chicago, where, with the financial aid of the Philadelphia traction kings Widener and Elkins, he soon got control of the major street-car lines on the North and West Sides. He replaced horse cars with cable cars, built new lines, drove all competitors off the streets by means of nuisance law suits, court injunctions, and raids on the stock exchange against their securities. He created a fantastic empire of holding companies, operating companies, construction companies. His corporations went through one financial reorganization after another, and each time he watered the stock liberally, and always the water flowed into his account.

The outstanding stock in his companies became more and

more excessive in relation to the physical value of his properties, but always he made enough profit to pay decent dividends
on the excessive capitalization. His victim was the ultimate
consumer. Yerkes covered a single route with two or more
companies, so that passengers paid a double fare. He used
gimcrack equipment and drove it at reckless speed. He ran
one street-car where the passenger load called for two. The
protests got louder and louder, and Yerkes said bluntly: "The
straphangers pay the dividends."

He could do all this for one reason, and one only: he had the
franchises. He got them from the city council. He paid cash
for them, not to the city, but to the aldermen. He was the
archetype of the political businessman. Every time he stole a
dollar from the passengers on his lines, the politicians got their
cut.

He bulldozed over opposition. The bankers hated him for
his manipulations, for his lack of prudence, for his dashing personal life. He hated them, but he borrowed heavily from them.
And in 1892 he got caught short again. He sought another loan
from a bank where he owed a million dollars. The bank refused him and insisted that they wanted the outstanding loan
reduced at once.

"Are you sure you do?" he asked. He was told yes.

He said: "All right. I'll be back in ten minutes."

He went to the safety deposit vaults in their basement, and
returned with a million dollars in government bonds. Then he
closed his account.

Now he really needed liquid assets. The rumor circulated
that he was on the verge of failure. Nobody would lend him a
cent.

Yerkes went to President William Rainey Harper of the new
University of Chicago. Yerkes said that he wanted to donate a
million dollars to the University to build a gigantic telescope
and an astronomical observatory. He had two conditions: the
gift must be announced at once by the president, but Yerkes
actually, and secretly, would pay no part of the money for sev-

eral months. The announcement was made. Yerkes' credit in town went through the roof. Later he paid the money, and the observatory was built at Lake Geneva, Wisconsin.

Once he sold a property to be merged with another. After the merger deed was signed by the other parties, Yerkes inserted a clause in it. He was summoned to a bank for a showdown. He was told, what he already knew, that his action was a criminal offense, and that he must make restitution or go to jail. He looked at the others, one by one.

"All right, gentlemen," he said, "but there is hardly a man in this room with whom I have not made similar deals, and if prison doors are to close on me, they will on you—and you— and you."

He left. He did nothing further. Nor did they.

He was sensitive only about the mottled reputation of his wife. When a Chicago newspaper that specialized in blackmail wrote a sensational story about Mrs. Yerkes, they sent it before publication to Yerkes. The reporter asked Yerkes if he had any comments to add. Yerkes read the story coldly and said to the reporter:

"You can accuse me of all the crimes in the calendar, and I won't have a word in reply. But you can tell your employer that if he publishes one line of lies reflecting on my wife, I will not stop for legal proceedings. Within twenty-four hours I will shoot him like a dog."

The story was never published.

He was like a plague that had stricken the city. When ceremonies were being planned to commemorate the Great Fire of 1871, "Mr. Dooley" asked in his daily column: "We've had manny other misfortunes an' they're not cillybrated. Why don't we have a band out an' illuminated sthreet cars f'r to commimerate th' day that Yerkuss came to Chicago? An' there's cholera. What's th' matter with cholera?"

It was left for a Chicago businessman of the next generation, Samuel Insull, to push to perfection—and to reform—the methods of corporate pyramiding and financial skullduggery invented by Yerkes. Insull was thirty-two years old when he left his association in New Jersey with Thomas Alva Edison to come to Chicago. The man who brought him was Robert Todd Lincoln, son of Abraham Lincoln and a corporation lawyer in Chicago, who thought him just the man to reorganize and run the Chicago Edison Company. He was. Brilliant at engineering, management, and finance, Insull was a ruthless despot. Hour after hour he stalked around the company with a cold cigar between his fingers, browbeating vice presidents and sweepers impartially. He had no pleasures. He knew only profit and efficiency. He was a full-bodied, silent man who seldom laughed. His only smile was a bitter one. When he went to the exclusive Calumet Club, he was usually alone. He sat by the pool tables and smoked and stared and kept his own counsel.

He once said: "My experience is that the greatest aid to the efficiency of labor is a long line of men waiting at the gate." Marshall Field, Swift, Armour, Yerkes—they would all have understood the wisdom of that. The persistence of some attitudes among Chicago businessmen is important; but equally important is the fact that Insull was of another generation, operating in a changed environment, using methods that often were quite different.

For three decades after 1861, the chief opportunities open to Chicago businessmen were local ones. Their chief energies went into the development of local firms, local industries. Capital and labor from the East and from Europe poured into Chicago to create new facilities. The chances to make money were, paradoxically, enhanced by the Great Fire of 1871, which forced the rebuilding of so much of the city. Field, Armour, Swift, the thousands of men who scoured the country and the world for them knew the sources of supply and the markets in countless towns. But none ever doubted that Chicago was the center of his business. His main plants were there, most of his employees were there.

But after 1890 this situation altered. Labor continued to

come to Chicago, but capital began to flow out. The local real estate market became less speculative, less buoyant. Men still made money in real estate, but now it was a long-term investment, not a quick killing. So the smart money began to look around in other areas. Chicago money owned street railways in St. Louis and Toledo, timberlands in the West, cattle ranches in the Southwest, real estate in the South; and the utilities empire of Samuel Insull was to spread in all directions.

Chicago business had reached maturity. Many of its firms now had a history to talk about. For a quarter-century or more, people had been buying dry goods from Marshall Field and Mandel Brothers, Brunswick Balke billiard tables, W. W. Kimball pianos, Rand McNally maps, Crane and Company valves, Lyon and Healy sheet music, Kuppenheimer men's clothing. Chicago was a city where a man could succeed greatly or fail miserably; you had to seize your chances quickly before somebody else seized them.

"The really influential men in America," said John Peter Altgeld in 1891, "are the successful private individuals—positive men, earnest, conscientious, thoroughgoing men. Take successful businessmen, successful manufacturers, leading railroad men, lawyers, physicians, and even preachers when they have sufficient independence to develop any individuality—these are the men who mould public opinion . . . secure legislation and shape the policy of the country."

But of course these men did not pass the laws or interpret them or enforce them. They just "secured" them from the men in public office, including the gray wolves in the city council of Chicago. They did it the way they did everything else that might influence their business—systematically.

"Uncle Joe" Cannon, member of the Federal House of Representatives, came from a rural district in downstate Illinois. His farmer constituents, most of them debtors, were pressing hard after 1890 for an inflationary monetary policy. They wanted free coinage of silver, so that they could pay their debts in cheap money. Cannon was feeling the pressure. But the businessmen did not want cheap money; they were the creditors to whom those debts were owed. J. Frank Aldrich went to Cannon and chided him for not leading the voters, for letting them push him around. Cannon, said Aldrich, should come up to Chicago more often and get to know the men of affairs. Cannon did so, joining the Union League Club. Aldrich was able to report a gratifying change in the Congressman's attitude after he had been a member for a little while.

Even "Bathhouse" John Coughlin, after a decade as alderman, was able to scoff at the reformers. "I'll be reelected," he said confidently. "I have the business interests with me. Because why? Because when anyone wants me to do anything I do it courteously. Marshall Field, Mandel Brothers, the First National Bank. They're all with me."

But Yerkes remained the prize performer. He got what he wanted. Alderman Johnny Powers explained why: "You can't get elected to the council unless Mr. Yerkes says so."

CHAPTER 5

The Women at Hull-House

Moral purpose must actually become incorporated in adequate social mechanisms if it is not to be frustrated and corrupted.

—Reinhold Niebuhr [*]

OPPOSITION TO Johnny Powers in his own Nineteenth Ward always centered in Hull-House, the social settlement on Halsted Street. In contrast to Powers' cynicism, the women living there were moralistic and virginal. But if they were highminded, they were also hardheaded. Out of their practical idealism came many specific reforms and the new profession of social work. These were women who never outgrew the ethical code that they had learned as girls about the time of the Civil War—a code they shared because, to a remarkable degree, they had been reared in similar families.

I

To most children of the nineteenth century, morality was a drab discipline, a tiresomely reiterated list of simple and foolish maxims. But Florence Kelley found real vitality in the preachments and practices that she observed in her Grandaunt Sarah's tranquil home in Philadelphia.

[*] *An Interpretation of Christian Ethics* (New York: Living Age Books, 1956), p. 164.

113

Aunt Sarah was a Quaker. She was also an abolitionist who had refused to use sugar in her tea and had substituted linen underwear for cotton, because, as she explained to her niece Florence, "these things were the products of slave labor." But the small girl heard more than recitations of things past. True, Aunt Sarah liked to read aloud the letters she had received from English liberals: Richard Cobden, John Stuart Mill, the Duchess of Sutherland, and Lady Stanley of Alderley. But she was more likely to discuss the goals yet to be achieved, such as woman suffrage, a single standard of morality for men and women, peace, free trade. She thought that evil could best be fought by recruiting the young to battle against it, and she found the frail, somewhat sickly Florence receptive to crusades. After all, the foster-great-grandparents of Florence Kelley had made the crossing to America with Joseph Priestley, the chemist and Unitarian minister who had to flee England after a mob wrecked his house, library, and scientific equipment because of his defense of the French Revolution.

Florence Kelley grew up four miles from Independence Hall. Her home was serene, even though her mother had lost five children. Florence's father, William Darrah Kelley, encouraged her lively curiosity, and together they explored many fields of knowledge. He was a self-made man who started in the printer's trade when only eleven years old, studied law at night, was admitted to the bar and then elected to the bench, where he served for nine years. In 1856 Judge Kelley was one of those premature Republicans, running unsuccessfully for Congress on the Free Soil ticket with Frémont, and in 1860 he was among the frenzied, cheering delegates who nominated Lincoln at the Chicago Wigwam. His political foresight then was rewarded with a seat in Congress, where he remained for twenty-eight years and (contrary to the free-trade teachings of Aunt Sarah) came to be known as "Pig Iron" Kelley through his championship of a high tariff for that booming Pennsylvania industry. Emblazoned on his political record was the inscription, "I knew Abraham Lincoln." For the daughter, as for a multitude of other Americans, this was akin to having touched the garment of the divine.

The uncertain health of the girl often interrupted her formal schooling, but her father's library provided a voluminous substitute, and she absorbed the English and American classics. One winter in Washington, D.C., she spent long hours in the Library of Congress. William Kelley, a supporter of equal suffrage for women, approved his daughter's enrolment at sixteen at Cornell, one of the few colleges which then offered equal education for women. Florence Kelley recalled those years: "Little did we care that there was no music, no theatre, almost no library; that the stairs to the lecture halls were wooden, and the classrooms heated with coal stoves. No one, so far as I know, read a daily paper, or subscribed for a monthly or quarterly. Our current gossip was Froude's life of Carlyle." A degree and a highly commended thesis on common and statute law dealing with children was followed, however, by frustration. She was denied permission to enter the graduate school of law at the University of Pennsylvania and turned instead to establishing an evening school for girls in Philadelphia.

The continuing desire for study led to a trip abroad with her elder brother. Again frustration. After a year of study at Leipzig she was denied a degree. Next she took a walking vacation in England in the summer of 1883, and saw the Black Country of the coal miners and the cottages of the sweated nailmakers and chainmakers. Going then to Zurich because she had heard that its university did not exclude women, she became acquainted with social revolutionaries, refugees from Russia, Germany, and Austria.

She already knew a little about their doctrines. In Philadelphia, a lace importer and friend of Karl Marx had brought Judge Kelley some red-bound agitational pamphlets, and the girl had found them "startling." Now in Zurich she attended socialist meetings, participated in debates, translated *The Condition of the Working-Class in England in 1844,* by Friedrich

Engels, into English, and married a revolutionist, Lazare Wischnewetsky, a young Polish-Russian physician. They had three children, a son born abroad and a son and daughter born in New York, where the family settled in 1886. Florence Kelley's interest in socialism continued in the United States, although her membership in the Socialist Labor party was an uneasy one. After a year she was expelled because the German and Russian "impossibilists" were suspicious of her "too fluent" English. And her marriage broke up. Dr. Wischnewetsky had virtually no medical practice. Debts were heavy and oppressive. Five years after her wedding Florence Kelley moved to Illinois where, on the grounds of nonsupport, she obtained a divorce, the custody of her children, and resumption of her maiden name.

A new way of life had to be constructed, and her attention came to focus on the problem of child labor. Deploring this exploitation had little effect. She developed the better weapon of research. Soon she was reading a paper at a convention of commissioners of labor statistics, publishing a paper on "Our Toiling Children." But this was mere guerilla assault; she wanted the efficiency of a regular battalion of reform. Hopefully, she approached the Woman's Christian Temperance Union, but it was concerned only with the demon rum. Then, shortly after Christmas of 1891, Florence Kelley enlisted in Chicago's new settlement, Hull-House.

There she met Julia Lathrop, whose ancestors had been in America even longer than her own. In 1634 the Reverend John Lathropp, an English nonconformist sent to prison for his beliefs, successfully petitioned for "liberty in exile," and emigrated to Boston, where he gained a reputation as "a sound scholar and a lively preacher." Julia heard the story many times from her father, and in adulthood she liked to claim that her kinsman "would have come over on the Mayflower but for the unfortunate circumstance that he was in jail at the moment that doughty vessel set sail."

Among John Lathropp's descendants, some drifted westward; William Lathrop, out of Genessee County, New York, settled in Rockford, Illinois, where by 1857 he was well established in the practice of law, and had a wife, and home, and $10,000 in the bank. The next year Julia Clifford was born, one of five children.

The girl was shy. In school she was reported a "good child" and a "smart scholar," but she felt an absence of understanding on the part of her teachers. What the school lacked, however, the parents supplied. At home the children were encouraged to express their opinions and, without interference from the adults, to develop their particular interests. William Lathrop held a tight purse but it opened readily when the proposal was for books or education. His accomplishments in politics and the law were instruction by example. In 1854 he helped found the Republican party in northern Illinois, and this activity brought about his election to the legislature where a former member of that body, Abraham Lincoln, once helped him in his search for a book at the library. The event was casual; the recollection permanent.

This was the period when Susan B. Anthony appeared before the Illinois legislature to advocate equal rights for women, when Dorothea Dix rode by wagon to Springfield from Chicago to plead for the humane treatment of the insane, when the author of the best-selling novel was a woman abolitionist, Harriet Beecher Stowe. The legal practice of the Rockford legislator reflected his exposure to these ideas. When a Mrs. Dixon shot her husband because she believed he intended to steal her baby from her, William Lathrop successfully offered emotional insanity as the defense, the first such plea in the history of Illinois jurisprudence. (Thus early are the origins of the type of legal argument that Clarence Darrow, a friend of Julia Lathrop, would use in dozens of murder trials.) He set another precedent in welcoming Alta M. Hulett to prepare for the law in his office while he drew up the bill permitting women to practice. She was the first woman admitted to the bar in Illinois.

William Lathrop probably was an agnostic, although for a time he bowed to his wife's interest in the Second Congregational Church and led the family parade to the pew on Sunday. He ended this concession when none of the children joined the church at the appropriate age; he was even gleeful over the failure of his rather unwilling example. Although Adeline Potter Lathrop did wish that her husband would conduct family prayers, she was not too disturbed by his indifference to religion. At least he gladly supported her in other fields—advocacy of suffrage and devotion to books which were discussed at the Monday Club, a circle Mrs. Lathrop had helped form. Moreover, he was concerned with his wife's school, Rockford Seminary (now Rockford College), and served it diligently as a trustee.

The daughter Julia, slender, sallow, and dark-eyed, enrolled at Rockford for a year after completing high school, with the intent of qualifying for Vassar. Her father was pleased at her ambition and employed German and mathematics tutors when it grew obvious that the girl was not adequately prepared for the eastern school. In 1880, after hard work and little fun, Julia Lathrop was graduated from Vassar. The college apparently did not inspire her for a particular vocation. Teaching held no appeal. She went into her father's law office as secretary, read a good deal of law with keen understanding, and displayed a head for business by becoming secretary for two different companies in which she had invested and profited. Manufacturing was growing rapidly in Rockford; the town was turning into a city.

In the winter of 1888-1889, the Lathrops were invited to a meeting at Rockford College where Jane Addams and Ellen Gates Starr, graduates of the school, were appealing for support of a new kind of project, a social settlement to be opened the coming fall in Chicago. There were many friendly questions about the enterprise that was intended "to make social intercourse express the growing sense of economic unity of society and to add the social function to democracy." To

William Lathrop this was as vaporous as most of the missionary enterprises hatched at the college, idealistic, but not very practical. Nevertheless, he interposed no objection when Julia Lathrop decided to join the settlement.

She had been at Hull-House six years when Dr. Alice Hamilton came. The newcomer was also a native of a small midwestern city, Fort Wayne, Indiana, where the streets were shaded by elms and maples, the sidewalks paved with red brick, the shops austere except for the drugstore with its flasks of colored water. Alice Hamilton lived as part of a clan in a cluster of houses: the Old House, grandfather Hamilton's, with its mysterious forbidden room without a floor; the brick Red House belonging to her uncle, more modern but without the dignity of the Old House; and her parents' place, the frame White House with wonderful places for solitude, the arm chair in the library, a refuge at the head of the attic stairs. Sociability too was a part of her growing years: in addition to the adults, the clustered family group included seventeen cousins.

Grandmother Hamilton was a descendant of English immigrants whose offspring had followed the well-worn trail from Virginia to Kentucky to southern Indiana. A "passionate" reader (Alice frequently saw her "in the library of the Old House, crouched over the fireplace where the soft coal fire had gone out, so deep had she been in her book"), she was elusive, impersonal, remote, but not so much so that she did not have as her guests Frances Willard, head of the Woman's Christian Temperance Union, and the suffragette Susan B. Anthony. The temperance cause was respectable, but to entertain Miss Anthony required audacity on the part of a hostess. Grandmother Pond, on the other side of the family, was a Victorian. Her morals and manners had been learned at Miss Lucy Green's very proper school in New York. She adored Byron but pledged herself never to read *Don Juan,* accepted the Bible literally, and never doubted the iniquity of the Roman Catholic Church.

Montgomery Hamilton, Alice's father, had run away from

Princeton to enlist in the Union Army at nineteen, but in later years he never mentioned the war except to denounce shoddy supplies sold by profiteers, to proclaim the foolishness of his enlistment through a boyish desire for adventure, or to declare that the South had a right to secede. Theology, primarily, and literature, secondarily, were his interests. Rigorously the father drilled four daughters and a son with his interpretations and preferences. He dwelt endlessly on Arianism, Socinianism, Gnosticism and other heresies, and the Westminster Catechism, "that heathenish production." "I suppose a sensitive child could have been profoundly affected by such horrible teaching," Alice Hamilton said, "but it made not a dent on us."

One aspect of the father's discipline did possess value. The children were not permitted to make a statement unless they were prepared to prove its validity. Information, Montgomery Hamilton reminded them, was available in the family library. But this, too, was distorted: when Alice at fourteen wanted to study physics the father had a simple answer: "It's all in the encyclopedia."

Father's reading tastes emphasized Macaulay, Froude, Addison, and Pope. The mother, Gertrude Pond Hamilton, drew more response from the children by reading aloud *The Mill on the Floss* and *Adam Bede* and by inducing Alice to memorize Gray's "Elegy Written in a Country Churchyard." Gertrude Hamilton neglected the fine points of theology, but she could speak with authority on such taboo subjects as pregnancy, childbirth, and sex. Virtue to her was not the same as fear of public opinion, and she brushed aside contemporary prudery. Interwoven with her beliefs was the capacity for indignation: against the lynching of Negroes, child labor, police brutality, and a system that permitted such injustices. Alice Hamilton frequently heard from her mother: "There are two kinds of people, the ones who say, 'Somebody ought to do something about it, but why should it be I?' and those who say, 'Somebody must do something about it, then why not I?'" The choice was obvious to the daughter.

Miss Porter's School in Farmington, Connecticut, a requirement for all the Hamilton girls, was Alice Hamilton's preliminary to the study of medicine at the University of Michigan. She chose this field of study, not because she was scientifically minded, but because she thought that as a doctor she would secure freedom from the restraints on women. At Ann Arbor the training was advanced, German-influenced, and included courses in biochemistry, bacteriology, physiology, and pharmacology. Above all, Ann Arbor offered emancipation. No one fretted about Alice Hamilton's hours; no one stood at the doorstep worrying about her safety.

Vacationing as well as schooling was in Michigan. The four sisters summered at Mackinac. Edith and Margaret, from Bryn Mawr, bubbled over Matthew Arnold, Walter Pater, and the Goncourts. Norah, studying at the Art Students' League in New York, taught Alice to sketch, a valuable help in her medical work. Judge Edward Osgood Brown of Chicago took long walks with the sisters and encouraged them to read George Bernard Shaw and Henry George's *Progress and Poverty*. He also startled them by his defense of the anarchists hanged for the Haymarket bombing. The Hamilton sisters had accepted the trial as one conducted by Judge Gary with complete objectivity with a just verdict against criminal violence. But Judge Brown offered facts in abundance, "new and upsetting," and if his ideas were true "we had to accept them. . . ."

Bacteriology and pathology appeared more attractive to Alice Hamilton than a general medical practice. From Ann Arbor she went for two brief unhappy months to the Hospital for Women and Children in Minneapolis. There she was left on her own to cope with typhoid fever and obstetrical cases, of which she knew little. Then came an opening at the New England Hospital for Women and Children on the outskirts of Boston. This, at last, was the big city. On the first evening she was called to a case some distance away in a poverty-ridden neighborhood. The patient lived above a saloon, and it was not until midnight that Alice Hamilton was ready to leave.

She immediately lost her way. Fearful of asking any man for assistance, she approached a pert little woman, a chorus girl, who laughingly gave her directions and added, "Just walk along fast with your bag in your hand, not looking at anybody, and nobody will speak to you. Men don't want to be snubbed; they are looking for a woman who is willing." The advice was sound, for the young Doctor Hamilton, going by night into sordid tenements and houses of prostitution, was never molested.

Visiting back in Fort Wayne, Alice Hamilton, now acquainted with the city slum, discussed socialism and settlements with sister Norah and cousin Agnes Hamilton. Agnes was an enthusiast for Richard Ely's Christian socialism and promptly converted Alice. One day Norah burst into the house with the breathless news that Jane Addams of Hull-House was to speak at the Methodist Church. Hull-House was about six years old, with a fame that had spread quickly. Both Agnes and Alice, absorbing every word spoken by Jane Addams, decided that some day they must become a part of settlement life.

First, though, Alice Hamilton needed status in bacteriology and pathology. For this, study in Germany was essential. In 1895 with her sister Edith she went abroad. The German schools were cold to women students. Degrees were impossible. At the University of Leipzig the sisters gained entrance but only upon the understanding that they were to be considered "invisible." Munich was conquered, too, after irksome and prolonged negotiations. It seemed impossible to achieve status; the next year Alice, back in the United States, was without a bid for her services. Bacteriologists and pathologists were not yet in demand, so when Edith became headmistress at the Bryn Mawr School in Baltimore, Alice accompanied her to study at Johns Hopkins. She found two of her old teachers from Michigan, W. H. Howell and John J. Abel, among the giants of the new medical school—William Welch, Simon Flexner, William Osler, Howard Kelly, John Finney, Franklin

Mall, and Lewellys Barker. It was Flexner in pathological anatomy who hammered ceaselessly on "that important part of research, the thorough and critical review of all that has been written on one's problem and the scrupulous care one must use to give credit where credit is due."

Eventually came employment in her field. The Women's Medical School of Northwestern University in Chicago, the Chicago of Jane Addams and Hull-House, asked her to teach pathology. She determined to live at Hull-House.

II

The cluster of hills around the village of Cedarville broke the flat sweep of the prairie in northern Illinois, and on one of these elevations pine trees flourished, grown from seeds planted by John H. Addams in 1844. Through the village a stream flowed, with caves eroded into its banks. In the summer the purple anemones were a daytime delight and at twilight the whippoorwill introduced an appropriate solemnity. In this setting the girl Jane Addams, born in 1860, found places for play and dreaming. She was slightly stooped, pigeon-toed, and bashful, perhaps because of a spinal curvature. In the crude surgery of the day her spine was seared with a red hot iron but the result, if not actually harmful, was without benefit.

The mother of Jane Addams had died when the daughter was a baby, too soon for even a vague memory to take root, and her father did not remarry for eight years. In that interval, however, there was no neglect or shunting aside of the questioning child.

Scene: *The Addams Home in Cedarville, Illinois*
Time: *About 1867*

> The little girl is having a "horrid night." Sleep will not come because that day she told a lie. She thinks of death, of a fiery furnace for sinners, of Satan in all his malevolence. How to get relief? One way has always helped. Go to father's room and

make full confession. She slips slowly from under the warm covers, eases her bare feet to the cold floor. She will have to pass the unlocked front door. Papa will never lock it. That's because he's a Quaker. She approaches the stairs, clutches the newel post for support. Now she darts down and, afraid to pause, rushes past the door and through the wide, black cavern that is the living room. Panting, wild-eyed, the girl blurts out her confession. Papa is calm; papa is always calm. He is glad she felt "too bad to go to sleep." She does not ask for forgiveness. She receives no absolution. There is a hug, a kiss. The trip back is nothing. She walks sedately, without fear, without noticing the cold. Bouncing into bed, she is asleep within a minute.

John H. Addams began work as a miller, but he went into politics because of his concern with the abolitionist movement, the formation of the Republican party, and the Civil War. It was politics in the highest sense. In his long service in the Illinois Senate, 1854 to 1870, he earned the distinction of never having been offered a bribe. Senator Addams brought his politics home. Jane Addams was not yet four when she entered her father's room one morning to find him in whispered conversation with a Negro. The fugitive was on his way to freedom in Canada and, young as she was, Jane Addams abided by her childish pledge not to talk about the slave's visit. A year later Jane Addams came home from play to find the two white gateposts of her home decorated with American flags and black streamers. Inside, the always calm father sat with tears on his cheeks. "The greatest man in the world has died," she was told.

That "greatest man" had often solicited the opinion of "My dear Double-D'ed Addams," as Abraham Lincoln liked to address him. One of the letters, carefully preserved by the Cedarville legislator, said that Lincoln knew Addams would vote according to his conscience but asked to know how the conscience "was pointing" on a particular measure. Jane Addams understood the moral enthusiasm of her Hicksite Quaker father for Lincoln and the issues for which he stood. She perceived something unique in the reverent admiration for Lincoln by his contemporaries. "They realized," she said, "that if this last tremendous experiment in self-government failed here it would be the disappointment of the centuries" and that if it was to succeed "it must be brought about by the people themselves; that there was no other capital fund upon which to draw."

Rockford Seminary, where her father along with William Lathrop served as a trustee, was a logical choice for Jane Addams in 1877. But the choice was made by the parent. Jane preferred Smith College. However, three sisters had attended Rockford, and John Addams believed that education should be near home followed by travel abroad. And Rockford was gaining a reputation. It was a school where intense effort was the norm. The education was a combination of classical reading and evangelical appeals. Translations of Plato, Aristotle, and Plutarch, readings of Carlyle, Ruskin, and Browning were occasionally interrupted by a lecture from visitors. One was Bronson Alcott, whose heavy cloth overshoes were cleaned of clay by a worshiping Jane Addams. Of mathematics there was a dash, of economics nothing, of oratory an abundance. In the last subject she had some skill, being selected to represent the school in a statewide oratorical contest. She placed fifth or "exactly in the middle," not a bad showing for the only woman entrant who was pitted against such wonders as William Jennings Bryan, who won second prize.

John Addams' promise of a European tour was fulfilled. In 1883 Jane Addams embarked on a journey that took her through England, France, Germany, Austria, and Italy and lasted two years. She was an indefatigable tourist, exploring the misery of East London, interviewing a Saxe-Coburg brewery owner who exploited women, spending a considerable sum for an engraving by Dürer, whose work was "surcharged with pity for the downtrodden." She prowled through the slums of Naples, strolled across the sunny Campagna into Rome. It was a nervous, maladjusted, intellectually confused

Jane Addams who returned home to Cedarville. She shuttled between there and Baltimore, where she received treatment of her spine (during her lifetime it required four major operations) and heard comforting lectures on Mazzini's philosophy. But she was shaken by mankind's resistance to the dictates of morality, and at the advanced age of twenty-five she joined the Presbyterian Church at Cedarville. She was seeking, not respectability, but "an outward symbol of fellowship, some bond of peace, some blessed spot where unity of spirit might claim right of way over all differences."

After another two years, Jane Addams sailed again for Europe. Some cities were revisited, others added to her itinerary. In a vague way she was thinking about renting a house in a poor city area back home where young women of comfortable circumstances might engage in social activity to overcome the one-sidedness of viewing life through books and foreign travel. The dream became clearer in Spain where she was traveling with her Rockford classmate, Ellen Gates Starr. Then in London the two young women saw the first settlement house in the world. Toynbee Hall was the conception of a young clergyman, Samuel A. Barnett, who wanted to remedy the undermining of the old parish system by the industrial revolution. Here at Toynbee in 1884 a colony of young men became a part of the community of the poor, organized clubs, lectures, and concerts, identified themselves with the aspirations and struggles of the dispossessed. Mutuality was to bring about class rapprochement. Practicality from below was to replace preaching from on top. Jane Addams had found the device she had been seeking.

Back in the United States, she and Ellen Gates Starr began looking in Chicago for a suitable building for their settlement house. On the first day of their search they stumbled upon the former country home of Charles J. Hull. This house on South Halsted Street was surrounded by tenements and factories, the area populated by immigrant Russian and Polish Jews, Italians, Irish, Germans, and Bohemians. Nine churches had 250 saloons as competitors. Life in the Nineteenth Ward was, for the most part, dominated by disease, poverty, vice, premature death, foul housing, blighted childhood, and crushing labor.

The old home, occupied on September 18, 1890, "responded kindly to repairs." Jane Addams had an income of her own, and this combined with contributions paid for restoration of the residence. It had been constructed in 1846 when builders believed in ample room. The lofty ceilings had elaborate cornices. The long drawing room had French windows and carved white mantelpieces. New furniture was brought in, other pieces were donated, and the house was decorated with knickknacks and pictures collected on European travels. The dining room was long and paneled, with chandeliers of Spanish wrought iron.

There was no perplexity over where to begin. The streets of the ward, crowded with children, suggested a kindergarten and clubs; in the first few weeks Ellen Starr organized a reading party for young women with George Eliot's *Romola* as the first selection. As time went on, a penny savings bank was established, a day nursery, an employment bureau, an orchestra, quarters for the organization of women's trade unions. Parties were frequent, although Jane Addams was taken aback by the refusal of a number of little girls to accept gifts of candy at Christmas. (They had been working in candy factories from seven in the morning until nine at night and "could not bear the sight of it.")

Julia Lathrop organized a Plato Club and soon had men like John Dewey coming on Sunday afternoons to lead uneducated immigrants in sessions about Greek philosophy. The discussions often wandered beyond that topic to embrace the whole of culture, and the allotted two hours stretched to five. Courses in arts and crafts resulted in an invitation to Frank Lloyd Wright in 1895 to lecture at Hull-House. But the handicrafts movement did not awaken a sympathetic response in Wright, now twenty-six years old and a newly independent architect who had finished his apprenticeship to Sullivan and Adler.

Taking as his subject "The Art and Craft of the Machine," Wright derided the revival of handicrafts that took its inspiration from the ideas of William Morris. Every age, he said, must do its work with "the tools most successful in saving the most precious thing in the world—human effort." It is foolish to do work with hand tools when machinery can be used. As new types of machinery and new materials become available to architecture, new designs and new types of beauty must be developed that are appropriate to, and take advantage of, the new opportunities. This had not been done. Rather did most of the audience own furniture "very likely carved by the machine, and fitted with curved arms and legs, with a tortured sprawl which you suppose artistic when it is nothing more than a nasty imitation of an erstwhile woodcarver's dream."

Wright tried to awaken his audience to some of the new resources for creating beauty. Steel had made possible an unprecedented handling of the tall building. Woodworking machines could handle wood in ways that brought out its native beauty as never before, its marking, texture, and color. In stone work the planer made it possible to use the material in thin sheets. The exteriors of buildings could be surfaced with burned clay, terra cotta, as Louis Sullivan had done so brilliantly. But the architectural and engineering schools remained blind to these new resources: not one school was trying to train the architect "to his actual tools, or by a process of nature study that develops the power of independent thought fitting him to use them profitably." Instead they taught men to copy designs that had originated hundreds or thousands of years earlier and that had no relation to modern life. (As Altgeld had said, the schools made minds into storehouses, not into workshops.)

Hull-House thus tried not only to relieve the physical want that stifled most residents of the Nineteenth Ward; it also aimed at ending their spiritual deprivation. And it did so with no hint of self-consciousness or uplift, because it rejected the distinction between intellectuals and workers. Greek philosophy and modern architecture were part of the common heritage of the human race, and one man had as much right as another to share in them. Nor were the women of Hull-House tainted with the earnest solemnity that made many reformers intolerable. "When men and women, boys and girls, work all day in sweatshops, they want to have fun," Jane Addams insisted. This sort of realism was repellent to the evangelists and romanticists who wandered into Hull-House, and for most of them a single visit was enough.

Wisely Jane Addams avoided a denominational or even a religious subscription from those who participated in the activity of Hull-House. She was wary of anything divisive. Religious spokesmen were welcome, although the reception they met was not always to their satisfaction. The Women's Club had as one of its first speakers a Christian Scientist who at the close of a lengthy address said: "Now here in this neighborhood, when you are out at night, just as the sun is setting and you go down to the river and notice the odors which arise from it, you must think of the pine trees and how they smell and say to yourself, 'Oh! what a lovely evening; how sweet everything smells!'" An elderly German woman, well acquainted with the slimy stream, arose and remarked: "Vell, all I can say is if dot woman say dot river smell good den dere must be something de matter with dot woman's nose." The club members roared with approval.

But Hull-House welcomed the nonconformist and the eccentric. An elderly anarchist, who probably shuddered at slapping a fly, preached violent revolution and assassination. But a self-styled Hindu Mahatma converted him to another way of life. The anarchist was instructed to lift his face to Heaven, to say, "I am divine," and to restrict his diet to garlic and popcorn.

Some anarchists were more dedicated. Marie Sukloff had attempted to kill the governor of Kiev with a bomb, been sentenced to life imprisonment in Siberia, and escaped via Japan to America and Hull-House. With Alice Hamilton she visited the penitentiary at Joliet and was horrified. "It is worse than any thing in Russia or Siberia," she said. "Russian prisons are dirty and the guards are often cruel, but they are human —they may hit you one minute but the next minute they talk to you as if you were their sister. In Joliet it is all whitewashed and still, it works like a machine, it is terrifying."

Sometimes the numerous crises of the poor caused Jane Addams to wonder if the higher purposes of the settlement were being lost. Once she and Julia Lathrop were called to help a young woman who was about to give birth unattended in a tenement. Neighboring women refused to help the girl because she was unmarried and because anyone calling a doctor might be held responsible financially. The two women from Hull-House hurried to the tenement and were initiated as midwives. As they walked back slowly to the settlement, Jane Addams exclaimed, "This doing things that we don't know how to do is going too far. Why did we let ourselves be rushed into midwifery?" Julia Lathrop's answer was never forgotten: "If we have to begin to hew down to the line of our ignorance, for goodness' sake don't let us begin at the humanitarian end. To refuse to respond to a poor girl in the throes of childbirth would be a disgrace to us forever. If Hull-House does not have its roots in human kindness, it is no good at all."

Under the impact of life in the Nineteenth Ward, the Toynbee Hall objective of class reconciliation, although never formally abandoned, dwindled to lesser importance than the host of problems tossed on the doorstep of Hull-House. And Jane Addams was learning, too, that there were various practitioners of class harmony. Alderman Johnny Powers, for instance, manipulated the workingman's vote for the service of the employer. Powers demonstrated to Jane Addams the reality of municipal government, the political science of making and manipulating friends. Jane Addams "soon discovered that approximately one out of every five voters in the Nineteenth

Ward held a job dependent on the good will of the alderman."
At the outset she did not grasp why there were so many street-
car and telephone company employees in the ward; then she
found out how franchises were secured.

On election day, Powers would drive to all the polling places,
including the one at Hull-House, his big bandwagon playing
"Nearer, My God, to Thee"; nickels would be tossed to the
kids, cigars to the men. He would see Jane Addams and call
out, "Miss Addams, if you ever want any little favor from me,
just tell me and I'll see to it." She would thank him, but if ever
a favor was needed, a legitimate request for a city permit, she
asked some other resident of Hull-House to run the errand.
Powers never failed to respond favorably. "How is she?" he
would ask and, when told "Pretty well," would say wistfully,
"Did she ask you to come?" Informed, "Oh, no, she just told
me she wanted it," Powers would sigh and comment, "Well,
Miss Addams is always O.K. with me, but I wish just once
she'd ask me and not fight me all the time."

Fight him she did, and in the third campaign against the
alderman, serious inroads were made into his majority. But
the many persons dependent on Powers' favors reacted, Jane
Addams noticed, "with the same sort of hostility which a
striker so inevitably feels against the man who would take his
job, even sharpened by the sense that the movement for reform came from an alien source." Such episodes made her
doubt, as she had doubted earlier in Baltimore, the strength
of moral suasion. (Could downtrodden immigrants afford to
scruple too finely when their very survival was so uncertain?)
To a close friend she gave the impression of "always being very
sad, as if the sorrows of the neighborhood were pressed upon
her."

To relieve those sorrows took money, and she had to get
money from people who had it. She was a regular visitor at
Bar Harbor, Maine, in spite of its wealthy snobbery and its
marked bias against women, because she found she could get
nearly as much in contributions in a summer there as she could

during the rest of the year elsewhere. But when employers offered money to Hull-House in the expectation that she would temper her program, she refused them, while wondering why she was offered bribes when her father never had been. It was one of the few subjects on which she was sensitive enough to lose her temper. Once when she was telling an audience of workingmen about the aims of Hull-House, a heckler interrupted to call out: "You won't talk like that when the millionaires begin to subsidize you." Stung deeply, she retorted: "I don't intend to be subsidized by millionaires or bullied by labor unionists."

It probably was in one of her periods of despondency that she investigated socialism. The outcome was that she recoiled from the contention that men's ideas originated in their class position. Nor could she accept class consciousness as desirable in an America where individuals could still rise out of one class into another. Hull-House, she came to resolve, must be built on the "solidarity of the human race" and on the premise that "without the advance and improvement of the whole, no man can hope for any lasting improvement in his own moral or material individual conditions." Based on this genuinely catholic acceptance of mankind, Hull-House was open to the most diverse viewpoints. What bound it together was the personality of Jane Addams.

From other states, from Europe and Asia, visitors came to examine this Chicago on Lake Michigan. For many, there were three attractions: the stockyards, the new university, and Hull-House. In 1893 Sidney and Beatrice Webb and Governor Altgeld were the guests of Clarence Darrow at Hull-House, where the visiting Englishwoman persuaded Jane Addams to try a cigarette for the first and last time. This was the year of the Exposition and prominent speakers were happy to lecture at Hull-House: Dr. Bayard Holmes discussed "The Conscience of the State," and Swami Vivehanande, "The Economic and Social Conditions of India." But that year marked more than the mushrooming growth of a settlement with a reputation. Following the recommendation of Henry Demarest Lloyd, who was completing his *Wealth Against Commonwealth,* Governor Altgeld appointed Florence Kelley as chief factory inspector of Illinois, a post created by a new law. Now the activity of the women of Hull-House was to spread into a far wider field. The core of this remarkable work was concern for the family: the unschooled child, the working mother, the exploited father. Within a few years the women of Hull-House recorded accomplishments that had never before been achieved by any group of American women—or equaled since.

III

A year after Hull-House opened, Florence Kelley and her children arrived on a snowy December morning. Already standing at the door ringing the bell was Henry Standing Bear, a Kickapoo Indian. The door was opened by Jane Addams. She had the cook's fat baby on her left arm while the right restrained a little Italian girl, whose mother was at a sweatshop, from dashing out into the snow. The next day a place was found for the Kelley children at the Winnetka home of Henry Lloyd, within easy reach of Hull-House.

At the time the sweating system of Chicago was being attacked by the Chicago Trades and Labor Assembly. Mrs. Thomas J. Morgan, wife of a socialist leader in the labor movement, had begun to expose the conditions in the garment industry, and a suggestion was made to the Illinois state bureau of labor that accurate statistical information be compiled on the industry. Florence Kelley was appointed to conduct the inquiry. So effective was her report that a special legislative committee was named to study the sweatshops. Then, with the women of Hull-House, the labor unions, and Governor Altgeld as the chief promoters, the legislature enacted the first meaningful factory law of Illinois. Although a weak measure, the law did prohibit the employment of children in factories, fixed

an eight-hour day for women, and, most important, provided
for factory inspectors.

Florence Kelley as chief inspector was provided with a staff
of twelve, several of whom were residents of Hull-House. Now
the settlement gained a reputation for reckless radicalism.
Businessmen associated its leaders with Altgeld, the pardoner
of the Haymarket anarchists, with the Trades and Labor Assembly and socialists, with agitation for and enactment of the
bothersome law. If this was to be a step in erasing class antag-
onisms, the manufacturing interests of Illinois wanted no part
of it.

The opposition of manufacturers, city authorities, and courts
was formidable. Florence Kelley brought before the state's
attorney of Cook County the case of an eleven-year-old boy
illegally employed at gilding picture frames with a poisonous
fluid. The youngster had lost the use of his right arm and Mrs.
Kelley sought the prosecution of the employer, who could be
fined $20 but otherwise not held responsible.

"Are you calculating on *my* taking the case?" the state's attorney asked with astonishment.

"I thought you were the district attorney," Mrs. Kelley said.

"Well, suppose I am. You bring me this evidence this week
against some two-by-six cheap picture-frame maker, and how
do I know you won't bring me a suit against Marshall Field
next week? Don't count on me. I'm overloaded. I wouldn't
reach this case inside of two years. . . ."

Indignation drove Florence Kelley to enroll the next day at
Northwestern University and by June, 1894, she had her law
degree.

A case against Marshall Field in person was brought by Mrs.
Alzina Parsons Stevens, one of the deputy inspectors who re-
sided at Hull-House. Mrs. Stevens discovered bales of cheap
women's coats and jackets in a smallpox-infected tenement
house and, before burning them, removed the Marshall Field
label. Armed with her evidence, the inspector confronted the
merchant. Field offered no excuse. He arraigned Mrs. Stevens

as a "termagant," "no lady," and "unsexed woman," and advised her to go home. According to a witness who heard what followed, never "did a guilty man take such a magnificent scorching of sarcasm and denunciation. . . ."

The supreme court of Illinois seized the first opportunity to declare the eight-hour provision for women unconstitutional. Florence Kelley rebelled at this manifestation of power by the judiciary. Constitutional government, she contended, could not endure unless the courts adjusted to social conditions, but she was not able to persuade all of her associates of the validity of this thesis. Julia Lathrop, for one, insisted that precedent must broaden into precedent, and she was not shaken from this stand even in later years when, as chief of the Federal Children's Bureau, she saw the United States Supreme Court strike down the child labor law.

Julia Lathrop, not inclined to charge headlong into battle like Florence Kelley, preferring the flanking attack instead, was appointed early in the Altgeld administration to the state board of charities. She astounded a stodgy officialdom by visiting each of the 102 county farms or almshouses. In one institution she abandoned her usual reserve and slid down a new fire escape to test its effectiveness. In her conservative dress, usually a blue tailored suit, Julia Lathrop made the dreary rounds of the poor, the epileptic, the insane, the unwanted. Most distressing to her was the treatment of delinquent children; those over ten years of age were handled in the same fashion as the adult criminal.

Back in Rockford the father who had doubted the Hull-House project took increased pride in his daughter. His expressions of approval were often oblique. Meeting one of Julia Lathrop's fellow workers at the Rockford railway station, he questioned her on the way home. "You don't seem to have anything the matter with you," he said, and then added: "Oh, well, when Julia asked me to stop at the station for you, I looked for someone who was lame or blind or insane or something like that! You know, we think she's only interested in people who are in trouble!"

Out of these experiences of neighborhood needs, welfare institutions, factory conditions, law and courts, the women of Hull-House wrought their change in social work. That change was to transform the social worker from an amateur to a professional and to shift projects, once public confidence had been won, from private to government hands. With Sophonisba Breckinridge, Julia Lathrop persuaded Edith Abbott to leave Wellesley College and help them establish a department of social research in the School of Civics and Philanthropy at the University of Chicago. The objective was to relate social research to the professional concerns of social workers and to educate a group scientifically trained in the public services. One of the first courses at the new school was given by Dr. William Healy, who introduced social psychiatry to the school of social work.

Jane Addams now was pushing the transfer of private charity to public bodies. Hull-House took on the function of an experimental pilot. If an enterprise proved its worth, the next step was to convince the city or state to enter the field. The playground, the public bath, the kindergarten—such projects instituted by Hull-House were year by year taken over by the city. The work was not always done as well by the municipality. Political appointees did not match the volunteers of Hull-House, but the weakness, Jane Addams insisted, was incidental to the greater step forward of public acceptance. In 1889, for example, the state had been persuaded to enact a law regulating private employment agencies. A poor, loopholed measure, it was policed by Grace Abbott, sister of Edith and superintendent of the League for the Protection of Immigrants.

John P. Altgeld was an ex-governor on the day Alice Hamilton arrived at Hull-House. That evening he was the guest of honor at a dinner where Jane Addams, Florence Kelley, and Julia Lathrop expressed their appreciation of his administration. It was not an occasion of jubilation. Florence Kelley had been dismissed from her post and replaced by an employee of the Illinois Glass Company, one of the most flagrant exploiters of child labor. Altgeld himself was under the heaviest attack of his career. But there was no air of defeat either.

Alice Hamilton was promptly put to work establishing a baby clinic. She had learned from books that babies should have nothing but milk until their teeth came, and she was startled when foreign-born women ignored her dietary teaching. An Italian-born woman explained how she had fed her robust three-year-old son, who had been difficult as a baby. "I gave him the breast and there was plenty of milk, but he cried all the time. Then one day I was frying eggs and just to make him stop I gave him one and it went fine. The next day I was making cup cakes and as soon as they were cool I gave him one, and after that I gave him whatever we had and he got fat and didn't cry any more."

Intimate association with ordinary people taught Alice Hamilton that "education and culture have little to do with real wisdom, the wisdom that comes from life experience," and that "the banal, the bromide and the cliché" can be used with complete sincerity. She came to know a widow who preferred to be a scrubwoman at night rather than turn her child over to an orphanage; a young eight-dollar-a-week Irish girl who shunned an offer of well-paid prostitution because "It would be selling my soul"; a woman who frankly said, "My sister's got it good. Her old man's dead."; a young Italian mother who paced the floor night after night with a sick baby until exhaustion warred with her love, and she exclaimed: "My God, if you're going to die, why don't you die?"

She learned, too, that her scientific knowledge could not always be applied when confronted with a person's sense of right and wrong. When she remonstrated with a woman who had taken a year-old baby into a room where a child was sick in bed with diphtheria, the shocked mother replied, "Do you think that God would punish me for going in to help Maria with her sick child? No, he would rather punish me if I did not." The baby did not catch diphtheria. "They never did when I said they would," Alice Hamilton remarked.

Life at Hull-House aroused an interest in industrial ailments, and Alice Hamilton acquired the background that enabled her to become a pioneer in industrial disease. She wrote a paper which held flies responsible for a serious typhoid epidemic in Chicago. The paper was a success; it provoked a public investigation and the complete reorganization of the city health department. Later she was to learn that her flies had little to do with the case. "The cause was simpler but so much more discreditable that the Board of Health had not dared reveal it. It seems that in our local pumping station . . . a break had occurred which resulted in an escape of sewage into the water pipes and for three days our neighborhood drank that water before the leak was discovered and stopped."

In these trial-and-error days for the young doctor, she escaped the narrowness which so commonly curses the specialist. She found time to listen to Bill Haywood expound his one-big-union philosophy, to hear Emma Goldman denounce government, law, police, religion, and moral codes, to chat with the young Upton Sinclair who was writing *The Jungle*. Much of what she found stimulating was far from respectable. Hull-House itself was under constant attack from those who dominated Chicago's affairs; the settlement was especially wary of reporters because any event there was likely to be twisted into a sensation. When an anarchist shot the chief of police, Hull-House was pictured as a "nest of anarchists" by reporters who learned that Jane Addams and her associates did not apply a political loyalty test to participants in its activities. Police, assigned to watch mass meetings at Hull-House, brought a sense of fear and possible violence. When a group of immigrants engaged in a loud discussion of political theory, a club-twirling policeman lectured Alice Hamilton: "Lady, you people oughtn't to let bums like these come here. If I had my way they'd all be lined up against a wall at sunrise and shot."

Hull-House, more and more, was offering adventure that

was both practical and exhilarating, a combination that helped to reconcile so many brilliant women to an unmarried, childless, career-cloistered life.

In the nineteenth century, Jane Addams observed, women could not combine a career, if that rare opportunity opened, with marriage. Men rejected the career woman as a matrimonial prospect, public opinion was hostile to the dual role, and the labors of homemaking took all of a mother's time. A professional woman usually had to have some independent income or financial patronage. But a career, for most of the women of Hull-House, possessed an attraction as powerful as the distant horizon that had lured restless Daniel Boone. In a new frontier, the city slum, these women found endless fascination.

There was a qualitative difference between the unmarried career woman and the wife who had a part-time interest in public or professional activity. For the first, her work was primary; for the second, her home. Society demanded a clear choice just as firmly as did the papacy that forbade priestly marriage to prevent dual allegiance. Since any wife was frequently forced to suspend her outside activities to minister to children, husband, and home, her attachments to those activities were tenuous. The church and organizations under religious influence were her usual centers, and these recognized and preached the priority of the family. The forms were varied: the missionary circle to the Woman's Christian Temperance Union, the Women's Refuge for Reform to the Daughters of the King. Occasionally there was an individual whose activity became demonstrative, like that of Fannie Gary, daughter of the jurist. For two weeks one summer she served as a substitute for a girl in a tailor shop so the seamstress might have a vacation. No doubt the gesture was kindly, but still a gesture in comparison with the professionally directed work at Hull-House to assist working women to form unions and gain vacations through collective effort.

If a young woman wanted a career, she knew in advance

that marriage would seriously impede it. Perhaps she had never seen a poor woman try to earn a wage and raise a family (and often fail at both), but she did see her own mother bound by the rigorous discipline of cooking, preserving, laundering, child caring, shopping, and sewing. She herself had done these tasks as an apprentice. The role of housewife meant muscle work, plus skill, plus organization—without benefit of electricity, modern plumbing, gadgets, prepared or packaged food. A sewing machine was an aid to the household, but no housewife able to take pride in her table resorted to "store bread" or "store cake." Even when the family income increased and servants became available, the housewife took on responsibilities of supervision which consumed the time released from physical labor. And larger incomes led to widening social obligations.

Many married women, eager to see vocations opened to women even though they themselves did not want careers, gave valuable aid to the single, professional women. Louise de Koven Bowen, a banker's wife, relieved Jane Addams of much of the management of the Hull-House budget. Mary Rozet Smith provided a refuge for Jane Addams and her associates with her spacious home on Walton Place, removed both from the troubles of the Nineteenth Ward and from the scorn of the leisure class. But these part-time auxiliaries could escape at will from the demands of the outside world. Not so with the woman who had decided to sacrifice family life for the loneliness of individual creativity. One explanation of the success of the women of Hull-House was the toughness of the step they took.

Although Jane Addams had her own ideas about what a woman gained and what she lost by wedding a vocation, she also sought the opinion of her friend Emily Greene Balch, for twenty years the head of the department of economics at Wellesley College. As career women grew older, Miss Balch noted, they admitted that not to have married and borne children was a serious loss. But they had made their choice, and they could live with it. Miss Balch saw "no evidence that they themselves or those who know them best find in them the abnormality that the Freudian psychoanalysists of life would have one look for. They are strong, resistant and active . . . they are neither excessively repelled nor excessively attracted to that second-hand intimacy with sexuality which modern science and modern literature abundantly display. It is, however, strange to them to read interpretations of life . . . that represent sex as practically the whole content of life; family feeling, religion and art as mere camouflaged libido, and everything that is not concerned with the play of desire between men and women as without adventure, almost without interest. If the educated unmarried women of the period between the Civil War and the World War represent an unique phase, it is one that has important implications which have not yet been adequately recognized by those who insist upon the imperious claims of sex."

In the growth of Hull-House two elements stood out with increasing clarity. One was its vision, forged from Puritan morality and Lincoln's humanitarianism. The other was its insistence on visible results, an insistence that love of mankind must make changes in the way men live. Love of mankind meant the preservation of the family, school instead of factories for children, destruction of the sweating system, a reduction of the abundant wretchedness in the homes of working people.

Henry Lloyd, early in the history of Hull-House, was sure that it would be remembered a long time. "While others speculated and theorized and patented complicated mechanisms for the perpetual motion of social harmony," he wrote, "this simple and living impulse offered itself as a sacrifice to prove that all men needed to do was to live together, and that it was not sacrifice, but delight, and honour, and safety."

Jane Addams lived with people from all ranks of society. Able to talk the language of businessmen and legislators like her father, she also understood the problems and hopes of the immigrant workers in the Nineteenth Ward. Because of her experiences, and her sympathy, she was one of the handful of Chicagoans who could sense the deeper meanings of the social cataclysm that ripped the city in the summer of 1894, when Eugene Debs and the American Railway Union did battle with George M. Pullman and the Federal army.

CHAPTER 6

A Compulsory Heaven at Pullman

In so far as philanthropists . . . are cut off from the great moral life springing from our common experiences, so long as they are "good to people" rather than "with them," they are bound to accomplish a large amount of harm.

—Jane Addams *

I

GEORGE MORTIMER PULLMAN was one of the great industrialists of the age, not just one of the most successful, but also one of the most creative. Inventor, strategist, executive, he was the perfect businessman. More than that, he recognized that the lives of his employees did not end when they left the shop at night. He had a vision of a richer existence for his labor force, and out of it he built the first model town in industrial America. It was a showplace. Visitors came from all over the world to admire it. Here was the solution to the labor question. But as the years passed, George Pullman's vision proved to be both more complicated and simpler than it had seemed at first. And in May, 1894, his heaven exploded.

Pullman was born in 1831 in a small town in upstate New York, one of the ten children of a general mechanic. He quit

* "A Modern Lear," in Graham R. Taylor, ed., *Satellite Cities* (New York: D. Appleton and Company, 1915), pp. 83-85.

school early to be a cabinetmaker, then became a street contractor. His work took him to Chicago, where he quickly found a chance to show his resourcefulness. In 1858 the Tremont House, a downtown hotel, seemed to be settling into a bottomless pit of mud. Although the structure was four stories tall and made of brick, Pullman vowed that he could raise it without breaking a single pane of glass or awakening a single guest. He put 5,000 jackscrews in the basement and assembled twelve hundred men. At a signal, each man gave a half-turn to his four jackscrews. Inch by inch the building was plucked out of the morass.

Pullman began to tinker around at building a sleeping car for the Chicago & Alton Railroad. But when it was finished, the railroads were loath to adopt it; so he wandered out to the newly opened mining fields in Colorado and ran a store. By 1863 he was back in Chicago and working in earnest on his invention. His basic design, the key to which was the hinged upper berth, was just like the modern Pullman. But he decorated the car lavishly: other sleeping cars were built for about $5,000; Pullman spent $20,000 on his. In order to accommodate the berths properly, he made the car a foot wider and 2½ feet higher than ordinary railroad cars. Any railroad that wanted to use Pullmans would have to alter its bridges and its station platforms. Pullman didn't care; he was going to build his car right. He focused on one thing: maximum comfort for the passenger.

And he won out. By 1867 orders were pouring in. On every hand railroads were altering stations, bridges, culverts. The Pullman Palace Car Company was incorporated in Illinois, and gradually plants were built from New York to California. Pullman made other inventions: the restaurant car, the dining car, the chair car. He made railroad cars on contract for the railroads themselves. But his sleeping cars he would not sell. His company operated the cars itself; the railroads simply hauled them around the country. Pullman paid his stockholders a straight 8 percent dividend each year, and the rest of the profits he kept in the firm as surplus. Shares in the Pullman Company rose to twice their par value.

More manufacturing facilities were needed. And George Pullman had his vision. Other companies were frequently beset by labor troubles. Strikes occurred at crucial times and crippled production. Men got drunk and stayed home to recover. Workers strayed off to other jobs as soon as they had acquired the skill you needed. But if you gave them a really decent place to live, you could get a better class of workmen, labor turnover could be reduced, unrest would turn into contentment. Above all, if you owned the entire town, you could insulate your employees from corrupting influences. The environment could be kept as controlled and sterile as an incubator, a church, or a prison.

Some of the Pullman directors objected to using corporate funds for such a purpose. Their business, they said, was manufacturing and operating railroad cars, not real estate. But George Pullman overrode them. A perfect site for the new shops was the prairie twelve miles south of the business district of Chicago. Here was the railroad hub of the United States, accessible to more major railroads than any other spot in the country. But it was a relatively isolated spot, far from the residential areas of the working class. The only way to get a labor force was to build the housing.

But George Pullman never thought of the town solely in terms of its indirect benefits to the company. He also thought about its direct commercial value. Every dollar invested in the town was expected to yield a 6 percent return.

In 1880 the Pullman Company quietly bought a solid tract of four thousand acres, nearly seven square miles, on the west shore of Lake Calumet. It was in the town of Hyde Park, a sprawling congeries of settled areas and huge vacant stretches which adjoined Chicago. The town of Pullman was erected on three hundred acres, surrounded by an empty *cordon sanitaire*. The little community was a beautiful place, especially when compared to the filthy industrial giant just to its north. One

tenth of the area of Pullman was taken by its parks. A minia-
ture lake was created for boating and swimming. An island
in the lake was used for many types of athletics.

Every street in town was paved with macadam. The sidewalks were paved too, usually with wood, and were lined with
shade trees. The front lawn of every house in town was land-
scaped by the company. The buildings were nearly all yellow
brick, made in Pullman itself of clay dredged from the bottom
of Lake Calumet. By 1885 the town had fourteen hundred
dwelling units. Most of them had five rooms, and they were
built as row-houses. The company kept them in good repair.
There were occasional complaints in cases where two families
had to use a single toilet, but in Chicago few tenements had
any indoor plumbing at all. In other respects, too, health conditions in Pullman were excellent. Sanitation was outstanding,
the company even furnishing garbage receptacles and empty-
ing them daily.

Pullman had a higher tax assessment for school purposes
than any other area in Hyde Park. The term lasted for two
hundred days, which was incredibly generous for that time.
Schooling was free through the eighth grade, the only condition being that all students had to be vaccinated for smallpox.
Another pioneering feature was the kindergarten for children
between the ages of four and six. An evening school taught
such commercial subjects as bookkeeping and stenography.

The cultural life of the town was quite varied. Besides the
extensive athletic program, there was a theater with one thousand seats, where the foremost actors and musicians of the
time performed during the 1880's. The library, luxurious with
its Wilton carpets and plush chairs, was opened in 1883 with
an initial gift of five thousand volumes from George Pullman.
The eighty-piece Military Band, good enough one year to win
the statewide competition, was composed entirely of men who
worked for the company. During the summer it gave free
weekly concerts.

This industrial Arcadia grew year by year. It hit its peak in

1893, just before the depression struck, when the population of the town was 12,600. At that time, employment in the Pullman shops was 5,500, with many of the workers living in surrounding towns. The town grew in value too. The land had cost $800,000 in 1880. Twelve years later, George Pullman estimated that it was worth $5 million. He had reason to congratulate himself.

But he had his problems with the town. The most serious was that it never earned the return that he had expected from it. For years it paid only about 4.5 percent. In 1892 and 1893 the return further declined to 3.82 percent.

Even to get that much, Pullman had to fight a continuing war against the town of Hyde Park about his tax rates. He took no interest in civic affairs outside his own town, but his business brought him into politics anyway. In order to keep foreign competition away, he was a high-tariff man, and that prompted him to contribute heavily to the national Republican party. And his desires to keep his taxes down and to be left alone to run his town as he saw fit—together they carried him deep into local politics.

Foremen at the Pullman shops openly solicited votes for the company-approved candidates in elections. Workers were discharged because they persisted in running for public office contrary to the orders of their superiors. When John P. Hopkins, a prosperous storekeeper in Pullman, organized voters for Grover Cleveland in 1888, his landlord made life so difficult for him that he had to move his store to nearby Kensington. The Pullman Company maneuvered and manipulated and coerced for years to prevent Hyde Park from becoming part of Chicago, but in 1889 it lost that fight, and thereafter George Pullman had to go into Chicago politics to keep his taxes low.

He was an irascible, pompous man who could never see any viewpoint but his own. He thought that liquor was bad, so he banned it from the town. He thought that prostitution was bad, so he banned that too. He kept his eye on everything. He had informers in every lodge, in every social group; sometimes it seemed that he had them in every parlor on Saturday night. He wanted to know everything that happened. The town was his, and he would run it his way. He believed in thrift and hard work and sobriety. He believed in individual responsibility and the other Puritan virtues.

But many of his workers came from other traditions. As early as 1884 more than half of the residents were foreign-born. Eight years later, 72 percent were, including 23 percent Scandinavian, 12 percent British, the same proportion of Germans, 10 percent Dutch, 5 percent Irish. Many of them could see no harm in a pint of beer. Many of them wanted to worship in their own faith.

George Pullman had his ideas about that too. There was one church building in town. Pullman owned it, just as he owned everything else. He was a Universalist who didn't care about doctrinal niceties, but the church was nonsectarian. It was part of the business; it too had to pay its way. The rent set on it by Pullman was so high that no congregation in town could afford to pay it. The Presbyterians tried it for a few years and went bankrupt. The resultant bitterness was summed up by one Presbyterian minister: "I preached once in the Pullman church, but by the help of God I will never preach there again. The word monopoly seems to be written in black letters over the pulpit and the pews." George Pullman didn't care.

From the very beginning, Pullman's high-handed ways aroused opposition. Prior to 1882 the shops had been expanded more rapidly than the housing facilities. Many employees were still living in Chicago, and they had to pay a round-trip fare of 20 cents a day on the Illinois Central to get back and forth to work. The company paid this fare. Then it announced that it would pay only half. A thousand men struck. The strike was broken; the ringleaders fired.

In March, 1884, a group of 150 men in the freight-car department struck against a wage cut. That strike was broken too. Then the company learned a new technique. In October,

1885, it instituted a wage cut of 10 percent. But the reduction was introduced first in one department, then in another; the workers were never unified against it. So a strike did not come until the following spring, when an estimated fourteen hundred workers at Pullman were members of the Knights of Labor. They joined in the general movement for an eight-hour day that was sweeping through Chicago, and to the general demand they added their own—a 10 percent pay increase, to recoup what they had lost. The company refused; the workers struck; within ten days the shops were reopened under guard.

George Pullman wanted no truck with trade unions—and for the next eight years there was no effort at organization in his plant. Small strikes occurred in 1888 and 1891, but they were hardly serious enough to be annoying. In 1893 the company could announce smugly: "During the eleven years the town has been in existence, the Pullman workingman has developed into a distinctive type—distinct in appearance, in dress, in fact, in all the external indications of self-respect. . . . ." A typical group of Pullman employees, said the statement, was "40 percent better in evidence of thrift and refinement and in all the outward indications of a wholesome way of life" than any comparable group in America.

The "outward indications"—Pullman could usually control those. But he could not legislate against the bitterness within. As one man protested: "We are born in a Pullman house, fed from the Pullman shop, taught in the Pullman school, catechized in the Pullman church, and when we die we shall be buried in the Pullman cemetery and go to the Pullman hell."

A year after the Company had congratulated itself, the inward bitterness of its employees burst forth in action, and the "distinctive type" of workingman proved that, if goaded hard enough, he could be an unruly ingrate like anybody else.

II

The financial policies of the Pullman Palace Car Company

throughout its history had been so sound that the firm was in excellent position to meet the depression in 1893; usual dividends could have been maintained for years out of the undivided surplus that had been accumulated. But businessmen care about current income as well as about liquidity, and the gross receipts of the Pullman Company fell drastically in 1893. Income from operating its sleeping and dining cars held up well, but much of the firm's manufacturing activity consisted in filling orders from other firms for various types of railroad cars. These outside orders now dried up almost entirely: no railroad adds new equipment when much of what it has is idle.

George Pullman was not a man to stand quietly with his hands in his pockets while his money seeped away. He responded vigorously with a program of lay-offs, reduced hours, wage cuts. In July, 1893, the shops at Pullman employed 5,500 men; the following May, only 3,300. Wage rates were slashed an average of 25 percent, but the pay cuts were far from uniform: machinists in the street-car department claimed that their wages had been reduced more than 70 percent. At a time when painters in Chicago—those lucky enough to be employed —were getting 35 cents an hour, the painters at Pullman were paid 23 cents an hour.

These policies were superbly effective, as the company's accountants had reason to know:

Year ending July 31	Wages	Dividends
1893	$7,223,719	$2,520,000
1894	4,471,701	2,880,000

The outlay for wages had been reduced 38 percent in a single year; but dividends were actually increased. And the company had an undistributed surplus for the year 1893-1894 of $2,320,-000!

During all this time, rental charges for housing in Pullman were not reduced. Renting houses was one thing; employing workmen was another; the two had no connection. And so long as the capital invested in the housing remained the same, why should rents be reduced? In regard to this, a Federal commission later concluded: "If we exclude the aesthetic and sanitary features at Pullman, the rents there are from 20 to 25 percent higher than rents in Chicago or surrounding towns for similar accommodations. The aesthetic features are admired by visitors, but have little money value to employees, especially when they lack bread."

As early as December, 1893, the Pullman Company felt constrained to issue a statement denying that extreme distress existed among the residents of Pullman. So the winter dragged on, and the workers and their families suffered. Since George Pullman had always managed the town arbitrarily, its institutions of local government were anemic. The town had no mechanisms for public relief, which was contrary to the owner's ideas of individual self-help. But the typical worker was hesitant to move away even after he had been laid off by the shops. House rents in Pullman were higher than elsewhere, but unemployment was everywhere, and the workers believed that residents of Pullman would be the first to be rehired. So destitution became unbearable; yet there was nothing to do except bear it. In some homes the children lacked the shoes and coats needed to go to school in the severe Illinois winter; in others they were kept in bed all day because there was no coal in the house.

And then came a voice of hope. A dim hope—yes, but still it was something. The previous spring, June, 1893, just as the depression was beginning, fifty railroad workers had met in Chicago to form the American Railway Union. Prior to that time the only trade unions on the railroads had been the various Brotherhoods, a separate one for each of the main occupations in railroading. The Brotherhoods of skilled workers, such as the Engineers, were the strongest and best organized, and they tended always to sneer at their fellow workers in the less skilled crafts—the switchmen, the brakemen, even the locomotive firemen—and they hardly recognized the existence of the men who worked on the railroads but had nothing to do with operating trains, such as the section hands.

The utter lack of cooperation, verging often on civil war, among the various Brotherhoods made it impossible for the unskilled crafts to bargain effectively with the railroads, and even the Engineers achieved many of their gains by ruthlessly sacrificing the interests of other crafts. Beginning about 1885, a movement developed in each of the Brotherhoods that aimed at bringing about joint action among them. Finally in 1889 the Supreme Council of the United Orders of Railway Employes was formed, consisting of the officers of several of the Brotherhoods. The organization for a time seemed to be working well, and it appeared that the other Brotherhoods would join and even that ultimately they might all merge into one big Brotherhood of railroad workers—one industrial union rather than many craft unions. But within less than two years, one of the member Brotherhoods conspired with the Chicago & Northwestern Railroad to destroy another of the member Brotherhoods. The Supreme Council collapsed.

The episode caused some of the more radical officials in the Brotherhoods to despair of their conservative fellows, who seemed determined to seek their own selfish ends and to block any moves toward unification of the different organizations. Chief among these dissidents was Eugene Victor Debs, secretary-treasurer of the Brotherhood of Locomotive Firemen since 1880 and editor of its magazine. When Debs took these jobs, the order was small and moribund, with sixty inactive lodges and a substantial debt. Twelve years later it was out of debt, had twenty thousand members, and was solidly established. Much of this progress was due to Debs personally: to his zeal, his dedication, his relentless drive, above all to his concern for the welfare of the poor.

Thirty-eight years old in 1893, he was a man of awesome vigor. His life was one perpetual organizing trip. Every day, day after day, he could travel two or three hundred miles, give a half-dozen speeches, and have energy left for a good deal of sociable drinking. His stamina welled outward from a tall, austere frame and a copious spirit. Debs was a visionary. He pictured a land from which poverty, whether of the body or of the heart, had disappeared, a land where violence was not even a bad memory, an America where everybody treated his fellows generously of his own will, because he could do no other, an America where everybody smiled and everybody sang.

But he knew that no man can smile with another's face or sing in a foreign language. Debs was no George Pullman, carrying a prefabricated Utopia around in his vest pocket. He spoke of the evils of this world and of the possibility of a better one. About the evils he was explicit: poverty, arbitrary power, treating men solely in terms of their cash value, one man imposing his will on another. But he never spelled out the details of the better life he was always talking about. He exhorted men to love one another; beyond that, they would have to find their own way. Men cannot be driven at all; and they cannot be led down a narrow and fenced road to a waiting corral. The job of leadership is to point a general direction and to awaken in men the hope that they can move in that direction. Debs could do this. When he talked, men came to life, and they moved. He was an agitator. To agitate, all that he needed was to feel sure himself of the general direction that men should go.

In 1892 he was sure. He was fed up with the internecine warfare of the Brotherhoods, which saw each of them cut the throat of the others for some selfish and short-term gain. He was gagging on the smug arrogance of the Brotherhood of Locomotive Engineers. He wanted to see an organization that would really protect the railroaders, all of them, against the tyranny and exploitation of the corporations. But when he declined to stand for reelection as secretary-treasurer of the Firemen in 1892, his plans were very general: "It has been my life's desire to unify railroad employees and to eliminate the aristocracy of labor, which unfortunately exists, and organize them so all will be on an equality." The following spring Debs was one of the founders of the American Railway Union, and became its president.

The ARU started its first local lodge on August 17, 1893. Thereafter a flash flood of members threatened to drown Debs and the two other full-time organizers. Within twenty days, thirty-four lodges had been chartered. Members were joining at the rate of two hundred to four hundred men a day. Entire lodges of Railway Carmen and Switchmen changed their affiliation to the ARU. Conductors, firemen, even engineers, joined the new industrial union. But most of the applicants were previously unorganized men in the less skilled crafts who had been excluded from the Brotherhoods. These were the engine wipers, the section hands, the most exploited and worst paid men on the railroads, who had formerly been left to suffer in isolation. Now they rushed toward the organization that had opened its ranks to them, rushed so eagerly that the ARU had eighty-seven local lodges by mid-November: for three months, a new lodge every day. The surge continued over the winter, and in the spring of 1894 it was vastly accelerated when the ARU won the first strike that any union had ever won against a major railroad.

James J. Hill's Great Northern Railroad stretched westward from Minneapolis clear to the Pacific. When its employees went on strike in April, direction of the walk-out quickly passed into the hands of Debs and his colleagues. After the entire line had been closed down nearly a fortnight, the St. Paul Chamber of Commerce demanded that Hill and the union should submit the dispute to arbitration. They did so. The award gave the strikers 97½ percent of their demands, an aggregate wage increase of $1,752,000 a year.

Although this victory was won in the Twin Cities, it was widely publicized in Chicago, where the ARU centered in many ways. Its national headquarters were there. Most of its local lodges were on roads running from Chicago westward. And it was there that Debs gave a fervent speech at the Columbian Exposition. It was in the autumn of 1893, before the dreadful winter at Pullman, and Debs did not mention George Pullman by name, but his speech contained an unqualified attack on Pullman's type of paternalism:

> The time is coming, fortunately, when we are hearing less of that old paternal Pharisaism: "What can we do for labor?" It is the old, old query repeated all along the centuries, heard wherever a master wielded a whip above the bowed forms of the slaves . . . We hear it yet, occasionally, along lines of transportation, in mines and shops, but our ears are regaled by a more manly query, . . . which is, "What can labor do for itself?" The answer is not difficult. Labor can organize, it can unify, it can consolidate its forces. This done, it can demand and command.

And in the spring of 1894, at the time of the victory over the Great Northern, the workers in the Pullman shops began to take Debs's advice. They were eligible for membership in the ARU because the Pullman Company operated a few miles of railroad leading to its shops, and, man by man, they joined. Their money was gone, and their patience with it. One blacksmith, when he worked six hours and was paid 45 cents, said that if he had to starve, he saw no reason why he should wear out his clothes at Pullman's anvil at the same time.

The workers went to the vice-president of the company and presented their demands. The official promised to investigate. The grievance committee held a meeting. Even though the top officials of the ARU urged delay, the committee voted a strike. Of the 3,300 workers in the factory, more than 90 percent walked out together on May 11. The company promptly laid off the others. Three days later, Eugene Debs was in Pullman. He had advised against the strike. But after walking through the town, hearing the stories, seeing the paychecks, he realized that it had been an act of desperation. Even the local leader of the strike said that they did not expect to win. They just didn't know what else to do.

The strike dragged along until June 12, when the first national convention of the American Railway Union met in Chicago. In one year, the organization had enrolled 150,000 members. The total membership of all the Brotherhoods was 90,000. But success had not gone to Debs's head. He knew that the union was loosely organized, that it was largely uncoordinated, that it had little money, that it was scanted for experienced leaders, especially in the farflung local lodges. The ARU had won its battle against the Great Northern; Debs was not sure it could win another against an equally powerful corporation.

A committee from Pullman appeared before the convention and made a plea: "We struck because we were without hope. We joined the American Railway Union because it gave us a glimmer of hope. . . . We will make you proud of us, brothers, if you will give us the hand we need. Help us make our country better and more wholesome." A seamstress at Pullman, thin and tired, came to tell how, when her father died, she had been forced to repay $60 back rent that he owed the company.

The sentimental delegates were swept by indignation. One suggested that the convention declare a boycott of Pullman cars. Debs, who was presiding, refused to entertain the motion. Using every recourse available to a chairman to thwart actions that he disapproves, Debs suggested a committee from the convention to confer with the Pullman Company. Twelve men, including six strikers, were chosen to go to the company and propose arbitration of the wage dispute.

The committee returned next day to the convention, to report that the Pullman Company had refused to confer with any members of the ARU. Again a boycott was proposed. Again Debs blocked it. A second committee, consisting solely of strikers, was sent to the company with a request for arbitration. The company said that there was "nothing to arbitrate." After voting relief funds for the strikers at Pullman, the convention set up another committee to recommend a plan of action. When the recommendation came on June 22, it was direct: Unless the Pullman Company agreed, not to a settlement, but merely to begin negotiations within four days, the American Railway Union should refuse to handle Pullman cars. Again Debs urged caution. But the delegates, in no humor for pussyfooting, adopted the committee's report.

Then the committee was sent back to Pullman for a final effort. The firm would concede nothing. Nothing. Its position was that wages and working conditions should be determined by management, with no interference by labor. So the ARU convention unanimously voted the boycott. Debs, his hand forced, devised the tactic: switchmen in the ARU would refuse to switch any Pullman cars onto trains. If the switchmen were discharged or disciplined for this refusal, all ARU members on the line would cease work at once.

III

The boycott began at noon on June 26. At once the union was opposed by the railroads, which took an active hand in the conflict. Here was their chance to cut the ARU down to size. Unified by the General Managers Association, the twenty-four railroads running out of Chicago—with a combined capital of $818 million, with 221,000 employees—declared that their contracts with Pullman were sacred and that they would operate no trains without Pullman cars.

Deadlock. By June 29, twenty railroads were tied up. An estimated 125,000 men had quit work. Agents of the General Managers were busy in Eastern cities hiring unemployed railroaders as strikebreakers. Leaders of the Railroad Brotherhoods were denouncing the ARU. Eugene Debs was sending telegrams all over the Great Plains advising his members to use no violence and to stop no trains forcibly; they should simply refuse to handle Pullmans. But the Illinois Central claimed that its property at Cairo, Illinois, was in danger, so Governor Altgeld, with the permission of the local authorities, sent three companies of the state militia there. A crowd stopped a train at Hammond, Indiana, and forced the crew to detach two

Pullmans. Two other trains were temporarily stopped by mobs in Chicago. But there were no major riots. No mail had accumulated in Chicago. As late as July 5, total strike damages to railroad property were less than $6,000.

But the facts were being misrepresented. The Federal district attorney in Chicago wired Washington on June 29 that conditions there were so bad that special deputies were needed. The newspapers were hysterical, with headlines like "Mob Is In Control" and "Law Is Trampled On." The real cause of concern was stated by the Chicago *Herald:* "If the strike should be successful the owners of the railroad property . . . would have to surrender its future control to the class of labor agitators and strike conspirators who have formed the Debs Railway Union." It became common for the press to refer to "Dictator Debs."

Then the Federal government took a hand. On June 30 the General Managers telegraphed Richard B. Olney, Attorney General of the United States, urging him to appoint Edwin Walker as special Federal attorney to handle the strike situation. Walker had been since 1870, and was, at the time of the strike, attorney for a railroad that belonged to the General Managers. But Olney didn't even pause to consult the Federal district attorney on the spot before making the appointment.

Olney, a man as tyrannical as George Pullman, also sent Walker some pointed advice: that the best way to cope with conditions was "by a force which is overwhelming and prevents any attempt at resistance." Olney believed that a national railroad strike was illegal by definition, and that the local and state officials in Illinois could not be trusted to handle matters. In his judgment, the strikers were impeding interstate commerce and the movement of the United States mails. On either score President Cleveland could have used the Federal army to remove the obstructions. But Olney doubted that Cleveland would act except to enforce the order of a Federal court. So the thing to do was to get such an order.

On July 2 in Chicago, Edwin Walker and the Federal district

attorney drafted an application for an injunction against the strike leaders. They were aided in its revision, before court opened, by Judges Peter Grosscup and William A. Woods. Satisfied at last, the two judges ascended their impartial bench and granted the application. The breadth of their order was breathtaking: the strike leaders were enjoined from any deed to encourage the boycott. They could not send telegrams about it, or talk about it, or write about it.

If the ARU leaders obeyed the injunction, the boycott would collapse; central coordination was essential. But if they did not obey it, all strikers would be in active opposition to the Federal government, and the leaders might well go to jail for contempt of court. Debs and his colleagues decided to ignore the writ. Debs declared bitterly, "The crime of the American Railway Union was the practical exhibition of sympathy for the Pullman employees." Sympathy was Christian, but practical sympathy was dangerous.

The Attorney General's plan worked out well. If the injunction was sweeping, enforcement of it was more so. An ARU official later testified: "Men have been arrested in Chicago because they refused to turn switches when told to; they were arrested when they refused to get on an engine and fire an engine." So by interpretation, the injunction forbade action by an individual as well as by the group, and required action in addition to forbidding it.

Olney hit a snag when he first proposed sending Federal troops to Chicago: the Secretary of War and the Army Chief of Staff both opposed it. But on July 3 he received a telegram saying that no agency but the army could protect the mails. There was no proof of the statement, but the telegram was signed by Judge Grosscup, Edwin Walker, and the Federal district attorney in Chicago. Now Grover Cleveland was ready to move. On the morning of Independence Day, by his orders, the entire command from Fort Sheridan turned out for active duty in Chicago.

The ARU was incensed. So was Governor Altgeld. The

Constitution gives the President power to send the army into a state "on Application of the Legislature, or of the Executive (when the Legislature cannot be convened)" in order to protect the state "against domestic Violence." Altgeld protested to the President that neither he nor the legislature had asked for help. Three regiments of state militia in Chicago could be mustered into active service, but "nobody in Cook county, whether official or private citizen," had asked for their help. The local and state authorities were adequate to what little violence had occurred. "At present some of our railroads are paralyzed," Altgeld told the President, "not by reason of obstruction, but because they cannot get men to operate their trains. . . . The newspaper accounts have in many cases been pure fabrications, and in others wild exaggerations." Lastly, Altgeld protested that "local self-government is a fundamental principle of our Constitution. Each community shall govern itself so long as it can and is ready and able to enforce the law."

The President's reply was brief. He wired back that the postal authorities had asked for the removal of obstructions to the mails, that Judge Grosscup had asked for help in enforcing the injunction, and that there was "competent proof that conspiracies existed against commerce between the states." Any of these conditions, Cleveland contended, was ample to give him power to order Federal troops into Illinois.

Altgeld reasserted his position forcibly and at length. The President closed the discussion curtly: "While I am still persuaded that I have neither transcended my authority nor duty in the emergency that confronts us, it seems to me that in this hour of danger and public distress, discussion may well give way to active efforts on the part of all in authority to restore obedience to law and to protect life and property."

Although Governor Altgeld had to yield to the power of the army, similar protests were made by the governors of four other states. And the dispute between state and Federal officials served to underscore an issue that was not merely constitutional; it was political and ethical also. Even assuming that the President had properly enforced the law as it existed at the time, his action seemed grossly partisan. The full thrust of Federal power was exerted to break the boycott, while nothing was done—nothing was said—to incline George Pullman or the railroads toward a peaceful settlement. Eugene Debs spoke for a sizable group when he telegraphed the President that "a deep-seated conviction is fast becoming prevalent that this Government is soon to be declared a military despotism." This issue of public policy could be resolved only at the ballot boxes and in the convention halls, and in 1896 John Peter Altgeld was to get his revenge against Grover Cleveland.

But for the time the army ruled—along with five thousand special Federal deputy marshals. Since these temporary jobs were unattractive to most men, they were filled by petty criminals, labor spies, riff-raff generally. Local officials told of special deputies who fired without reason into crowds, wantonly killed bystanders, stole property from railroad cars, cut fire hoses while cars burned. The result was chaos. On July 5, the day after the army reached Chicago, violence there was more serious than before. The next day it reached its peak; railroad tracks were blocked, dozens of railroad cars were burned—a crime for which nobody was ever indicted. Total damage in the one day was $340,000, although on no other day was it more than $4,000. If the army and special deputies were meant to keep the peace, their immediate effect was just the opposite.

Eugene Debs, continuing his efforts to prevent violence, again told the strikers: "Our men have the right to quit, but their right ends there. Other men have the right to take their places, whatever the opinion of the propriety of so doing may be. Keep away from railroad yards, or right of way, or other places where large crowds congregate. A safe plan is to remain away entirely from places where there is any likelihood of an outbreak." Debs repeatedly argued that the rioting was being done by hooligans, not by strikers. During the entire boycott, not a single ARU member in Chicago was killed or wounded by the law-enforcement authorities.

The outbreak of violence was distressing; the propaganda about it was chilling. In Chicago, headlines read:

Unparalleled Scenes of Riot, Terror and Pillage
Anarchy is Rampant
THIRSTY FOR BLOOD
Frenzied Mob Still Bent on Death and Destruction
Violence on Every Hand

Newspapers and ministers charged that Debs was a dipsomaniac. A Brooklyn cleric declared: "The soldiers must use their guns. They must shoot to kill." One of the most prominent religious leaders in the country revived the themes of a year earlier by calling Governor Altgeld the "crowned hero and worshiped deity of the Anarchists of the Northwest."

On July 10, with the boycott obviously on its last legs, a Federal grand jury in Chicago delivered another blow by indicting Debs and three of his colleagues for conspiracy to obstruct a mail train on the Rock Island Railroad. Arrested at once, the four men were released on bail within a few hours, but their freedom made little practical difference. The next day trains were moving even in California, where the boycott had been most effective. The mayors of Chicago and Detroit made a futile call on the vice-president of the Pullman Company to again request arbitration. They found him unyielding. "The issue at question, which was simply that of reopening the shops at Pullman, and carrying them on at a ruinous loss, was not a proper subject for arbitration," he was reported to have said.

The boycott dragged along another week, while at Pullman the leader of the original strikers announced that they were being starved into submission. Then, on July 17, Debs and his associates were again arrested, this time for violating the July 2 injunction. They refused to post bail and were imprisoned. Twenty-four hours later a notice was put up on the gates of the Pullman shops: "These gates will be opened as soon as the number of operatives is sufficient to make a working force in all departments." It was the end.

Of the men now hired at Pullman, one of every four had not worked there before the strike. Every applicant was forced to sign a pledge that he would not join any union. A thousand former employees were left destitute. Governor Altgeld appealed to the Pullman Company to help them. He got no reply. Altgeld then called upon the public for a relief fund. Even the Chicago *Tribune* cooperated in raising it.

In January, 1895, the ARU leaders were brought to trial on the conspiracy charges. For nearly a month their lawyers, Clarence Darrow and S. S. Gregory, used the proceedings as a forum to indict the prosecution. Eugene Debs, seeming very much a benign and immaculate businessman, testified at length about his career on the railroads. Leaders of the General Managers were called to the stand, where they could "not remember" what had happened at their meetings. Then a juror became ill. After four days Judge Grosscup discharged the jury and continued the case until May. It was never reopened.

But Debs went to jail anyway, for six months, for having violated the injunction. The case went all the way to the United States Supreme Court, where the union leaders were represented by Darrow, Gregory, and the aging Lyman Trumbull. The Court decision virtually ignored the Sherman Act, on which the injunction had been based. Instead the Court unanimously ruled that the equity powers of Federal courts could be used to prevent interference with the mails and with interstate commerce. An injunction, regardless of the validity of its provisions, must be obeyed. Violation could be punished by a jail sentence. And it was.

IV

The end of the boycott did not end the shouting and pondering about what it had meant. President Samuel Gompers of the American Federation of Labor, in sending Debs a contribution to his legal defense, said the money was intended "as a protest against the exercise of class justice, and as a further protest against the violation of rights guaranteed by the Constitution and the Declaration of Independence." In opposition to this was the New York *Tribune,* which charged that Debs was a self-seeking dictator and warned the working people against "surrendering their liberty and prosperity into the hands of a single individual."

A Federal investigating commission appointed by President Cleveland, after hearing testimony from railroad officials, strikers, union leaders, public servants, denounced Pullman's refusal to arbitrate the dispute. The report urged compulsory arbitration as insurance against future strikes on the railroads. Ultimate responsibility for the Pullman boycott, said the commission, "rests with the people themselves and with the government for not adequately controlling monopolies and corporations, and for failing to reasonably protect the rights of labor and redress its wrongs."

Four years later another governmental body, the supreme court of Illinois, passed judgment on one element in the situation that had led to the Pullman strike. Holding that the corporation had no right under its charter to construct the town of Pullman, the court ordered the Pullman Company to dispose of all property not required for its manufacturing activities. Company towns such as this, said the court, were "opposed to good public policy and incompatible with the theory and spirit of our institutions."

The poet Eugene Field, a Chicago newspaperman during the strike, was concerned with the characters of the men involved: "If ye be ill, or poor, or starving, or oppressed, or in grief, your chances for sympathy and for succor from E. V. Debs are 100 where your chances with G. M. Pullman would be the little end of nothing whittled down."

But it was left for Jane Addams, in a speech before the Chicago Woman's Club, to give the most searching interpretation of "the shocking experiences of that summer, the barbaric instinct to kill, roused on both sides, the sharp division into class lines with the resultant distrust and bitterness." All this, she declared, could be endured only if it resulted in some "great ethical lesson."

Like Eugene Field, she was impressed by "the manifestation of moral power" in the efforts of the American Railway Union to aid the strikers at Pullman, men who had done nothing to help the union but were helped by it. Here was evidence that the workingmen were beginning to act on new watchwords: "brotherhood, sacrifice, the subordination of individual and trade interests to the good of the working class." Nor was George Pullman open to indiscriminate condemnation. His standard for treatment of his employees, "exceptionally liberal in many of its aspects," had been close to the ideal of "the best of the present employers." Pullman had manifested that ideal more fully than the others. "He alone gave his men so model a town, such perfect surroundings." His policies, in fact, had seemed to many businessmen a case of intemperate sympathy for the lower classes.

But Pullman had been utterly blind to the "touch of nobility" in the ARU sympathetic boycott. He could recognize nothing as virtuous except the individualism that he had learned in his youth, the ruthless self-reliance that had brought him to the top of the heap. And ironically, he had actually succeeded in teaching part of that morality to his employees at Pullman, so that throughout the strike they were "self-controlled and destroyed no property."

Pullman's failure, then, was the failure of an ideal. The magnitude of his indulgence was matched by the magnitude of the disaster it engendered. He was—and here Jane Addams took her title—"A Modern Lear." King Lear too was lavish in his gifts. Only he had kingdoms to give, and he gave them. But he demanded from everybody the acknowledgment that all gifts flowed from him. He insisted on his right to do things for people, and denied them the right to do things for themselves. He demanded the right for his will to impose itself on others.

Similarly George Pullman, insisting on his right to be a benefactor, had grown away from "the power of attaining a simple human relationship with his employees, that of frank equality with them." Pullman had ceased to be a part of "the great moral life springing from our common experiences," and by setting himself above the common run of men he had done an immense amount of harm. He had failed to sense "that the social passion of the age is directed toward the emancipation of the wage-worker; that a great accumulation of moral force is overmastering men and making for this emancipation as in another time it made for the emancipation of the slave; that nothing will satisfy the aroused conscience of men short of the complete participation of the working classes in the spiritual, intellectual and material inheritance of the human race."

But in this noble effort the workingmen must not become selfish or vindictive. The story of King Lear holds a lesson for them, too. At the beginning of the play Cordelia seeks her salvation alone. She demands her right to be herself, but her vision is not broad enough to include her father. By the time her conscience has reached out to enfold the blinded Lear, "the cruelty and wrath" had become "objective and tragic." Only then, on their way to prison and probable death, do Lear and Cordelia find salvation together. The Pullman strike should be a warning that "the emancipation of the working people will have to be inclusive of the employer from the first or it will encounter many failures, cruelties and reactions."

Jane Addams called on all would-be philanthropists to remember "the old definition of greatness: that it consists in the possession of the largest share of the common human qualities and experiences, not in the acquirements of peculiarities and excessive virtues." The greatest of all Americans was the man who had gathered to himself "the largest amount of American experience": Abraham Lincoln. Seeking to draw out the vital center of Lincoln's life, Jane Addams concluded:

The man who insists upon consent, who moves with the people, is bound to consult the feasible right as well as the absolute right. He is often obliged to attain only Mr. Lincoln's "best possible," and often have the sickening sense of compromising with his best convictions. He has to move along with those whom he rules toward a goal that neither he nor they see very clearly until they come to it. He has to discover what people really want, and then "provide the channels in which the growing moral force of their lives shall flow." What he does attain, however, is not the result of his individual striving, as a solitary mountain climber beyond the sight of the valley multitude, but it is underpinned and upheld by the sentiments and aspirations of many others. Progress has been slower perpendicularly, but incomparably greater because lateral.

CHAPTER 7

Anti-Monopoly

Republicans . . . are for both the man and the dollar, but in
case of conflict the man before the dollar.
—Abraham Lincoln to H. L. Pierce and others,
April 6, 1859 *

I

IN THE DECADES after the Civil War, most political conflicts
were mere jockeying for party advantage. But the dispute
about government policy toward the Pullman boycott was un-
usual in being almost a pure conflict of principle. The public officials involved were all Democrats: Cleveland, Olney,
Altgeld, and John P. Hopkins, who had been run out of Pullman in 1888 only to be elected mayor of Chicago at a special
election in December, 1893. And the dispute about principle
prompted Altgeld to begin a bitter, sustained effort to wrest
control of his party from President Cleveland and the Eastern
conservatives.

This effort was especially presumptuous because Altgeld's
influence was often slight in the Democratic party of his own
state. The legislature in 1893, although the Democrats were
the majority, had ignored most of his recommendations; Clay-
ton Crafts, who had become speaker of the lower house with

* In P. Stern, ed., *The Life and Writings of Abraham Lincoln* (New York:
Modern Library, 1942), p. 539.

168

Altgeld's support, had openly combined with a few other members to block all laws on which they could not make money for themselves. "No measure to in any way regulate corrupt corporations could be passed," Altgeld declared. "In fact, the corporations ran the legislature and Mr. Crafts was simply a convenience for them, while thus using his power to prevent the passage of any labor measure or any other measure of value." It had been common talk in Springfield in 1893, said Altgeld, that Crafts had made $50,000 that year.

Altgeld's power with the legislature was even less after the 1894 elections. Yerkes wanted to get renewals of several key Chicago street-car franchises well before they expired in 1903. He therefore spent money lavishly in buying control of the nominating conventions (both parties, of course) in the legislative districts in 1894, with the result that most of the Democratic nominees were friendly to his wishes. Partly because of that, partly because of disgust nationally with the Democrats, the Republicans swept the election. They won substantial majorities in both houses of the legislature. They won twenty of the Illinois seats in Congress to only two for the Democrats.

Altgeld was not deterred from presenting a broad program to the legislature, but he never expected most of it to pass. Soon after the election he wrote a friend: "Don Quixote you remember attacked windmills. I have attacked a good many things and will probably fare as he did." The Governor explained that he was going to agitate for many reforms, hoping that some of them could be achieved in later years. He did exactly that, and, considering the obstacles he faced, he also achieved a surprisingly good record of practical results.

The legislature passed a law setting a maximum workday of eight hours for women. But the state supreme court invalidated it: by forbidding women to work more than eight hours a day, you were depriving them of life, liberty, or property without due process of law, in violation of the Fourteenth Amendment. Florence Kelley and her subordinates in the state factory inspector's office forced many factories to cease hiring child labor and to correct unsafe or unsanitary conditions. In the summer of 1895 Altgeld called the legislature into special session and asked it for machinery to arbitrate labor disputes. The board that was set up was quite different from what he requested: it had three permanent members representing labor, employers, and the public. In its first seventeen months the board was able to mediate thirty-eight of the forty-one disputes in which it took an interest. In the three other instances, the employer refused to recognize the board, which had no powers of compulsion.

The Governor was able to make realities of some of the visions he had announced in *Our Penal Machinery and Its Victims*. His efforts led to the establishment of indeterminate sentences and the parole system. The term of probation was set at six months, after which the prisoner might be discharged for good. If he violated his parole, he went back to prison to serve the maximum term for his offense. Prison inmates were given plain gray suits in place of stripes. A new reformatory for girls was established. Altgeld sought, largely in vain, to establish new industries inside the prisons so that inmates would learn a trade and be useful members of society—an effort that was steadfastly opposed by trade unions.

His attempt to reform the court system also failed, although he repeatedly called attention to unjust delays, biased grand juries, and the abuses in Chicago police courts. He granted pardons in all cases where it could be shown that the trial had been unfair. But what he aimed at was strict justice, not softhearted mercy; several of his predecessors had been more liberal in granting pardons and commutations than he was.

The Governor ordered that competitive bidding be instituted for all purchases of supplies by state agencies. He required the annual publication of detailed payrolls. Previously custodians of state funds had been allowed to keep the interest on such funds for themselves; now they were required to pay the interest into the public treasury. The legislature even passed a bill authorizing cities to set up civil service systems if the voters approved the law by popular vote. Less than two weeks after the law became operative, it was adopted by Chicago, but it was only mildly successful in eliminating the spoils system.

In accord with Altgeld's demands during his campaign in 1892, the Edwards law was repealed. Kindergartens were added to the public school system, and a state pension fund for teachers was established. But Altgeld's chief contribution to education was in building up the University of Illinois. When he took office it was a trivial school of agricultural and mechanical arts: twenty-six professors, fewer than six hundred students, an appropriation for the preceding two years of only $96,000. The first biennial appropriation under Altgeld was three times that. By 1897 the University had established a law school, a medical school, and a school of pharmacy.

The Governor used his power to extend the public parks of Chicago. Most of the shore of Lake Michigan south of the Chicago River had fallen into private hands and was contaminated by industrial filth; Altgeld determined that the Lake Front on the North Side must be preserved and developed for the rest and recreation of Chicago's citizens. When the board of commissioners of Lincoln Park showed itself hostile to this aim, he demanded that half of its members resign, including some of his own appointees. His actions resulted in the extension of the park as he wished.

Altgeld's aim was to reduce special privileges and to foster equality of opportunity. His method was to vastly expand the powers and activities of the state government and use it to improve the lives of ordinary people. Obviously this would require increased tax revenues. Therefore when the Supreme Court of the United States in 1895 ruled that a Federal income tax was unconstitutional, Altgeld declared that the Court had "come to the rescue of the Standard Oil kings, the Wall Street people, as well as the rich mugwumps." On the state level he pressed unsuccessfully for fairness in the assessment of property values, citing the Pullman Company and the Chicago

Tribune as beneficiaries of favoritism. Under his urging the legislature also levied the first inheritance tax in Illinois.

With this program, Altgeld was pioneering a basic realignment of American politics. Most upper-class reformers emphasized a reduction of taxes, elimination of graft, and efficiency in government. These measures had no appeal for the workingman: efficiency was too heartless and could mean cutting him off the city payroll; elimination of graft would make it impossible for the ward boss to be so liberal with the dispossessed; reduction of taxes would mean reduction of public services. To win these voters away from the bosses (or, as actually happened, to force the bosses to take up reform in order to hold their constituents), reformers had to advocate positive measures such as workmen's compensation and factory legislation. (Progressives were slow to learn this lesson, but Franklin Roosevelt understood it well: during the New Deal the government took over many functions that had formerly belonged to the political machines.)

But when all this is said, perhaps Altgeld's main achievements as governor were negative ones. He was outstanding less for what he did than for what he prevented. In the Haymarket case he thwarted a continuation of injustice. In the Pullman strike he denounced biased use of Federal authority and the infringement of States' rights. And twenty-three times he vetoed acts of the legislature as being destructive of the public interest. Among the vetoed acts were the Eternal Monopoly bills.

The city council of Chicago in February, 1895, granted a franchise to the unknown Ogden Gas Company, authorizing it to charge 90 cents per 1,000 cubic feet. The existing company in Chicago, the so-called Gas Trust, charged $1.25. Everybody suspected that the Ogden Gas Company had no intention at all of producing and selling gas: that it was purely a scheme of Mayor Hopkins and Roger Sullivan, well on his way to becoming Democratic boss of Illinois, to blackmail the Gas Trust into buying from them their nonexistent property.

And to sew up their scheme, they had a bill introduced in the legislature providing that no city council could grant a gas franchise until the recipient of the franchise had the consent of a majority of the street-frontage on each block where it proposed to lay gas mains. Since the Gas Trust could always stymie these permissions for at least one block, the law was equivalent to saying that no franchise could be granted to a new company. And the legislature passed the bill.

At the same time Yerkes collected his reward for his lavish expenditures in the 1894 elections. In 1874 the Illinois legislature had decreed that no city could grant a franchise to any street railway for a term longer than twenty years. But now the Humphrey Act floated (on a generous stream of boodle) through both houses of the legislature. It extended several of Yerkes' key franchises for a full ninety-nine years—without providing for any payment at all by the companies to the city of Chicago. And the bills needed only Altgeld's signature to become law.

Altgeld by this time was almost destitute. He had tied up all of his capital in the Unity Block and had borrowed besides. His rental income had fallen disastrously during the depression. He was hard pressed to meet the interest payments on the bonds he had issued. The banks were denying him further loans. He sat alone in the executive mansion in Springfield. A story reached him that a large quantity of bonds of the gas company had been placed in a security vault in Chicago; a man would deliver the key to him if the gas act was signed.

One evening an agent of Yerkes walked into the Unity Block. He was carrying a valise. He asked for Altgeld's cousin, John Lanehart. He and Lanehart talked privately. They went together to the vault of the building with the bag. This was Yerkes' offer. The amount was probably $500,000.

Altgeld vetoed the bills, prompting Yerkes to exclaim: "I admire that man!" But he still wanted his franchise extended. Now began a furious effort to pass the Eternal Monopoly bills over the veto.

Scene: *The Lobbies of the Legislature, Springfield*
Time: *Late Spring, 1895*

John W. Yantis, secretary of the state Railroad and Warehouse Commission, is working with Altgeld to hold the legislature in line. Yantis approaches a leader of the legislature and asks:

"You are not going to vote against the Governor, are you?"

"It is going to pass anyway," the man replies, "and ten thousand dollars looks good to me."

"But how are they going to get enough fellows?" Yantis asks. "They can't afford to pay that kind of price to get enough fellows."

"Oh," the legislator says, "they've got a lot of cheap skates lined up."

Thinking it over later, Yantis gets an idea.

He goes to another legislator, who had voted for the bills originally.

"What are they giving you?" Yantis asks.

"Two hundred dollars."

"Don't let them make a sap out of you," Yantis says. "They are paying as high as ten thousand dollars!"

The man is indignant. "Why, the crooks told me that two hundred was the top!"

The legislator passes the word to several of his colleagues who have sold themselves cheap. They become angry and refuse to vote for the bills.

The veto is sustained by one vote.

II

These were the achievements on which Altgeld would run for reelection in 1896. But they were not enough, for most of them had little appeal to voters outside of Chicago. He had to have an issue that would draw farm votes into a coalition with the working classes of the cities.

That issue was ready-to-hand: the free coinage of silver as well as gold. For a generation the American economy had been growing prodigiously, and the supply of money had not grown as rapidly. The general level of prices had been sagging constantly. Output of such staple crops as wheat and cotton rose precipitously, and American farmers lost part of the world market as production also expanded abroad. The result was a persistent decline in the prices at which farmers could sell many of their crops: a drop of about 50 percent from 1870 to 1896. To complete the squeeze, much of the Southern and Western farm land was mortgaged. Debts that had been contracted when money was worth little had to be repaid when it was worth much more in relation to goods—especially in relation to farm products. Inevitably a persistent cry arose from rural areas to increase the quantity of money in order to reduce its value. Sometimes it was a demand for the issuance of paper greenbacks; sometimes, for the coinage of silver as well as gold. But always it was a demand for inflation.

Always the business classes fought the demand: creditors wanted to be repaid in money that was worth as much as possible. And the major political parties, although making occasional concessions to the debtor farmers, stood generally with the business groups. After Congress in 1890 provided for the regular purchase by the Treasury of a moderate quantity of silver each month and the issuance of notes against it, President Cleveland in 1893 forced repeal of the law. The Democratic administration had joined the Republicans in hostility to the just demands of ordinary farmers: that was the cry, and farmers gave more than a million votes in 1894 to the new People's party, the Populists.

Altgeld's strategy was simple. He would win labor and reformers by a broad program of social reconstruction. He would use the silver issue to win farm areas and the silver-producing states of the West. With the support of these groups he would oust the Eastern conservatives from their own party, and the Democracy would once more stand proudly in the anti-monopoly tradition of Jefferson and Jackson.

And he did it. In June, 1895, a special convention called by the Democratic party of Illinois declared for the free coinage of silver. For the next year Altgeld diligently organized the free-silver forces throughout the Ohio Valley, and in 1896 he was chosen chairman of the Illinois delegation to the Democratic national convention. When that convention met in Chicago in July, he was the most influential man present. Plank after plank in the platform bore the mark of his thinking, and around this document, the Chicago Platform of 1896, would swirl the struggles for a full decade thereafter for control of the Democratic party in Illinois and in the nation.

The demand for free coinage of silver, although vital in winning support, was a minor part of the platform, which also called for an income tax and criticized the Supreme Court decision of 1895 invalidating the earlier one. In reference to the Pullman strike, it denounced President Cleveland's action in sending troops into Illinois, charged that "government by injunction" was "a new and highly dangerous form of oppression," urged strict adherence to civil liberties, urged arbitration of labor disputes affecting interstate commerce. It declared that "as labor creates the wealth of the country, we demand the passage of such laws as may be necessary to protect it in all its rights."

An amendment was offered: "We commend the honesty, economy, courage and fidelity of the present Democratic National Administration." The amendment was rejected, 564 to 357. The most popular Democrat since Andrew Jackson had been repudiated by his own party. It was reported that the President was "dazed" when he read the platform.

Altgeld's victory over Cleveland would have been total if he had also won the Presidential nomination, but he was disqualified by his birth in Germany. The call went instead to William Jennings Bryan, only thirty-six years old, a former Congressman from Nebraska, whose Cross of Gold oration during the debate on the platform is the most famous speech ever made to a party convention. Bryan's superb voice and gestures mesmerized the delegates into supporting him, but it was not so clear that he knew what he was talking about. Altgeld doubted that he did. The day after Bryan indicted the Cross of Gold, Altgeld said to Clarence Darrow: "I have been thinking over Bryan's speech. What did he say anyhow?"

Darrow and Henry Demarest Lloyd had even graver doubts, and their faith in the conversion of the Democratic party was far from unqualified. At the convention of the People's party, they tried to hold the delegates to an independent course in order to exert radical pressure on the Democrats. But their efforts were unavailing; Bryan got the Populist nomination also, and the People's party for all practical purposes merged with the Democrats.

Bryan campaigned with unprecedented vigor: he traveled eighteen thousand miles and spoke to an estimated five million people. But his campaign was limited to the single demand: free coinage of silver, while in Illinois Governor Altgeld campaigned for the entire Chicago Platform. The business classes regarded Bryan as an irresponsible child; the really dangerous man was Altgeld. They were terrified at the thought of Bryan in the White House with Altgeld and Eugene Debs as his chief advisers—a result the newspapers intimated was certain if Bryan won. Bryan, screamed *Harper's Weekly*, was only a tool in the hands of "the ambitious and unscrupulous Illinois communist," Altgeld.

The Republican campaign was managed by the astute Mark Hanna, a wealthy Cleveland industrialist, who used the fear of Altgeld and Bryan to raise an enormous campaign fund: estimated as high as $7 million. The lowest estimate, $3½ million, was more than ten times what the Democrats reported spending. The Democratic total was only slightly more than the contributions of one company, Standard Oil, to the Republicans. Hanna's party distributed more than 100 million tracts and pamphlets—about five for every voter. In the closing weeks of the campaign the Republicans had eighteen thousand speakers in the field. Meanwhile William McKinley, the candidate, sat quietly on his front porch in Canton, Ohio, saying the same thing tirelessly to the voters who pilgrimaged there: only the Republican party can bring back prosperity.

The Republicans campaigned with special fury in Illinois. One after another of their top orators came into the state to speak. One man alone, John W. Gates, President of the Illinois Steel Company, put $50,000 into the campaign fund. Industrialists threatened to close their factories if Bryan were elected. Trade union leaders were coerced or bribed or persuaded into endorsing McKinley and John Tanner, the Republican nominee for governor. The socialists were attacking Altgeld from the other side, deriding him as a mere reformer. To make matters worse for the Democrats, the rural demand for inflation was blunted during the final weeks, when crop failures abroad brought an increased demand for American products: just before the election the price of wheat almost doubled.

By October the situation looked so bad that Florence Kelley had almost lost hope. Altgeld's friends seemed few indeed when he needed them, she wrote to Henry Lloyd: "And if the working people allow him to be defeated now, in the face of his record, surely they deserve to have no other friend until this generation dies out and another and better one takes its place." Two weeks later she wrote Lloyd: "I think the state is lost. . . . There may be more moral courage among the wage earners than I'm calculating upon. But I see no reason for expecting much."

Her fears were accurate. In spite of the efforts of Altgeld and his supporters, the Democratic campaign had been narrowed in voters' eyes to the single demand for free coinage of silver, and that reform had little appeal to the urban workers, who justifiably felt that inflation might injure them instead of helping them. The rest of the Chicago Platform had little appeal to farmers. On election day, while the votes were being cast, Altgeld was sure that he would lose. He did, overwhelmingly, and so did Clarence Darrow in his race for Congress, and so did Bryan. McKinley's popular majority was the greatest since 1872. Bryan carried only the mining regions and the staple crop areas where prices were lowest. He lost every state in the Old Northwest, where diversified corn-hog farming had already begun to bring a new prosperity.

In Chicago many workingmen did not bother to vote at all. And many men voted who had never bothered to be born. The following spring over sixty thousand names of nonexistent persons were found on the election registry in Chicago. Altgeld claimed that 100,000 fraudulent votes had been counted in Illinois, and that the falsifications elsewhere were so great that actually Bryan had won. But Mark Hanna had his victory, no matter how.

"Exit Altgeld!" was the exultant heading on the Chicago *Tribune*. But Altgeld threw the words back. Only six months earlier, he declared, the Democratic party had been prostrate, "betrayed into the hands of the jobbers and monopolists by President Cleveland." But the party "cut loose from the domination of the trusts and syndicates, . . . repudiated the men who betrayed it," and "again proclaimed democratic principles and espoused the cause of toiling humanity." During the campaign "it was confronted by everything that money could buy, that boodle could debauch, or that fear of starvation could coerce." In spite of that it had revitalized itself and fought a good fight. And by an honest count, it had won.

Altgeld went into semi-retirement, his health shattered, his fortune gone, virtually a bankrupt, and the Republicans went into office, and the businessmen were repaid for their campaign contributions. Down to Springfield went Yerkes' men again with their bags of gold, and the legislature passed the Allen bill which authorized the city council of Chicago to grant street-car franchises for terms up to fifty years. Governor Tanner—no Altgeld, he—signed it into law.

III

The outcry in Chicago against the Allen Act was so fierce that even Yerkes, with all his boldness, decided to wait before pressing for extension of his franchises. John Peter Altgeld personally picked the son and namesake of former Mayor Carter H. Harrison as the Democratic nominee for mayor in the spring of 1897, and young Harrison was elected to City Hall on a platform pledging to protect the public interest in any franchises to street-car companies.

Altgeld and Harrison fell out almost immediately. The new mayor appointed to office some of his patron's worst enemies in the Democratic party, including Gold Democrats and men who had opposed Altgeld's actions during the Pullman strike. The new administration connived at the evasion of the civil service act by naming "temporary" appointees to all vacancies. Harrison's obvious purpose was to unite with the Democratic ward bosses in building an unprincipled machine in Chicago, and then to reach out to New York for an alliance with Richard Croker, the Tammany boss, so that they could control the Democratic national convention in 1900. Harrison and Croker were convinced that the Chicago Platform—by frightening the business classes and alienating all men capable of making big campaign contributions—would never bring victory in a national election. What they cared about was office and the rewards of office.

The chief issue dividing Harrison and Altgeld was how to cope with the burgeoning monopolies. Altgeld, after he left office, became increasingly persuaded that public ownership was the only answer. When Henry Demarest Lloyd wrote him asking how the monopolies would be compensated when their property was taken by the public, Altgeld replied that public ownership could be achieved by condemnation proceedings, with a jury fixing the value of the property.

"I have no doubt," he wrote, "that in some cases corporations would get much more than they are entitled to, but even then it would be the last steal and would be better for the public than the perpetual robbery we now have. A straight-out steal from the treasury does not hurt our people so much as the process of ceaseless bleeding. . . . Further by taking the monopolies—no matter at what price—the people will again get control of their government . . . and this is far more important than all monetary considerations."

So Altgeld opposed any extension of street-car franchises to private companies in Chicago; what he wanted was city owner-ship and operation. Mayor Harrison, on the contrary, said that he would negotiate with the companies after the Allen Act was repealed. Altgeld wanted an immediate reduction of street-car fares from a nickel to four cents; Harrison wanted to leave the fare at a nickel but force the companies to pay 10 percent of their gross receipts to the city. Harrison's pro-posal, Altgeld charged, was merely a device to tax the poor people who rode street cars in order to reduce taxes on the wealthy property owners.

In the fall election of 1898 Harrison and the ward bosses picked the Democratic candidates, and many of their nomi-nees disgusted Altgeld. But the election results did have the result of forcing Yerkes' hand: every member of the legislature who had voted for the Allen Act was defeated. It seemed likely that the new legislature would repeal the Act. If Yerkes wanted extensions of his franchises for fifty years instead of a mere twenty years, he had to move fast. In December, 1898, the extension ordinances were introduced in the city council.

Altgeld pointed out that the ordinances could be passed by the votes of forty-six aldermen. Their passage would certainly add $40 million to the market value of the outstanding stocks and bonds in the traction companies. If a third of this profit were divided among forty-six aldermen, each would receive $300,000, and Yerkes and his stockholders would be left with a profit of $25 million. The time had come, Altgeld said, for the people to "rise up and buy ropes."

They did exactly that. Protest meetings were held night

after night, with Altgeld and others calling for city ownership. Masses of indignant men marched in the streets. On the night when the vote was taken in the city council, City Hall was surrounded by a mob—armed with nooses and guns. The vote went against Yerkes. No longer in Chicago could a public utility openly and proudly debauch the city government. In January the city council resolved that the Allen Act should be repealed, and in March the legislature followed this recommendation almost unanimously.

Already Altgeld's friends had persuaded him to enter the race for mayor against Carter Harrison in the spring of 1899. Although his health was miserable, he declared: "If there is no other way to rescue the Democratic party from the treachery of City Hall I will run for mayor, or even for constable." The Democratic party must win as the liberal party or not at all. But he refused to enter the Democratic primaries, calling them "a brace game" that Harrison could control by using "the police force and saloon element." Petitions were started to make him an independent candidate for mayor.

Not one of the nine Chicago dailies supported Altgeld. Two were impartial. Only two supported the Republican nominee, who had roughly the same traction program as Harrison. Five were for Harrison, including the two owned by President McKinley's chief supporter in Chicago. This irregularity was engineered by Mark Hanna, the national Republican leader, who wanted to build up Mayor Harrison so that he and Tammany would control the national Democratic convention in 1900. Hanna felt sure that these office seekers would put forward a conservative Democratic nominee and platform in 1900, which the Republicans could beat easily, thus avoiding the need for another huge campaign fund.

To get his message known, Altgeld relied on the newly organized Municipal Ownership League and on "family circles" which his friends organized to meet in private homes. He also spoke to a series of giant meetings. Nightly for the last six weeks of the campaign at least a thousand people, sometimes as many as six thousand, jammed a hall to hear Altgeld and Darrow denounce the mayor's traction program as a sell-out. They almost ignored the Republicans; the real enemies were the renegade Democrats. The City Hall group fought back hard. They used the police and the saloon-keepers and the ward bosses. They used the City Cab Inspector to mobilize the hack drivers to campaign for Harrison. They used strong-arm men to muster support in the trade unions. But most of all they counted on Republican bolters to reelect their man. None of the Harrison campaign literature mentioned the word "Democratic"; if any label at all was used, it was "nonpartisan."

Altgeld's effort failed. For every vote he got, the Republican candidate got two, and Carter Harrison got three. In 1899 a straightforward demand for city ownership could not muster a majority of the voters of Chicago. And the man whose arrogance might have helped to promote radicalism, Charles Tyson Yerkes, left the city soon after the election. He did it in his usual arrogant, and profitable, way.

First he formed the Union Traction Company, which had no assets whatever. The new corporation leased all the property and franchises of Yerkes' two operating companies, agreeing to assume all obligations of both and to pay the stockholders of one of them a dividend of 12 percent annually, of the other a dividend of 6 percent annually. Then Yerkes persuaded two Philadelphia traction magnates that Union Traction would earn much more than enough to meet these commitments. They bought out his entire interest in Chicago street cars. As a final gesture of contempt for the ordinary man, Yerkes made public his business accounts, and left for his Fifth Avenue mansion in New York. With him he carried $15 million in cash.

IV

The great issues of foreign policy at the turn of the century were also seen by Chicago liberals as conflicts between two

visions: equality and monopoly. This persistent stance served
to unify views that might otherwise seem contradictory.

Even while he was still governor, John Peter Altgeld had
compared the Cuban struggle for independence from Spain to
the American Revolution. In an article written at the request
of William Randolph Hearst for the New York *Journal,* he
urged American intervention to help the Cubans. Spanish
atrocities in Cuba, he wrote, were worse than "cannibalism and
the slave trade"—instances where "the moral sense of the civilized world" recognizes the right of a nation to intervene in a
foreign country. Henry Lloyd took the same position in May,
1898, when he wrote to a friend: "I believe that a nation should
be a gentleman, . . . and no gentleman would stand by while
a Spanish brute was kicking the life out of a Cuban baby."

Ten days earlier, Congress had declared war against Spain.
The chief advocates of this action had been liberals, including
Hearst and his newspaper rival in New York, Joseph Pulitzer.
On the other hand Marshall Field and six other leading Chicago citizens had told the President that they would "deprecate
war with Spain except as a last resort." The United States was
just clearly emerging from the depression that had begun in
1893, and most businessmen were fearful that a war would
endanger the new-found prosperity by spawning unforeseen
and unstable elements in the economy.

But if they had opposed the war itself, they quickly came to
favor retention of the fruits of the war. They were persuaded
that China especially would soon become a huge market for
American goods; the Philippines were the gateway to China;
therefore the Philippines must be kept. Altgeld in July, 1898,
at the height of the war, endorsed this policy—up to a point.
He warmly supported the war, and even sought to claim credit
for it for the Democratic party. He favored annexation of
Puerto Rico as part of the war indemnity, and of Cuba, Haiti,
and Santo Domingo whenever the people of those countries
wanted it. He urged that the United States keep permanently
"a number of the best harbors in the Philippines and any other

good harbors we can get." But he drew the line at any effort
by the United States to rule the Philippines. And on this point
he separated himself from the Republicans and from the conservative Democrats: Carter Harrison favored keeping the
Philippines, and Croker of Tammany Hall urged "holding
whatever possessions we have gained by annexation, purchase
or war."

Altgeld made a fundamental distinction between expansion,
—movement into nearby territory that would become states in
the United States—and imperialism—the seizure of distant areas
that would be held as colonies. He attacked the men who said
that "this people or that people are incapable of self-government." (Any clear-headed citizen of Illinois might well suspect
the argument: Could any election in the Philippines be more
corrupt than the 1896 Presidential canvass in Chicago? Could
any Manila alderman be more corrupt than "Hinky Dink"
Kenna or Johnny Powers? Could any legislature in the Pacific
islands show less regard for the public interest than the Illinois
legislature had shown in passing the Allen Act?)

In spite of all arguments, soon after Spain was defeated,
President McKinley began the forceful conquest of the Philippines, an effort that would take three years and cost more than
the war against Spain. And in January, 1899, the Senate by a
narrow margin ratified the peace treaty, which gave the United
States custody over the Philippines, Puerto Rico, and Guam.
These American actions were vehemently denounced by the
Chicago liberals. Thus Clarence Darrow, now Altgeld's law
partner, told a mass meeting at the Chicago Auditorium in
July that he would not give up "the republic of Jefferson" to
gain "the empire of McKinley." No government was just, he
said, unless the governed consented to it. Therefore he called
on the President to leave the Philippines in peace: "to take
away his lawless crew, remove his Christian cannon from those
far-off shores. . . ."

Altgeld and Darrow fought imperialism because they
thought it a perversion of the political ideal of democracy.

They also thought the same monopolies that had been bleeding the American people would now be the chief beneficiaries from foreign markets. Finally they feared that the colonies would serve as an excuse to build up the American army, which would then be used to destroy social protest in the United States, as the Federal troops had been used in the Pullman boycott. There was no doubt that powerful citizens were thinking along these lines: at a parade welcoming Admiral Dewey to New York, a corporation lawyer was heard to exclaim, "The best thing about this parade today is that it will show these anarchists and socialists that there is an armed force in this country able to defend property against the rabble." Nor were the liberals slow to identify American policy in the Philippines with the concurrent British effort to subjugate the Boers in South Africa. They had always regarded England as the foremost colonial power in the world, as the former tyrant over the thirteen American colonies; now Altgeld charged that American policy in the Philippines had been dictated by Great Britain.

Altgeld in 1900 had no official position in the Democratic party of Illinois, but this did not prevent him from exerting great influence nationally. He did so, as in 1896, by forming the strategy of the campaign and converting countless Democrats to it. The chief issue, he said, was imperialism. The next most important was to find a substitute for the Sherman Anti-Trust Act as a way of subduing the trusts. "Jefferson," said Altgeld, "would abolish all monopoly and all special privileges." But how to do it? The only way was for the people to own and operate "all necessary monopolies." But was not this contrary to Jefferson's view that the functions of government should be restricted to a minimum? Not at all, said Altgeld; Jefferson was thinking of his own day when government was distinct from the people. But Jefferson, like Lincoln, had faith in the people and wanted to refer all questions to them. Therefore he would have wanted government ownership in the present age when the people can control the government. "Experience has shown that a corporation standing between the people and the state will, when possible, plunder the one and debauch the other, and is therefore a constant menace to free government."

Altgeld also wanted to keep the free-silver plank in the platform, even though the great expansion of gold production since 1896 had inflated the currency and thus made the issue much less important. Referring to the alleged need to win back the Gold Democrats who had bolted the party four years earlier, he said that he was ready to welcome home the prodigal sons, but he would not permit them to write the menu and select the calf.

The Democrats nominated Bryan again, by acclamation, and Altgeld traveled New England speaking for him. But in November, McKinley's popular majority was 850,000, even larger than in 1896. The result, said Altgeld, proved "that money can control the American election." ("This people or that people are incapable of self-government.")

But Altgeld would not give up his fight to hold the Democratic party to the anti-monopoly flag. In 1901 he even supported the reactionary Republican nominee for mayor in order to break Carter Harrison's hold on the Democratic party, but Harrison won anyway. Altgeld went to many other cities in the East and the Midwest, speaking against imperialism and the trusts. Repeatedly he declared that "Were Jefferson alive today, his voice would be heard from ocean to ocean demanding that the people themselves must own the monopolies."

On March 11, 1902, Altgeld spent the day in court in Chicago defending a trade union. That evening he went to Joliet, thirty-five miles away, to speak at a meeting called by sympathizers of the Boers. After his vigorous oration he staggered on the stage. A violent attack of vomiting began. He had suffered a cerebral hemorrhage, and he died early the next morning. Clarence Darrow took the body on the train back to Chicago, where it was buried.

Altgeld was dead, and many of his ideals seemed prostrated.

Imperialism was the official policy of the United States. The power of the giant trusts seemed greater than ever. Chicago liberals delighted in a poem commenting on the situation. The poem told how a man came to an enormous mill and was told: "It's Morgan's." A railroad system stretching all over the country proved to be Morgan's, as did a "monster fleet" of ships.

> I dwelt in a nation filled with pride;
> Her people were many, her lands were wide;
> Her record in war and science and art
> Proved a greatness of muscle and mind and heart.
> "What a great old country it is!" I cried;
> And a man with his chest in the air replied:
>   "It's Morgan's."

Heaven had become Morgan's "Private Park." Hell was his, too.

CHAPTER 8

Education Comes from Life

You cannot make progress against the trust phalanx unless
you overcome the admiration of the American people for the
individuals who are the leaders of the trusts.

—Louis D. Brandeis to Edwin D. Mead, November 9, 1895 *

I

In 1897 Daniel Burnham, the city's ruling architect, crowned
with honors for his role in the Columbian Exposition, came
forward with his Chicago Plan for the improvement of the
Lake Front. This step was urgent, he said, because the city
had become such a miserable place to live that everybody who
could afford to move elsewhere did so. "We have been running away to Cairo, Athens, the Riviera, Paris and Vienna because life at home is not so pleasant as in these fashionable
centers." Retail trade in Chicago would benefit enormously if
the city were made attractive enough to keep its millionaires
at home. Even more might be done; Chicago could be made
so delightful that retired businessmen from the entire Missis-
sippi Valley and the West would come there to live.

Burnham had sound business reasons for wanting to keep
Chicago's millionaires near at hand: at home as abroad, they
spent money on a fabulous scale. A pioneer in extravagance

* Henry D. Lloyd Mss., Wisconsin Historical Society.

was Potter Palmer, the tycoon of State Street real estate after he sold his dry-goods store to Marshall Field. In the Great Fire of 1871, he lost ninety-five buildings on which the rents totaled $220,000 a year. One was the lavish hotel, the Palmer House. Palmer was left without enough cash to pay his taxes, but he borrowed $1,700,000 from an insurance company on his signature alone. Up went a new and more sumptuous Palmer House—with silver dollars embedded in the floor of its barber shop.

Palmer's brownstone home on the North Side was a forest of balconies and turrets. Finished in 1885, it had no door-knobs on the outside; nobody could enter unless a servant opened the door. Each caller's card had to pass through the hands of twenty-seven servants before a decision was made whether he would be seen. Mrs. Palmer's best friends were required to write for appointments.

Mrs. Palmer finally abdicated as society leader of Chicago by spending increasing amounts of her time in Europe. The diadem passed to Mrs. Harold McCormick. Harold was the son of Cyrus, the reaper magnate; his wife was the former Edith Rockefeller. Their gray-stone mansion at 1000 Lake Shore Drive was run with indomitable ostentation. Printed menus, in French, were provided for every meal. When two persons had lunch, four menials were needed to serve. Mrs. McCormick never spoke to any member of the enormous staff except her secretary and the chief steward. Since she would not allow herself to talk to the coachman, he was given instructions for the entire trip before it began. One wonders what Mrs. McCormick would have done if she had become suddenly ill during a drive; perhaps even her physiology could not depart from protocol.

Chicagoans bought so many precious stones that Otto Young, a wholesale jeweler, was himself a millionaire by 1892. He became famous for allegedly giving his daughter, Mrs. Louis Kaufman, a million dollars for every baby she had. Others indulged in the pleasures of the flesh on the same grand scale.

John W. Gates, who started as a barbed-wire salesman, was head of the Illinois Steel Company. The original idea for the formation of U.S. Steel was his, but J. P. Morgan elbowed him out. The grounds? Morgan thought Gates was personally gross: a devastating judgment since Morgan's own proclivities were hardly effete.

One day in August, 1902, Gates went to the race track at Saratoga. He lost heavily by pyramiding his bets. He went to Canfield's Club House, the famous gambling house, for dinner. After dinner he began playing faro in the downstairs gambling room. By ten o'clock he had lost $150,000. Then, at his request, the limits were raised to $5,000 on case cards and to $10,000 on doubles. By midnight he was even. The game ended at 8 A.M., with Gates $150,000 ahead.

Associated with Gates in many deals was Cornelius K. G. Billings, a Chicago broker and officer of the Gas Trust. Billings once gave a banquet where the guests sat on horses to eat.

Their hobbies were varied. In spite of the financial beating that young Joseph Leiter took from Philip D. Armour, the Leiters had enough money to collect English titles. Joseph's youngest sister married a major of the Central India Horse, a cousin of the Duke of Argyll. The next oldest married the nineteenth Earl of Suffolk and the twelfth Earl of Berkshire. The oldest married George Nathaniel Curzon, eldest son of the fourth Baron Scarsdale; their daughter was to marry Sir Oswald Moseley, founder of the British Union of Fascists.

But much of their money, as Daniel Burnham well knew, went into architecture. Charles Tyson Yerkes had medieval stained-glass windows in his office. But Yerkes came from a family of wealth and culture; most of his counterparts were of honest middle-class origins and had been too busy acquiring wealth to puzzle much about esthetics. Cyrus Hall McCormick lived in a castle of Lake Superior sandstone. In the Second Empire style, it had a grand library of ebony set off with silver. Not far away was the home of Perry H. Smith, a vice-president of the Chicago & Northwestern Railroad. "The style is Greek

Renaissance, with proportions of Italian palace architecture,"
reported the Chicago *Tribune* approvingly. Made of marble,
the house had an ebony stairway enriched with gold. In the
butler's pantry there were three faucets: for hot water, cold
water, and iced champagne.

Such practices prompted Herbert S. Stone, editor and pub-
lisher of *House Beautiful*, to print a series in 1904-1905 on
"The Poor Taste of the Rich." The first three articles described
specific homes, each one named. Two were in New York, one
in Boston. The fourth article described specific rooms—in un-
identified homes, city unnamed. It is easy to suppose that
Stone was being prudent about insulting the upper class in
his native Chicago. But in the magazine he printed photographs of rooms which verged on libel. One room he analyzed
objectively:

> Here the Moorish and the Turkish, the Japanese and the Chi-
> nese, fight for supremacy, assisted by a collection of Indian
> blankets. . . . There is not a square inch of plain space. Walls
> are covered and tables are loaded. Everything runs riotously;
> dragons writhe, bronze figures flourish swords, and painted
> dancing girls wave tambourines. It is as restful as the outskirts
> of a battlefield during an active campaign, and just about as
> safe. One false step would annihilate a costly Chinese vase, a
> bit of Venetian glass, or a trumpery American lampshade. . . .
> And the money spent on this nightmare of a room would build
> a dream of a cottage.

There was the point. The clearest statement of it came, not
from any millionaire, but from Detective Stephen Muchowski,
who in 1904 was the official art censor of the police department. His job was to tour the art stores, hotels, and saloons
to make certain that no pornographic pictures or statues were
displayed. But how did he know whether a given nude was
art, or was pornography and thus subject to destruction? His
standard was simple: "If a picture or statue costs $50 it is be-
yond all question a work of art. If an artist devoted sufficient

time to make it cost $50 it stands to reason that his motive was high."

Men who had made their family fortunes were often aware of their own narrow backgrounds and sought to give their sons the advantages of college, travel, luxury, and art. But, seeing their own careers as models for everybody, the fathers also expected the sons to begin a life in business as laborers or clerks. Thus Philip Armour's son Ogden returned to Chicago disenchanted by a trip to England. Philip explained later: "Ogden thought there would be something he would like to do instead of grubbing for money. He thinks I should retire. I told him to be at the yards in his working clothes at seven on Monday morning." And Ogden did settle down and spent his life grubbing for money, serving as head of Armour & Co. from 1901 to 1923.

In other instances, "it didn't work," testified Frazier Jelke, whose father had made a fortune from oleomargarine. Where Cyrus McCormick had died whispering "Work, work," his son Harold became patron of the Chicago opera and an international playboy. The estrangement of father from son could be almost total. When George Pullman died in 1897, his estate was some $17 million. But he left each of his twin sons a mere $3,000 a year income, saying that neither had developed the sense of responsibility "requisite for the wise use of large properties and considerable sums of money."

II

"Poor taste and riches do not always go hand in hand," declared the final article of the *House Beautiful* series. "Occasionally people of moderate income furnish their homes in a manner as execrable as that of the millionaires." Just why this was true had been explained, six years earlier, in a book called *The Theory of the Leisure Class* by Thorstein Veblen. Already forty-two years old in 1899, Veblen was only an instructor, the lowest academic rank, at the University of Chicago. This lowly status was no reflection on his scholarship: he was managing editor of the *Journal of Political Economy,* and he had published two penetrating articles belaboring his predecessors in economics.

The body of classical economics, Veblen wrote, rested on the interplay of "natural" scarcity and "personal" desires. It also assumed that a man faced with an economic choice would try to maximize his pleasures and to minimize his pains. Pleasure was defined as monetary profits; pain as individual exertion or work. In a convoluted prose that oozed irony from every word, Veblen stated this view of human nature: "The hedonistic conception of man is that of a lightning calculator of pleasures and pains. . . . He has neither antecedent nor consequent. He is an isolated, definitive human datum, in stable equilibrium except for the buffets of the impinging forces that displace him in one direction or another."

All this, said Veblen, is nonsense. The scarcity of goods is not "natural" and desires are not "personal"; both are socially determined. Man is not a passive thermometer; his chief characteristic is that he does things. What he does will depend on his temperament, and his temperament is the result of "his life up to the point at which he stands." The key fact is habit, announced *The Theory of the Leisure Class.* A man's habits are shaped by two sets of forces: the aptitudes he inherits and the society that molds those aptitudes. The chief innate trait of any human being is his need to respect himself, and "the usual basis of self-respect is the respect accorded by one's neighbours." The apparent exceptions to this rule go only to prove it: they are usually devout men who "fall back on the putative approbation of some supernatural witness of their deeds." The grounds on which a person comes to have self-esteem depend, then, on common opinion in the community. And so they shift from one culture to another.

Under primitive savagery, wrote Veblen, the output of any group was so small that all individuals had to work alike to wrest a bare subsistence from nature. But as the output of the group rose above this level, the surplus was not distributed equally. A few men seized it all for themselves, either by force or by fraud. The age of "predatory barbarism" begins. In this early age, physical violence is the ordinary mode of seizure; the leisure class is composed of those who are extraordinarily adept at warfare or hunting. But competence at fraud brings rewards too, as the leisure class also includes those who are engaged in government or religion.

Thus the leisure class and private ownership arose together. While most people continue to work at industrial activity (meaning "all effort directed to enhance human life by taking advantage of the non-human environment"), the leisure class engages in the "acquisition of substance by seizure." No longer are all men equal, and they learn to think in terms of "invidious comparisons." Society is a hierarchy, and a man's place in the hierarchy determines how he is regarded by his neighbors (and how much he respects himself). From the beginning, private ownership had no motive except securing social position, status, for the owner.

Technical knowledge and equipment continued to accumulate, and therefore the society's output of goods continued to rise. As the industrial age dawned, the usual mode of acquiring property shifted from force to fraud. Perhaps generals and athletes continue to get "the highest popular esteem," but money becomes "the basis of commonplace reputability and a blameless social standing." The touchstone is simple: How much do you own?

Men must have ways to exhibit their wealth. Under predatory barbarism the usual way is to show that your time is your own, that you are not forced to work. The highest goal is to show that your entire life has been one of conspicuous leisure: you can do this by acquiring certain capacities that obviously took much time to learn but that are useless for purposes of industrial activity. In "our time," said Veblen, looking at the curriculum and social practices of his own University, this might mean "knowledge of the dead languages and the occult

sciences; of correct spelling, of syntax and prosody; . . . of the
latest proprieties of dress, furniture, and equipage; of games,
sports, and fancy-bred animals, such as dogs and race-horses.
. . ." Also ". . . what is known as manners and breeding, polite
usage, decorum, and formal and ceremonious observances."

But as the society grows more wealthy, too many men are
exempt from industrial activity for that to serve as adequate
ground for social distinctions. The honorable man must now
show that his wealth is so great that he can throw it away with
both hands. He calls in others to help him at this task: while
one group of his dependents produces goods for him, another
group helps him to consume the goods. At first this may mean
only a favored wife; later it comes to mean hordes of retain-
ers, even artists to whom he serves as patron. A splendid device is the ball or other formal entertainment, when you call
in your competitors to consume your goods in your honor. The
requirements of conspicuous leisure and conspicuous consumption explain why, even at a fairly high point in the social scale,
you often find a man "applying himself to work with the ut-
most assiduity, in order that his wife may in due form render
for him that degree of vicarious leisure which the common
sense of the time demands."

All standards, even esthetic ones, must conform to "the law
of conspicuous waste." Moreover, the standard of decent expenditures for any class is set by those in the next higher class,
so standards for the whole society are influenced by the standards of the highest leisure class. In all classes but the very
lowest, the "conspicuously wasteful honorific expenditure" may
be more indispensable than satisfying the "lower" physical
needs; a family may economize on food in order to buy a sleazy
and vulgar lampshade. At the top end of society, as the society
becomes very wealthy, the ability to throw money away becomes so common that it too loses its value as a ground of discrimination; in this privileged group, "nonpecuniary canons of
taste" may assert themselves, but more probably the group will
develop private and transient "styles" peculiar to itself. And

in all classes, conspicuous waste must struggle against the instinct of workmanship, which "disposes men to look with favour upon productive efficiency and on whatever is of human use." Thus nobody can ever admit to buying things merely because they are costly; rather does the fact of expense help to mold the standards of beauty.

With exquisite irony, Veblen ranged Chicago for examples. He noted how natural trees and flowers stood in worse repute than "topiary work and conventional flower-beds." All classes in the city much admired what had been done with the former grounds of the Columbian Exposition—a clear case of "the dominance of pecuniary beauty over aesthetic beauty." Useful animals were not counted beautiful; the beautiful animals were the dog ("the filthiest of the domestic animals in his person and the nastiest in his habits"), the race horse, and the cat ("less reputable than the other two because less wasteful"). For centuries, canons of womanly beauty had emphasized delicacy, that is, unfitness for work: "delicacy of the hands and feet, the slender figure, and especially the slender waist" (not to mention the bound feet of the Chinese). But by 1899 the upper classes were so wealthy that nobody would suspect them of working, and standards were shifting back toward "a woman of the archaic type that does not disown her hands and feet, nor, indeed, the other gross material facts of her person."

(On this last topic Veblen was a man of sound qualifications. In spite of his habit of mumbling his words, something about him—his large slouching frame, his long drooping hair and mustache, his dour manner—was irresistible to many women, and his academic career was scored with amatory scandals. "What is one to do," he asked, "if the woman moves in on you?")

Architecture afforded a marked instance of pecuniary canons of taste: "The endless variety of fronts presented by the better class of tenements and apartment houses in our cities is an endless variety of architectural distress and of suggestions of expensive discomfort." The mania for "hand-made goods was to the same effect. Especially ludicrous was the example of books, where, although every advantage of serviceability was with the machine-made kind, volumes were issued "edited with the obsolete spelling, printed in black-letter, and bound in limp vellum fitted with thongs." The fact of wastefulness was further enhanced by printing them in "limited editions."

Veblen's prize exhibit was clothing. The most honorific dress must be obviously expensive and must obviously disqualify its wearer for work. Thus the reputability for men of "the patent-leather shoe, the stainless linen, the lustrous cylindrical hat, and the walking-stick." But the absurdity of men's dress came always against a limit. Pecuniary strength brought honor because it was evidence of superior personal capacity, so men's clothing that was so absurd as to suggest the "incapacity or marked discomfort" of the wearer could only defeat its own purpose.

With women, this limit was removed. The life of women was a vicarious one, lived not for themselves but for their masters; their dress did not need to show their personal capacity but only the wealth of their husbands. "The high heel, the skirt, the impracticable bonnet, the corset, and the general disregard of the wearer's comfort which is an obvious feature of all civilised women's apparel, are so many items of evidence to the effect . . . the woman is still, in theory, the economic dependent of the man, . . . still the man's chattel." This held true, too, for the expensive and uncomfortable livery worn by servants. And also for a third group, the uniformed clergyman, who was "a body servant constructively in attendance upon the person of the divinity whose livery he wears." Priestly vestments, said Veblen, were "evidence of a servile status and a vicarious life."

But economic advance brings changes. When the number of people wealthy enough to be immune to the charge of working has grown large, this group may develop its own standards and become indifferent to the opinion of others. With them the corset had fallen into disuse by 1900; among the upper classes it survived only—he looked at his own Chicago—in "those American cities, for instance, which have recently and rapidly risen into opulence." The upper class of older cities developed subtler standards, such as deprecating "loud" dress, and its standards gradually spread to the lower classes.

Commodities do not originate because they are conspicuously wasteful; on the contrary, they nearly always have some ostensible justification. But they do survive for this reason. Much as the law of adaptation selects certain species of animals for survival, so does the law of conspicuous waste select certain types of commodities for survival. "Any consumer who might . . . insist on the elimination of all honorific or wasteful elements from his consumption, would be unable to supply his most trivial wants in the modern market."

In an elaborate pose of objectivity, Veblen regretted that the word *waste* carried "an undertone of deprecation." That is not my purpose, he proclaimed; in "the view of economic theory," one expenditure is just as valid as another. He then stated his own view while pretending he was stating common opinion: "The popular reprobation of waste goes to say that in order to be at peace with himself the common man must be able to see in any and all human effort and human enjoyment an enhancement of life and well-being on the whole." It is not enough that a given expenditure is useful to the individual; perhaps his needs are destructive and should not be satisfied. The proper standard is "the generically human": the right experiences are those that help to develop the best capacities of man. In *The Theory of the Leisure Class*, Veblen's ethic is stated repeatedly—but always in an offhand way: The good is whatever makes for "added physical comfort and fullness of life." He, no less than the women of Hull-House, was concerned chiefly with the quality of human existence, but where they were straightforward, he was oblique and ironic.

In relating this ethic to economic affairs, Veblen distinguished two types of economic institutions: industry and business. The former had to do with producing goods and services;

the latter had to do with acquiring ownership of the goods and
services that were produced. One dealt in material things, the
other in pecuniary affairs. Business was preoccupied with status; industry was noninvidious. Industry contributed to the
general welfare; business was aimed at personal success and
was destructive of the general welfare.

Economic progress arises from any of three basic sources:
advances in technical methods of production (which increase
man's control of nature) or in forms of industrial organization
(which are often needed before the best technical methods
can be used) or growth of population. When advances of
these types occur, it is industry that puts them to use to produce more goods and services at lower cost. In contrast, "the
economic function of the propertied class or of the captains of
industry . . . is of a parasitic character, and their interest is to
divert what substance they may to their own use, and to retain whatever is under their hand. The conventions of the
business world have grown up under the selective surveillance
of this principle of predation or parasitism. They are . . . de-
rivatives, more or less remote, of the ancient predatory culture."

Under primitive savagery, the struggle for existence was a
struggle of the group against its natural environment. But with
the advent of predatory barbarism, when private ownership
began, the struggle for life became in large part a struggle between groups. The qualities that made for survival were "freedom from scruple, from sympathy, honesty, and regard for
life. . . . It is only within narrow limits, and then only in a
Pickwickian sense, that honesty is the best policy." The same
traits continued in the industrial age to be the ones that made
for personal success, but "fraud and prudence, or administrative ability," tended to displace physical violence as the common instrument. However, Veblen warned, "this substitution
of chicane in place of devastation takes place only in an uncertain degree."

As examples of the persistence in modern times of "the fighting propensity proper," he cited war and dueling. Enthusiasm for settling disputes by force was strongest in two classes: the leisure class and "the lower class delinquents." Members of both groups showed "a persistence into adult life of traits that are normal to childhood and youth, and that are likewise normal or habitual to the earlier stages of culture." A third example was sports, addiction to which "in a peculiar degree marks an arrested development of the man's moral nature." The total effect of sports was to promote "ferocity and astuteness," neither of which had any value "for the purposes of the collective life."

In modern society, industrial efficiency is the quality that best promotes the common weal. But modern technology does not depend on manual skill, as handicrafts had done; it depends rather on coming to understand certain mechanical processes so that we can control them. The man best able to do this is the man who habitually thinks in matter-of-fact, common-sense terms, who thinks always about mechanical sequences of cause and effect. Modern industry is also a collective undertaking, which requires "honesty, diligence, peacefulness, good-will, an absence of self-seeking." In short, the individuals involved must cooperate and not compete. But what promotes the group interest is contradicted by the requirements of personal success. To succeed, a man must be adept at "shrewd trading and unscrupulous management." The traits that promote the group interest are a handicap to the individual: they divert his efforts to other goals than making money; even when he tries to make money, he will do so "by the indirect and ineffectual channels of industry, rather than by a free and unfaltering career of sharp practice." (Clarence Darrow three years later, in his memorial address for Altgeld, declared: "Men have money not because they are smarter than other men, but because they have devoted such intellect as the Lord gave them to the base purpose of acquiring wealth.")

Veblen conceded that the creation of giant industrial organizations was an economic achievement of the first order. But he denied that the captains of industry were entitled to any credit. At most, the typical tycoon merely allowed these achievements; he did not institute them. "The mechanically effective details of production and of industrial organization are delegated to subordinates of a less 'practical' turn of mind, —men who are possessed of a gift for workmanship rather than administrative ability ["administrative ability" means, of course, a gift for "fraud and prudence"]."

The "economic man," who thinks only of profit for himself, "is useless for the purposes of modern industry," which "requires an impersonal, non-invidious interest in the work in hand. . . . This interest in work differentiates the workman from the criminal on the one hand, and from the captain of industry on the other." But the traits admired by the pecuniary classes tend to spread even to those engaged in industrial occupations, so that the distinctions between classes are not clear-cut.

In yet other ways the influence of the upper class worked for a perpetuation of barbarian attributes and habits of thought. Men are naturally conservative: "All change in habits of life and of thought is irksome." But members of the industrial classes were forced to change because of economic pressures, whereas the wealth of the leisure class sheltered it from these pressures and allowed it to be conservative. Since conservatism is characteristic of the most reputable class, it tends to become itself honorific, and members of other classes emulate their betters in this regard. Since the leisure class grabs for itself so much of the social output, it leaves many persons absorbed by the constant struggle to earn their subsistence, and therefore conservative "because they cannot afford the effort of taking thought for the day after tomorrow." And as people rose above the subsistence level, they often diverted their surplus "to the purpose of a conspicuous decency, rather than to added physical comfort and fullness of life."

But Veblen found a few signs that leisure-class standards might be decaying. The sense of status and of personal subservience seemed to be waning. Futile activities were generally disapproved, as was unmitigated selfishness and lack of regard for others. The decline of these traits was a blessing, since they were survivals from the earlier predatory barbarism and were incompatible with the efficiency of an industrial society.

"Both as a whole and in its details," wrote Veblen, "the industrial process is a process of quantitative causation. The 'intelligence' demanded of the workman . . . is little else than a degree of facility in the apprehension of and adaptation to a quantitatively determined casual sequence." Lack of this facility made workmen stupid, and enhancement of it "is the end sought in their education—so far as their education aims to enhance their industrial efficiency." (The modern school must "be a workshop," as Altgeld had argued, so that it will train students to understand the processes of production in industrial workshops.)

III

Meanwhile one of Veblen's colleagues at the University of Chicago, John Dewey, was trying to bring formal education into a living relation with modern industry. "It is our social problem now," wrote Dewey, ". . . that method, purpose, understanding, shall exist in the consciousness of the one who does the work, that his activity shall have meaning to himself. . . . How many of the employed are today mere appendages to the machines which they operate!"

Where Veblen was an academic failure, Dewey was a startling success. Two years Veblen's junior, he joined the Chicago faculty in 1894 as chairman of the department of philosophy, psychology, and pedagogy, and in 1896 he founded the Elementary School of the University. Here he explored the practice as well as the theory of the interaction between society and school system.

When Dewey set out to buy desks for the new kindergarten and primary school, he could not find what he wanted. Finally one dealer in school supplies told him: "I am afraid we have not what you want. You want something at which the children may work; these are all for listening." Exactly so, said Dewey, and that is what's wrong with traditional education. It appeals too strictly to "the intellectual aspect of our natures." A large majority of the school population left at or before finishing the fifth grade, only 5 percent got to high school. To these people, no subject, not even reading and writing, was a liberal art; all were practical tools for earning a living. The problem of the school was to end the separation of "cultured people" and workers, of theory and practice. The ordinary man's focus on practical matters must be accepted: to this innate interest the more intellectual aspects of learning must be tied.

In the pre-industrial age, children took part in the production of goods. This trained their characters in discipline, in order and industry, in responsibility to do something useful in the world. The child became acquainted with natural materials, and he learned how to manipulate them. This developed his powers of observation, of planning, of analysis. But in the modern city, goods were produced in factories and stores. No longer was the child in touch with spinning and weaving, with the sawmill and the forge. But any child is an active animal: he wants to do things, not merely to sit quietly while a teacher chants prefabricated knowledge for him to memorize, and this is especially true where the knowledge has no relation to the child's interests or to his daily experience outside the school.

The Elementary School was based on its shops: a kitchen, a sewing room, a carpentry shop. Here the children actually worked with food, with cloth, with wood and metal. They made things. Even more important, they made things together. They learned to cooperate in a common task. This was the exact opposite of traditional education. If school work consists of absorbing information, the success of the individual does not bring any clear social benefits. The only motive for learning is the competitive one in the worst sense, and the child is taught to be selfish and self-seeking. But where active work is going on, mutual aid becomes necessary, and the school gains a chance to "affiliate itself with life."

Dewey made clear that he was not aiming at manual training alone. If a child simply cooks an egg by dropping it in water for three minutes and taking it out when he is told to do so, he is not educated by the activity. But he is educated if he first experiments with various temperatures of water, and their varied effects on the egg. He learns not only how to cook an egg; he learns also the underlying properties of water and of eggs. If a child learns the many processes, from the simplest to the most complex, by which man can make cloth, he is led naturally into learning about the history of these processes. He comes to understand more and more deeply the central problem in every age of mankind: "how to master and use nature so as to make it tributary to the enrichment of human life." By working with the different types of fibers from which cloth can be made, the child learns botany. By studying where each process for making cloth originated, and why, and where all the fibers are grown, he learns geography.

Recognizing that young children have many of the interests of primitive man, the Elementary School imagined a primitive tribe. It was a hunting tribe, with bows and arrows. What environment would these people live in? This brought in geography. Then the children made arrowheads of various materials, thus learning mineralogy. The Iron Age was discussed, and the children built a smelting oven, thus learning the principles of combustion. And laced through the entire sequence of activities was training in anthropology, in the history of the human race.

In such a school the library was the place where the child went with his own problems to see what light the experience of others would throw on them. He also brought those problems to the recitation room for discussion. This type of education, said Dewey, recognizes "the organic relation of theory and practice; the child not simply doing things, but getting also the idea of what he does; getting from the start some intellectual conception that enters into his practice and enriches it; while every idea finds, directly or indirectly, some application in experience and has some effect upon life. This, I need hardly say, fixes the position of the 'book' or reading in education. Harmful as a substitute for experience, it is all-important in interpreting and expanding experience."

Dewey's pedagogy, like Veblen's economic anthropology, was based on the new knowledge of human psychology. Just as Veblen had scoffed at the classical economists' assumption that man was an inert animal, a mere "lightning calculator of pleasures and pains," so did Dewey object that traditional education was wrong in assuming that mind was purely intellectual, when it also involved emotion, purpose, action, a union of thought and practice. Both men insisted that mind was not individual but social, "requiring continual stimulus from social agencies," as Dewey wrote, "and finding its nutrition in social supplies." In a good school, it should be shown in regard to all facts that "they had been generated out of social situations and represented the answers found for social needs." Finally, both men insisted that mind is not static but is a process of growth. The child, Dewey said, is not a small man; he is a child, with his own peculiar capacities and interests.

These capacities and interests must be disciplined by using them to maintain "the cooperative living" in the school, especially by reproducing on the child's level the occupations of the adult world. These occupations were an immense part of each child's present environment, and they also repeated the past experiences of mankind. The instincts expressed in them were permanent and central to human nature. "Men have had to work in order to live. In and through their work they have mastered nature, they have protected and enriched the conditions of their own life, they have been awakened to a sense of their own powers."

Education based on the "psychology of occupation" was not

at all the same as training for a trade or profession. The latter aimed at external utility, often at teaching routines until they became habitual to the student. But sound education aimed at the internal growth of the student, at a maximum of consciousness, of planning and verification. It was the job of the teacher to know what capacities in the child were trying to express themselves at each stage in his growth, and to stimulate the activities that would help the child to discover and develop these capacities in himself. The aim is constant: the child must be "carried on to a higher plane of perception and judgment, and equipped with more efficient habits; so that he has an enlarged and deepened consciousness and increased control of powers of action. Wherever this result is not reached, play results in mere amusement and not in educative growth."

The young child, said Dewey, simply abandons himself to whatever he is doing; he is incapable of *conscious* effort. But there is a gradual development, at about age eight, of voluntary attention, which the ordinary school tried to stimulate by forcing the child to memorize ready-made answers to somebody else's questions. This tactic was futile, Dewey argued: a teacher cannot command a child (or an adult, for that matter) to be interested in a specific fact or question. All education must take as its starting point "the instinctive, impulsive attitudes and activities of the child." The teacher must discover a problem that has captured the attention of the pupil. He must then help the pupil to learn how to answer that question by disciplined activity: by planning an action, carrying it out, observing the results, correcting his action. He must use the answer to the original question to help the pupil formulate a new, more advanced question. He must guide the pupil in building a stock of knowledge and in developing powers of judgment and discrimination.

Such were the aims and methods of the University's Elementary School. Dewey emphasized that it was not a model school but a laboratory school, whose purpose was to experiment, to test carefully some hypotheses that might become part of a general approach to education. He wanted to show how the school system could be unified by relating it intimately to everyday life and by basing its activities on a sounder knowledge of human nature.

CHAPTER 9

The Criminal Law

Can it be possible that Jesus, & St. Francis, & Tolstoi, & Darrow & Whitlock & Jones and the unnumbered apostles of love are all wrong?

—Mayor S. M. Jones of Toledo to Brand Whitlock, August 30, 1903 °

I

THE GROWTH OF industrial cities, while challenging the foundation of traditional education, also threatened to pervert the courts into a tool of injustice. In an America of farms and small towns, like northeastern Ohio, where Clarence Darrow lived from his birth in 1857 until he moved to Chicago in 1887, enforcement of the law was often tempered by mercy. A man was likely to be known, at least by reputation, to all of his neighbors for miles around. Thus, if he were accused of a crime, he would be arrested by friends, relatives, and acquaintances, indicted by them, tried by them, sentenced by them. The men who enforced the law were often constrained in some degree to imagine themselves in the position of the man charged with having violated it.

But even before he left Ashtabula for Chicago, Darrow read

° Whitlock Mss., Library of Congress.

Altgeld's *Our Penal Machinery and Its Victims* and learned that law enforcement in great cities showed little of this compassion that arose from equality and uniformity. Chicago had a million citizens, of dozens of nationalities, of widely variant economic and social standing, of divergent political creeds, holding to contradictory religions and moralities. In this situation, stereotypes flourished. A man so much as accused of having broken the law was instantly cast out by many citizens from the common humanity and labeled as one of the "criminal classes."

And as the size of the city increased, the amount of crime seemed to increase more than proportionately. In 1893 in Chicago, one arrest took place for every eleven persons. The most common charge was disorderly conduct, which had increased more than six times in fifteen years. The second most common charge was assault: an indication of the growth of violence. The murder rate in 1898 was four times as high as in 1880.

In this situation the Chicago police were edgy in their actions, a predilection often increased by their own prejudices. Near Hull-House one spring day in 1897 a Polish-born patrolman, John Baginski, came upon two Italian workmen who were sitting on the wooden garbage box in front of their tenement chatting. He ordered them to move on. They refused. An argument started. He drew his revolver and shot them both. One died. Great community indignation finally resulted in the indictment of Baginski, who was quoted in the newspapers as saying: "The Italians who live in that neighborhood are vicious." But more than a year passed before he came to trial, and he was acquitted; many Chicago jurors were unwilling to limit the police in dealing with the "criminal element."

Such outrages could spring from personal prejudice; they could also spring from the deliberate policy of the police department. Anarchist meetings were systematically suppressed. Every time Albert Parsons' widow attempted to give a public speech in Chicago she was arrested, taken to the police station, charged with disorderly conduct, and promptly released. This procedure lasted for years after the Haymarket episode. As late as 1900, the police notified the owner of a hall where Mrs. Parsons was scheduled to speak that they would hold him responsible for any disturbance at the meeting. He therefore refused to open the doors. Mrs. Parsons and the few persons who appeared then gathered across the street. Although there was no effort at oratory and no breach of the peace, twenty detectives attacked the party with clubs and arrested five persons.

Other minorities were unable to get the police protection they wanted. In 1901 anti-Semitic assaults on street peddlers were estimated at twelve a day. Peddlers told how they had been beaten, vilified, and had their goods stolen or destroyed, mainly by gangs of teen-age boys. Jane Addams pointed to the police failure to prevent these assaults as one aspect of a general failure to enforce the law in Chicago. Clarence Darrow counseled the Jewish peddlers to demand their rights as citizens: "You cannot get others to help you until you organize and help yourselves."

But when a crime aroused widespread fear, the police were so zealous to identify the culprit that, contrary to the constitutional provision about self-incrimination, they forced him to identify himself; they assiduously used the sweatbox technique to extract confessions. Thus in 1902 the body of a young woman was found, shot in the head. Two days later the mother of her lover, William Bartholin, was found buried. Bartholin had disappeared. But a friend was arrested, held at the police station without being booked, and grilled relentlessly for six days. On the sixth day Darrow and another lawyer filed a petition for a writ of habeas corpus in his behalf. Now the police brought the prisoner into court and announced that they were ready to book him for murder. The judge held him to the grand jury and refused to set bail, but the prisoner was at least transferred to the county jail where he would not be subject to more sweatboxing. Three weeks later Bartholin was found dead in an Iowa field, obviously a suicide. Beside his body was a signed confession saying he had had no help in his crimes. Three Chicago dailies ran heated editorials against the sweatbox practice, but their heat subsided, and the police continued with the time-saving technique.

After the police arrested a man, the next step depended on the prosecutor. In Cook County, the state's attorney was not paid a salary; he earned only fees. For every felony conviction secured by his office he got $20; for every misdemeanor conviction, $5. He also got 10 percent of all bonds that were forfeited. On March 1, 1900, he was owed $15,000.

The lowest courts were presided over by justices of the peace. Elsewhere in Illinois these officers were elected by popular vote, but in Cook County they were appointed by the governor, and all sorts of political chicane entered into the appointments. Each justice had jurisdiction throughout the county, so that a man who lived at its southern limit could be sued at the northern one and the hour of trial fixed at 8 A.M. When the defendant did not appear at the proper time, a judgment by default was entered against him. (Often the justice got his share of the award. Of course, he passed part of it along to the ward boss who had persuaded the governor to appoint him.)

Indictment for serious crimes rested with the grand juries— and the trade unions consistently charged that the grand juries were not representative of the citizenry of Chicago. In 1900 a grand jury was impaneled to look into charges that the building-materials companies had conspired to fix prices and to discriminate against contractors who hired union labor. Of the twenty-three members, five were contractors or executives in building-materials companies. No indictments were returned. The secretary of the AFL Building Trades Council reported: "I visited the office of the jury commission and learned several things. I'm beginning to understand how the laboring men get the worst of it every time. The chief clerk of the commission admitted to me that he had a good deal to say as to whether a man served on the grand jury. If he looked intelligent and wore good clothes he might be certified for grand jury service."

From April to September, 1904, 135 men served on grand juries in Chicago. Eighty-five of them were business executives. Five were industrial workers.

Two years later the Chicago *Tribune* charged editorially that Mayor Edward F. Dunne, a liberal Democrat, had appointed boodlers to the school board. The board and the mayor demanded that a grand jury investigate and indict the grafters, if any, or indict the *Tribune* for criminal libel. The grand jury heard the *Tribune's* evidence, said it was trivial, and then neglected to indict the paper or any of its employees. Mayor Dunne, who had served since 1892 on the bench of Cook County, declared that grand juries had outlived their usefulness, and Louis F. Post's *The Public* agreed. Originally, said that journal, the device had protected men against baseless prosecutions by royal appointees. Since its purpose was to test the prosecutor's good faith and his ability to make a prima facie case, the grand jury heard only his evidence, and heard it in secret. But now the grand juries had become, not a check on the prosecutor, but his eager accomplices, and their secrecy had become "a dreadful agency of injustice."

After a man was indicted, he had to await his trial, which might not come for several months. If he could not post bond, he spent those months in jail. To further complicate matters, the clerk of the criminal court did not prepare a calendar of when cases would be called for trial; every afternoon at 2 or 3 p.m. a list was posted of the cases to be tried the next day. Since the sheriff would not serve processes presented to him after 2 p.m., a defendant was often unable to get his witnesses together in time. When the case was called, he had to ask for a continuance. In November, 1901, the county jail held sixty persons who had been there awaiting trial for more than six months because they had not been ready when their cases were called.

The judges themselves were a motley bunch. Some were decent men with common sense and a sound knowledge of the law. But none was on the bench for that reason. To be a judge, a lawyer needed either skill at getting along with the machine politicians, or he needed intimate connections with the business leaders and the newspaper publishers. Many judges were former corporation lawyers who had spent their days working with business executives, and who still associated with them evenings at the Union League Club. Such men were likely to have small patience with immigrant working-men, and even less with agitators like Eugene Debs.

After the Pullman strike, when Debs served six months in jail for violating an injunction issued by the same judge who sentenced him, Stephen S. Gregory wrote to Henry Demarest Lloyd: "It seems strange to me, except that it has been ever thus, that the railroads did not realize as well as public officials how it would disarm Debs to treat him justly—to show that the courts and Judges whom he denounced as corporate tools could yet . . . , calm and unruffled, administer the law justly, unmoved by the demand of the wealthy and influential classes for vengeance upon him. They in my judgment, and perhaps unconsciously, failed in this—and thus to a large degree justify him. . . ." Gregory had been one of Debs's lawyers in this very case, but he had also been a law partner of the Chief Justice of the Supreme Court of the United States, and subsequently he was president of the American Bar Association.

Another of Debs's attorneys, Clarence Darrow, persistently argued that the judiciary was biased. On the one hand, judges issued labor injunctions which had all of the force of statutes; on the other, they invalidated laws setting maximum hours of work for women. "It is no exaggeration," Darrow declared, "to say that nine-tenths of the laws are made nowadays by the judges and that they are made in the interests of the rich and powerful and to destroy the poor. . . . The judge is the most powerful official in the machinery of modern civilization, for he can override statutes and even the constitution whenever necessary."

Of course every defendant was entitled to a lawyer to protect him, but, Darrow pointed out: "The good lawyer does not defend poor criminals; he defends the rich ones—gas companies and railway corporations. It would be singular for the poor to win many of their cases."

If a man lost, he had the legal right to appeal his conviction. For the poor, said Darrow, this right was empty: "There is one court for the poor—the first court in which a case is taken—and all courts for the rich, who are able to appeal their cases. Justice is like sugar or salt. . . . The amount you get is regulated by the amount of money you have."

If the machinery of arrest and trial was harsh and often unjust, attitudes toward punishment were more so. Influential men, whether from hysteria or from ignorance, continuously argued that severe retribution would deter men from crime. In 1904 William Pinkerton, head of the detective agency in Chicago and the strikebreaker favored by some of its largest corporations, was asked how to stop an alleged crime wave. "The whipping post is the thing," he said. "Instead of regarding the bandit as a hero, the youth of today would hardly look with admiring eyes upon a cringing, whining criminal who had been publicly flogged."

At the extreme, criminals could be hanged, as had been done with four of the Haymarket defendants. It was not uncommon. During Altgeld's first two years as governor, seven men were hanged in Illinois. At the end of those two years Altgeld, in his message to the legislature, urged the abolition of capital punishment.

II

To Clarence Darrow, as to John Peter Altgeld, killing another man was wanton arrogance—men pretending to be God—even if the killing were done according to the form of the law. But ironically, Darrow used the existence of capital punishment as a way of reforming other parts of the law. From evil, good can come.

The criminal law, said Darrow, does many criminal deeds. This will be changed only if people take an interest and determine to change it. But who can care about outrages in the abstract? Reform will seem urgent only if men see how the abuse affects a human being. The problem must be personified, and dramatized, and nothing is more dramatic and personal than the statement that this defendant—this very person, this crazy Patrick Prendergast, this child Thomas Crosby—might be hanged by the neck until he is dead. Unjustly.

Prendergast did what no sane man would ever do: he assassinated one of the most popular mayors Chicago ever had. Carter Harrison the Elder, five times mayor of Chicago, had a flamboyance and tolerance that appealed to most of the voters. In 1893 he won handily over his Republican opponent even though all of the city's newspapers were against him except the one he owned.

Saturday, October 23, 1893, was American Cities Day at the Columbian Exposition, and Mayor Harrison gave one of his typical speeches boosting Chicago. He then returned to his home on the near southwest side. When his doorbell rang, he answered it himself. A young man dressed in working clothes stood on the porch. The visitor angrily stated that he had come to get satisfaction, drew a revolver, and shot the mayor three times. Seventeen minutes later, Harrison was dead.

The early magazine stories about the shooting said that the assailant, Patrick Eugene John Prendergast, was crazy. Although he had no legal training, he had filed an application to be appointed as corporation counsel to the city, and he was infuriated when the mayor neglected to reply to his request. *Harper's Weekly* also reported that Prendergast had written to Harrison on other topics in ways that showed his "mental disorder." But Chicago was aroused and wanted vengeance. Prendergast was brought to trial only five weeks after the shooting—legal processes can be unusually prompt when justice calls for delay—and was convicted of first-degree murder. The death penalty was mandatory. Two months later, on February 24, 1894, Prendergast's motion for a new trial was denied, and his execution was fixed for March 23. The state supreme court declined to interfere with the sentence.

At this stage other lawyers, including S. S. Gregory and Clarence Darrow, took an interest in the case. First Darrow went to Springfield to ask for commutation of the sentence, but Governor Altgeld was out of the state, and his powers of commutation were in the hands of Lieutenant Governor Joseph B. Gill. Gill was a decent man, but he knew what had happened to Altgeld for pardoning the Haymarket defendants, and he could read the newspapers, and he refused to act. Now there was only one chance to save Prendergast, a chance so slim that it was hardly a chance at all, but Darrow grabbed it. Illinois law provided that no stage in the trial, sentencing, or execution of a criminal could move forward while a criminal was insane, insanity meaning an inability to tell right from wrong. But the question of Prendergast's sanity up to February 24 had already been legally determined.

So Darrow went into court to stop the execution because Prendergast was unable to tell that he was being hanged because he had done a wrongful act. Prendergast is crazy, said Darrow—and his condition has become materially worse since February 24. To bolster this argument, Darrow introduced a technique that he would develop to perfection by the time of the Loeb-Leopold trial thirty years later: he introduced fourteen physicians, several of them specialists in the study of insanity, to testify to the mental condition of Prendergast. Darrow then used this testimony as raw material for his oral argument to the court.

Darrow claimed that his expert witnesses stood in the highest ranks of the medical profession, and that they had testified from no other motive than a desire to see justice done. But he ridiculed the expert witnesses for the prosecution. Of one: "If Dr. Bluthardt had on a white apron, we would all take him for a butcher. He looks like it—he testified like it." Dr. John C. Spray, who had been superintendent of the Dunning Insane Asylum for eleven years, was described by Darrow as "the man that had the white mustache and the jag." He dismissed them all as side-show performers, who should have practiced their trade on the Midway Plaisance at the Columbian Exposition.

Darrow denied that Prendergast had willed to do his deeds. Since the defendant had no freedom of will, he had no responsibility. His deeds were the fault of "the infinite power that made him the object you find today." But Darrow reminded the court that it was not like Prendergast; it could do as it chose. If it hanged the defendant, it would have to bear the responsibility.

> Your verdict will go toward making history. It will count for civilization or barbarism . . . It means much to him and his poor mother and his brother and friends, but it means more to this great State which we love: whether in this day and generation we shall put to death a man of the mental caliber of this. The question of insanity is largely a modern one. In ancient times lunatics were chained and imprisoned . . . They were confined in filthy pens. They were loaded with chains. All sorts of indignities were heaped upon them. But we have builded asylums; we have learned something of humanity; we have become more civilized and enlightened as the years have moved along; and we have recognized insanity as a disease, and treated kindly and patiently and carefully those who have received this terrible affliction from the hands of God.
>
> They tell us his life is not worth saving; that he may be insane, but what of it? Hang him anyway! Gentlemen, I cannot tell what harm would come from hanging a crazy boy. . . . But I do know . . . that not a drop of human blood is shed except it creates an impression on the world and I believe, gentlemen, that to lead this poor lunatic up the steps of the scaffold, to sew him in a shroud, to tie a rope around his neck, to drop the scaffold from his feet, to leave him dangling in the air, . . . would work infinite harm to infinite human beings on the earth. I know there is no power on earth to tell how many hearts would be calloused, how many souls would be wrecked, how many blood stains would come upon the conscience of men.

But the argument did not save Prendergast: the proposition that he had become insane in the preceding month was too absurd. He was hanged—the only client that Darrow ever lost to an executioner.

Five years later, in the trial of Thomas George Crosby, Darrow confronted an even more extreme instance of indictment for first degree murder. Crosby was a thirteen-year-old boy who lived with his aged foster-mother, Mrs. Marjorie Crosby. Some years earlier, when Mr. Crosby was ill, Mrs. Crosby had mortgaged the home she owned and lived in so that she could lend $14,000 to a firm in which Mr. Crosby was a partner. After Mr. Crosby died, the firm had denied that it owed anything to Mrs. Crosby. She brought suit to recover the money. While the suit was pending, proceedings were started to foreclose the mortgage on her home. Mrs. Crosby consulted an attorney, who told her—so she claimed later—that he had arranged for her to remain in her home for an additional sixty days, until January 7, 1899. Young Thomas was told by his mother that the attorney had advised them to shoot anybody who tried to molest them. They barricaded themselves in the house, sealing the windows with boards nailed to the frames.

On December 22, 1898, three days before Christmas, Thomas thought that his mother had gone downtown and that he was home alone. Somebody came onto the porch and knocked. The man then began knocking boards off a window. Thomas went to the window, holding a revolver in his hand, and called, "Go away or I'll shoot." The warning went unheeded. The boy pulled the trigger. He had never shot a gun before, and it did not fire. He then pushed the gun up to a hole in the window where a pane had been knocked out and fired again. He took no aim and saw nobody. This time the gun went off. He went into the hallway, where, to his surprise, he met his mother. He told her what he had done. He then went to the Lake View Water Works and telephoned the police.

He was arrested at home and taken to the police station. There he learned that he had shot and killed a deputy sheriff,

Frank E. Nye, who was trying to serve a writ of ejection from
the home on Mrs. Crosby. Both mother and son were indicted
for murder.

When the trial began in April, 1899, with Darrow and William Prentiss for the defense, the prosecution stated that it
would not ask the death penalty for young Crosby. But the
jury could impose it. Illinois law provided only that persons
under ten years of age could not be executed. Crosby was all
of thirteen. Persons under fourteen were presumed to be incapable of crime, but if such culpability could be shown to the
satisfaction of the jury, the death penalty could be inflicted.

Darrow and Prentiss went all out in the trial. They put
Thomas Crosby on the stand, where he made an excellent impression. They put Mrs. Crosby on the stand and let her
weep: she sat with bowed head, her cheeks trembling, the tears
running down her face. They talked indignantly about one
business firm stealing money from a widow while another business firm stripped her of her home. They railed at the inhumanity of a law that would allow a thirteen-year-old boy to be
hanged. When Prentiss said that if all boys were like Tommy
Crosby, there would be no need for courts and juries, three
women applauded—and a startled courtroom watched while
the judge ordered the three women taken to jail for contempt
of court.

Darrow in his final argument seemed downright reckless,
but was not; he had incredible talent for feeling what a jury
was feeling, and that told him how far he could afford to go.
Now he leveled a flat challenge: "Gentlemen of the jury, rather
than have you send this boy to the penitentiary or to the reform school, to be incarcerated among criminals, where his
young life would be contaminated and blasted, I would have
you sentence him to death on the gallows."

The jury deliberated for eight hours, while the defendants
were held in jail. Thomas Crosby, when interviewed in his
cell, was calm and cheerful. He said that if he were acquitted,
he thought he would study to "be a lawyer, so I can get a

chance to choke off some of these bad lawyers. I won't go around trying to take their homes away from widows. I'll defend them and I'll do it for nothing."

Darrow's intuition proved sound. Thomas was found not guilty. His mother was convicted of manslaughter and sentenced by the jury to a year in prison. Six weeks later, the appellate court in Chicago affirmed a court decision requiring the late Mr. Crosby's company to pay his widow the $14,000, plus interest.

III

By his dramatic appeals for justice for specific defendants, Darrow drew public attention to ways in which the law was itself guilty of inhumanity. Thus he helped to enlist or to neutralize public opinion in the campaigns for practical improvements. Of these reforms, none was more important or more successful than the changes in the judicial treatment of children.

Under English family law, a father had many rights and few duties: in most matters, his word was law. But the king was also "father of his country," who sometimes could act in place of the natural parent. In the United States, comparable authority was in the hands of the states, which usually acted by means of equity proceedings, thus allowing a judge some flexibility in dealing with specific cases. As early as 1831 in Illinois, the law provided that for certain offenses the penalties for minors might differ from those for adults. Thirty years later, the legislature allowed children accused of petty offenses to be put on probation or sent to reform schools. But in 1870 the state supreme court ordered one Michael O'Connell released from the reform school of Chicago on the ground that his confinement there without benefit of trial infringed his personal liberty and the right of the parent "to the care, custody and assistance of his child." There were great differences of opinion, said the court, as to the proper way to rear children; before the parental right is infringed, "gross misconduct or almost total unfitness on the part of the parent, must be clearly proved."

A law of 1879 set up industrial schools where dependent children could be sent, and the supreme court refused to invalidate the act, ruling that the restraint imposed in such schools was not excessive. "Such a degree of restraint as is essential to the proper education of a child," said the court, "is in no sense an infringement of the inherent and inalienable right to personal liberty."

But the total body of statutes dealing with children was still much too rigid. In the industrial school, children guilty of no offense whatever mingled with children who had been reared by hooligans, whores, and pimps. Humane judges minimized the more serious offenses of children in order to send them to the industrial school; otherwise any child ten years old or more would be arrested, tried in the police courts, and confined in prison. In 1898, there were 575 children locked up in the Cook County jail. About one hundred boys a month were being committed with adults to the house of correction.

It was the laws, not the judges, that were basically at fault. Indeed, baffled judges were known to resort to almost any expedient, so long as they could find some legal sanction for it, to avoid doing an injustice to a child.

Scene: *Probate Court of Cook County*
Time: *About 1898*

> The judge has asked Julia Lathrop, as a member of the state board of charities, to come to a private hearing in his chambers. She is present.
>
> The case involves a twelve-year-old girl. Five years ago she was legally adopted by a drudging woman who owned a little, cheap hotel. Since that time, the girl has been made to tend the furnace, take care of the house, wash limitless piles of dishes half the night. A short while ago a female guest in the hotel, upset at the mistreatment, persuaded the child to accompany her into another county. The foster mother made efforts to recover her ward, who was found living with her new friend in

a brothel. Now both women are present in the judge's chambers. The child waits outside while her fate is decided.

The judge is perplexed. Although the prostitute has concealed from the girl all knowledge of the trade being practiced in the house where they have lived for three days, obviously the child cannot be left with her. Nor can the foster mother retain custody, since a doctor has pronounced the child neglected and dangerously anemic. Nor can the girl be sent to an industrial school for dependent children, because it is unclear which county is responsible for her upkeep. The judge asks Julia Lathrop if she will accept legal custody. Although the child is a complete stranger to her, although she did not have any intention of adopting anybody, she agrees.

The judge turns to the two offending women. He berates the foster mother, but she cannot understand wherein she has erred: she was a "bound girl" herself in childhood, she has been grossly overworked since becoming an adult, and she regards it as the mark of a virtuous family that all members should work as hard as they can. The judge hints that the prostitute may be a procuress, and she is devastated at the accusation: she insists that she was "merely trying to be good to an accused child whose spine was growing crooked from lifting great shovelfuls of coal too heavy for her."

Neither of the women is threatened with any punishment by the judge, but neither is content to escape. Each feels that her intentions were only good and that she is utterly misunderstood. "Self-deception is one of the meanest tricks Fate plays upon us," Julia Lathrop comments later. "How simplified life would be if we could judge people by what they think of themselves!"

Julia Lathrop continued for many years to feel responsible for this girl, but not even the women of Hull-House could care personally for all of the dependent children in Illinois. The problem had to be taken over by some formal arrangement, and the new institution had to be given full discretion to deal with individual cases; it had to be able to act with flexibility and subtlety.

Together with Jane Addams and a few other women, Julia

Lathrop became aroused about the more than five hundred children confined in the Chicago house of correction. They raised the issue in the Chicago Woman's Club, which induced the Chicago board of education to set up a school for the boys in the jail. They raised the more general problem of dependent children at the meeting in November, 1898, of the State Conference of Charities. That body asked the Chicago Bar Association to draft a bill for a juvenile court. Even though there was no similar court anywhere in the United States, the Association took up the measure and drafted the bill. With such conservative origins and potent support, the bill made its way through the legislature; on July 1, 1899, it became law.

The law directed the circuit court judges in Cook County to designate one of their number to hear cases involving boys under seventeen and girls under eighteen. A complaint about the care of any child could be made by any person in the community, not merely by law-enforcement officers. A defendant was to be brought directly into juvenile court. If he was ruled dependent, neglected, or delinquent, he became a ward of the state. Then the judge could place him on probation with his parents, or place him under a guardian, or send him to whichever state institution was deemed most suitable. (The law was drafted carefully: when it was finally tested in 1913, the state supreme court ruled it constitutional in all respects.)

In the new juvenile court, the old rules of criminal procedure did not apply. Nobody was present to prosecute the child, nobody to defend him. There was a hearing, not a trial between adversaries. The idea of punishment was replaced by the aim of promoting the healthy growth of the child. All concerned were trying to find out what could be done in his behalf.

As if to emphasize its unique status, the juvenile court was not located downtown in the county courthouse. It had its own building, diagonally across Halsted Street from Hull-House. The building also held the detention home, which had its own schoolrooms and gymnasium; it was so well furnished that opponents of the juvenile court called it a "swell boarding-house for boys."

The law had provided for the appointment of probation officers—but the legislature had not provided the funds to pay them. Julia Lathrop and her friends took care of that; they organized a private Juvenile Court Committee, and, with the aid of several wealthy women in the Chicago Woman's Club, they raised the money for salaries. But what kind of person should be appointed to the job, and what should his duties be? Nobody knew: there was no literature at the time about probation officers or juvenile courts. As one woman prominent in the committee wrote: "Those of us who had the selecting of these officers had to fall back on our own knowledge of human nature." Their knowledge was sound. The first probation officer was Mrs. Alzina Parsons Stevens.

A New Englander by birth, she went to work in a cotton mill when only twelve years old, and promptly lost a finger due to, so the employer said, her "carelessness." She arrived in Chicago soon after the Great Fire of 1871, learned to set type, and became a member of the printers' union. She became prominent in labor circles, and in 1893 Governor Altgeld named her assistant state factory inspector, under Florence Kelley. In that post Mrs. Stevens proved her courage by clashing head on with Marshall Field. She repeatedly showed her humanity: when the despairing Eugene Debs went on a prolonged drunk after the collapse of the Pullman strike, it was Mrs. Stevens who smuggled him away to her suburban home and kept him under cover where the newspapers could not learn his condition. But she was no soft-headed apologist for everything workers did: when a resident of Hull-House tried to condone a dishonest labor leader, Mrs. Stevens flared, "That is the worst kind of snobbishness to assume that you must not have the same standards of honor for working people as you have for the well-to-do."

Turned out of her state job when Altgeld left office in 1897, she went to live at Hull-House, and began voluntarily going to court every morning to present cases of delinquent boys to the judges. Often they gave the boys into her custody, although there was no legal sanction for doing so.

In 1898, when the issue became timely in Illinois, she went to Boston, where she studied the truant schools and the judicial treatment of children. She presented this material before committees of the Massachusetts legislature; and the Illinois legislature used it in 1899 in considering the juvenile court bill. Mrs. Stevens had other qualifications for her new job: She was said to know by name nearly all the families in the Seventeenth Ward. She had been chairman of the industrial committee of the Illinois Federation of Women's Clubs, president of the Hull-House Woman's Club for two years, and a member of numerous reform societies. She also belonged to the Hull-House Anti-Cigarette Club, which had forty members.

When she was recommended by the Juvenile Court Committee, the judge who had been assigned to the new court cheerfully appointed her. Although she died less than a year later, already by that time she was the senior of six probation officers, and the outlines of this unprecedented role had been defined.

The juvenile court law improved the treatment of deprived children, but it did nothing to prevent children from lapsing into this state of need. To solve this more basic problem, the women of Hull-House had long been conducting a double-edged campaign: to ban children from gainful employment and to require children to go to school. And at the turn of the century, just when the juvenile court was being established, they also finished the job of erecting a fairly effective statutory web that would ban child labor and put the children into school.

As early as 1855 Illinois had accepted the principle of free tax-supported schools. The first compulsory-attendance law was passed in 1883, and other statutes on the subject were adopted in 1889 and 1893. But they did little good. None of them required attendance for more than sixteen weeks a year, and a child could virtually attend at the convenience of his parents: go to school a week, stay out two weeks, go another week. The 1889 law required every school district to appoint at least one truant officer, but this feature was made permissive rather than mandatory in 1893. Most important of all, so long as child labor was not banned, parents had a strong mercenary reason to ignore the compulsory-attendance law, and they did so by the thousands. A child-labor law was enacted in 1891, but it was riddled with loopholes.

Not until the child-labor law of 1893, which required the appointment of factory inspectors, was there machinery to chase the children out of the factories. Florence Kelley and her assistants did that, but they found that they were merely driving children out of the workshops onto the pavements. The law did not prohibit children from working in stores and warehouses, from shining shoes, peddling newspapers, hawking fruits and vegetables in the streets. Year after year in her annual reports Mrs. Kelley railed against the situation. She told how in Chicago, which did have truant officers although the state law did not require them, unruly children were expelled from schools so that teachers would not have to trouble with them. She told how principals of schools sent to the factory inspectors children only eleven years old, with the request that the child be given a work permit because he was "incorrigible" in school. The compulsory-attendance law, so she declared in 1896, was "a dead letter." She excoriated the Chicago city council because it cut school appropriations by $2 million for 1896-1897, thus checking the construction of school buildings.

Due in large measure to her protests, the legislature in 1897 extended the child-labor law to ban employment in "offices, stores and mercantile establishments" as well as factories. It also made the appointment of truant officers mandatory again. Two years later, it required all cities to establish the long-desired parental schools. Now a child who was a persistent truant, or who behaved so badly in his public or parochial school as to make his presence intolerable, was not merely expelled from school. Instead he could be committed by the juvenile court to the parental school for custody, discipline, and training.

In 1903 the last major gap in the statutes was plugged. A new compulsory-attendance law required every child between seven and fourteen to attend some school during the entire period it was in session, and required that this period should be at least 110 days a year of actual teaching. It provided that no child could be exempted from this requirement for any reason except physical or mental incapacity. No longer could a board of education permit a child to work because his earnings were needed to support his family.

Still other reforms were made in the treatment of children. In 1903 a widow was hailed into court. She was so poor that she could not bring up her little child properly. The child would have to be sent to an institution. But the mother testified that she could not live without her child. The judge was distraught. Although women were banned from serving on juries, he invited a group of women to advise the male jury. The women decided that if the child was dependent, so was the mother. Let them both be sent to an institution where they need not be separated. The official jury so decreed.

Step by step, with infinite stamina and practicality, the women of Hull-House reshaped the state institutions that dealt with children. But they did not rest there. They probed into the day-by-day administration of the new institutions they had helped to create. And always they gathered facts, facts, and more facts, and they analyzed the facts until they had gained deep and general insights. While Julia Lathrop was urging the partial truth that delinquency was mainly due to poverty, Edith Abbott and Sophonisba Breckinridge were already collecting the data that would yield a better theory. They made a statistical study of cases that came into juvenile court, not just a few, but thirteen thousand cases. They showed that a third of the cases came from broken homes. They showed further that delinquency was far more common in some areas of the city than in others, and that the difference could not be explained solely on the ground of differences in income.

Another woman in their school at the University of Chicago did the first intensive case studies of juvenile delinquents. This work, reinforced by a conversation with William James, gave Julia Lathrop an idea, and she induced Dr. William Healy to open a psychopathic clinic at the juvenile court in 1909—the first child-guidance clinic in the country. From that day forward, the emphasis in dealing with children was on mental hygiene, and the aim in each case was to take account of all the biological, economic, social, and emotional forces that molded the child's behavior. By that year, 1909, more than twenty states and the District of Columbia had set up juvenile courts.

The juvenile courts ramified in all directions. As judges were called on to deal with specific problems of indigent mothers, many of them came to advocate mothers' pensions or mothers' assistance programs. Several states started such programs, and thirty years later the Federal government came to subsidize aid to dependent children.

Of even more sweeping import was the changed attitude toward the law. Prior to 1880, the received dogma was that the function of the judge was to decide cases on the basis of earlier cases, of precedents. But now arose the competing doctrine that the law must take account of social facts and must be shaped to solve social problems. This sociological jurisprudence found its most complete application in the workings of the juvenile court, but adult offenders also benefited in the adoption of probation, parole, and the indeterminate sentence.

Much had been done; more remained to be done. In 1911 the Juvenile Protective Association, the successor at Hull-House to the Juvenile Court Committee, reported that nearly all of the city's dance halls—by far the most popular recreation with Chicago adolescents—were run for the benefit of adjoining saloons. These dance halls were licensed by the city, and policemen were on duty in most of the ones observed by the Association. But in six instances the policemen themselves were found drinking, and minors were drinking liquor in more than half of the halls. In 75 percent of the halls, liquor was sold. In these it was nearly impossible to get a drink of water, and almost all of the boys showed signs of intoxication by midnight. The windows were often boarded up in order to keep the temperature high and the dust thick. Dances were brief; intermissions extended.

In Chicago the saloon-keepers, like the industrialists and the aldermen, knew how to create the main chance.

IV

In contrast to the success of efforts to secure legal protection for children, little was achieved by the campaign to restrict the issuance of injunctions in labor disputes. The issue came to prominence during the Pullman strike of 1894, when a Federal judge ruled that Eugene Debs and his associates had violated an injunction and sent them to jail for contempt of court. Thereafter in strike after strike the employer got an injunction from a judge, and then used it to prevent picketing and to facilitate the hiring of strikebreakers. Repeatedly Altgeld and Darrow and the leaders of trade unions denounced this practice as "government by injunction." They were especially incensed that single-handed a judge could jail a man for violating an order that he himself had issued; they contended that men accused of contempt were in all cases entitled to the constitutional right of trial by jury, unless the contempt was direct, that is, had actually been committed in a courtroom and thus interfered with the administration of justice. But employers continued to ask for injunctions, and judges continued to grant them and to enforce them.

In 1900 a bill was pending in Congress to prohibit the issuance of injunctions in any labor dispute involving interstate commerce, and Darrow went to Washington to testify for it. As the chief witness for the bill, he urged that labor injunctions should be abolished altogether, but said it would be just as good to guarantee a jury trial in contempt cases. He also argued that no injunction should be issued to restrain any act that would be punishable under Federal or state law. But the members of the committee were hostile to his position, and the bill got nowhere in Congress.

Three years later, when Darrow was a member of the lower house of the Illinois legislature, he led the fight for a state law regulating labor injunctions. The bill guaranteed trial by jury for indirect contempt. It also provided that, if a body of workingmen had the name of their attorney on file with a court, the court could not issue an injunction until the attorney had been notified and a hearing held. But the bill never came to a final vote in the house and was never sent to the senate.

As soon as this session of the legislature adjourned and Darrow returned to Chicago from Springfield, he became involved in one of the most turbulent strikes that had yet occurred in Chicago. Early in May, 1903, two employees of the Kellogg Switchboard Company refused to join the toolmakers' union. The union demanded that they be fired. When the company refused, 900 of its 1,100 workers struck. The company obtained an injunction against picketing from Judge Holdom and proceeded to hire six hundred new workers. Soon sixteen strikers were cited for contempt of court. When they came before the judge for trial, an indignant Darrow was with them. He declared that the judge's decision would have no effect on the future conduct of his clients. They had been engaged in peaceful picketing, he asserted, and their actions had been entirely legal. If all of the union men were sent to jail for this reason, he would continue their actions himself.

Judge Holdom saw it differently. He ruled that the union's demand for a closed shop, which had set off the strike, was on its face unlawful. The pickets had been calling everybody who worked during the strike a "scab," which was not peaceful picketing. He fined each of the defendants and hinted at more severe penalties if the violations were repeated. They were. Ten days later another twenty-one strikers, eleven of them women, were cited for contempt. The judge sent a business agent of the union to jail for ninety days, and he refused to stay the sentence to allow time for an appeal.

But the injunction did not preserve the peace. Riots were a daily occurrence. By the end of June, the Kellogg plant was in a state of siege. Pickets were on every corner within six blocks of it, questioning anybody who came into the neighborhood to determine if he was a strikebreaker.

Confronted by this chaos, the judges of Cook County acted to remove one of the worst features of the situation. Every employer seeking an injunction had consistently schemed to have his motion come before a sympathetic judge. Darrow and the other labor lawyers had consistently moved to have the injunctions modified, and then schemed to have their motions come before judges known to sympathize with unions. This parody of justice led to anarchy, as judges engaged in public disputes with other judges on the same court. Now the judges adopted a new set of rules, under which a specific member of the bench was designated to hear all motions for three months, when he would be succeeded by another member.

The very day this reform was announced, Chicago had its wildest riot since the Pullman strike; one thousand men and women strikers systematically stoned the Kellogg plant and broke hundreds of windows. When police tried to disperse the crowd, they were stoned too. Dozens of strikers were clubbed by the police, and thirty-seven were arrested.

Clarence Darrow, on this day of carnage and devastation, astonished his friends by getting married to a vivacious journalist only half his age. The ceremony was performed by his favorite ally on the Cook County bench, Judge Edward F. Dunne. After a champagne breakfast at the home of the wealthy inventor of shorthand, John R. Gregg, the couple secretly boarded a train for Montreal. Strike or no strike,

Darrow and his bride spent three sybaritic months on the Continent.

His departure left the defense of the strikers in the hands of his partner, Edgar Lee Masters. Already more interested in writing poetry than in practicing law, Masters nonetheless attacked the contempt cases with passion. He wrote a heated pamphlet denouncing labor injunctions, which he called "The New Star Chamber." He carried his challenge of Judge Holdom's injunction all the way to the state supreme court, only to have that court uphold it.

Insult was piled on injury. Just after Darrow fled the city, a new grand jury was instructed to inquire into the Kellogg strike. The foreman of the grand jury was Enos M. Barton, president of the Western Electric Company, which controlled 60 percent of the stock of the Kellogg Switchboard Company.

Even this was not the bottom. A local of the press feeders' union had become a chartered corporation. The local went on strike. Judge Holdom issued an injunction against it. He then ruled that the injunction had been violated, and he fined the union for contempt of court. When the union failed to pay the fine, another judge placed it in receivership.

When five members of this union came before Judge Holdom for picketing, he sent them to jail for contempt. "Pickets," he declared, "are not entitled to any more consideration in the eyes of the law than is the military spy. Their act is akin to that of the thief who secures employment for the purpose of robbing his employer."

CHAPTER 10

Leisure-Class Reform

There is a considerable body of sentiment in the [leisure] class going to support efforts of reform and amelioration.

—Thorstein Veblen [*]

I

NOT UNTIL 1925 did the Illinois legislature pass an anti-injunction statute; a similar Federal law had to wait until 1932. This reform was so belated, compared with the earlier success of the movement for legal protection of children, because the issuance of labor injunctions did not arouse much sympathy outside the ranks of the unions themselves. No reform could succeed in Chicago fifty years ago unless it enlisted support within the ranks of the leisure class, since the workers were not sufficiently unified and powerful to secure it alone.

But where were they to look for allies? Not, it seemed, among the clergy. The Sunday after the Haymarket bombing, the pulpits of Chicago rang with diatribes against labor. Workingmen in general were denounced as communists who should be hunted down like "mad dogs." Ministers called for a strong militia and for the prohibition of any meeting where inflammatory speeches might be made. Nor was this simply antipathy to violence. One Protestant minister proclaimed that

[*] *The Theory of the Leisure Class* (New York: Modern Library), p. 234.

labor was just another commodity, that wages were regulated by the laws of trade, and that any effort to evade those laws by collective action was vain. Another said that strikes were wrong by their nature, regardless of the cause, and that the strikers should pray to God instead of taking matters into their own hands. The Reverend Frank Gunsaulus, the most popular minister in Chicago's history, never tired of eulogizing Philip D. Armour—hardly an idol of the workingman.

Gradually in the 1890's, sermons more frequently discussed the sweating system, the jobless, women and child workers. But Protestant ministers had to make a special effort to understand these matters, because their personal acquaintance with the lower classes was slight. When a worker belonged to any church, it was nearly always the Catholic one. The Church knew that its adherents were chiefly immigrant workingmen, while nearly all the businessmen were Protestants. Especially after 1891, when Pope Leo XIII's encyclical urged a sweeping program of social reform, Catholic clergymen were often sympathetic to wage-earners. Already by that time there were more than 250,000 Catholics in Chicago, while the seven major Protestant denominations combined had only 100,000 communicants.

But many workers stayed away from all churches. When W. T. Stead was going to speak at the Trades and Labor Assembly in 1893, he was warned in advance not to mention religion. "Not five percent of these men ever go to a place of worship," he was told. "If you say anything about God or Christ or the churches, you will be hissed off the platform." Seeking to explain this estrangement, one minister placed the blame on conspicuous consumption and the leisure-class canons of life: "There is no place in the average Chicago church for the poor man . . . surrounded by individuals who not only regard poverty as a disgrace, but by their vulgar display endeavor to perpetually remind the poor man of his poverty."

Thorstein Veblen had another explanation. Religion, he wrote, was "a survival from an earlier phase of associated life

—a mark of arrested spiritual development." Industrial workers would increasingly spurn all forms of supernaturalism because contact with modern industry tended to breed the habit of thinking in terms of material, impersonal causes. The most devout groups were the groups least exposed to this influence: Southern Negroes, lower-class immigrants who had not yet penetrated into the factories, much of the rural population, "the leisure class proper," and "the lower-class delinquents." Women of all classes were more devout than men, partly because women were shielded from the industrial process, partly because they were subjected more rigorously to "the patriarchal relation of status."

But if their existence inclined some women to piety, it spurred others to rebellion. Veblen pointed out that this result was especially common among the well-to-do. Lower-class women were tied to a life of drudgery, which gave them "something tangible and purposeful to do" and occupied their lives so fully that they had no time or energy for revolt. But upper-class women were forced into a life of vicarious leisure to honor their husbands; the canons of good repute excluded them from all useful work and condemned them to spend their days in "ceremonial futility." In these circumstances the "ancient habit of purposeful activity," the instinct of workmanship, began to assert itself, and some women sought to fashion for themselves a mode of life that had meaning.

Their effort ran against harsh barriers. Women could vote in only one election in Illinois: once every two years they could help to elect a woman as trustee of the state university. Some critics sought to abolish even this right. The woman president of the Chicago Anti-Suffrage Society complained that the advocates of woman suffrage were seeking to make "the individual the unit and not the family the unit," and that their foolishness was destructive of marriage and the home. When another critic pointed to the declining registration of women as evidence that they did not want to vote anyway, a suffragette called attention to a recent election in Evanston in which only men were eligible to vote. The population of the election district was more than 25,000; the number of votes cast, 141.

There was a constant danger that women would lose ground they had already gained. In 1899 the Chicago Theological Seminary became the first Congregational seminary in the country to admit women on equal terms, but in the same year the Chicago Education Commission recommended that married women be eliminated from teaching posts in the public schools, that women teachers be replaced by men in the upper grades of the elementary schools, and that men be paid more than women for teaching in these grades. The chairman of this Commission was President William Rainey Harper of the University of Chicago, and three years later his own school acted upon his philosophy. The trustees of the University, by a vote of 13 to 3, voted to segregate instruction for men and women. When Sophonisba Breckinridge was graduated from the university law school in 1904 with the highest average in her class, *The Public* tartly commented that her superiority was "another argument against co-education"—but not one likely to be used by the apostles of discrimination.

The drive for equal rights was stimulated by the actions of John Peter Altgeld as governor of Illinois. One of his first official acts was to appoint two women to state boards: Julia Lathrop to the state board of charities and Florence Kelley, the first woman factory inspector of Illinois. He named the first woman trustee of the University of Illinois. He insisted that every state institution holding women or children should have a woman doctor. Thus he helped to create in women a sense of their own worth. Having gained a little, they wanted more. But it was hard to get more. If the women of the leisure class wanted to remake society, the men did not: by 1893 more than two hundred women were registered as doctors, but a decade later a proposal to admit women to the Physicians' Club of Chicago was rejected by a heavy majority.

By 1899, when Veblen published *The Theory of the Leisure Class*, the reform activities of women were apparent on every hand; his achievement was to see the facts clearly and explain them cogently. But he failed to notice that the legal profession was also fertile in recruits to the cause of reform. Veblen had little use for lawyers. In recording the social hierarchy of occupations, he set down the reasons why the practice of law ranked high in reputability, just beneath captains of industry and bankers.

> The profession of the law does not imply large ownership; but since no taint of usefulness, for other than the competitive purpose, attaches to the lawyer's trade, it grades high in the conventional scheme. The lawyer is exclusively occupied with details of predatory fraud, either in achieving or in checkmating chicane, and success in the profession is therefore accepted as marking a large endowment of that barbarian astuteness which has always commanded men's respect and fear.

In fact the average lawyer in Chicago had reason to be dissatisfied with the way the pecuniary scheme of life was working out. By 1900 there were four thousand lawyers in the city. And their number was growing rapidly: whereas in 1891 the United States had 58 law schools with six thousand students, by 1902 there were 120 schools with fourteen thousand students. But, said one Chicago judge, men chose this occupation not because it offered the best road to wealth, but because it was the quickest path to political influence.

While the number of lawyers was increasing, several changes were reducing the demand for their services. The rash of business mergers in the last decade of the nineteenth century brought a concentration in industry, and that brought a similar concentration in legal practice. When twelve business firms combined into one, eleven lawyers lost their clients. The monopoly trend created so much resentment among lawyers that it even penetrated into the American Bar Association: at the 1903 convention the committee on commercial law brought in a report denouncing trusts and advocating radical measures to restore competition. But the report was not passed; already attorneys for the big corporations were the policy makers of the association.

The fact was clear: the independent lawyer engaging in general practice just could not compete with a giant law firm that had dozens of attorneys, each of them a specialist in a narrow branch of law. Nor could he compete with several other new institutions that were stripping him of his livelihood. Real-estate law, formerly 30 percent of legal practice, was passing into the hands of abstract companies and title-insurance firms which, doing business on a large scale, were satisfied with fees that a lawyer could not accept. The settlement of wills and the management of estates, another 10 percent, could be done more efficiently by trust companies and the trust departments of banks.

Collection of debts, another 20 percent, was being grabbed by collection companies. These agencies could pay their employees $10 a week, hardly a suitable income for a lawyer, and Illinois law gave them a further advantage: justices of the peace, who heard most of the collection cases, in Chicago were paid in fees rather than in salaries. Therefore they were likely to be partial to anybody who repeatedly brought them business —such as the collection companies. Business firms quickly learned that the private attorney was not the best man to represent their interests.

Corporation and commercial work, another 20 percent, was cut in various ways. Big companies often had their own legal departments. The new Federal and state bankruptcy acts both reduced the amount of law business. Insurance companies indemnified against risks that once had required the services of attorneys. Fidelity and casualty companies handled an increasing portion of the accident and negligence suits, another 10 percent of legal practice.

To magnify all of these evils, business firms and individuals alike were making more strenuous efforts to settle their conflicts out of court. If the problem was urgent, a private settlement was the only recourse: a case filed in the Cook County courts in 1904 would not come up for trial for at least two and a half years, and perhaps not for five.

The small lawyers clamored and clamored for legislation to protect them, but their clamor did not result in major reforms. Some legislators regarded these grievances as merely a chance for boodling. In 1903 a Chicago representative, Anton J. Cermak, introduced a bill that would have made it unlawful for trust companies to act in the settlement of estates. But officers of the firms declared that the proponents of the bill had no intention of passing it, but merely wanted to be paid for not passing it. Certainly the Chicago trust companies were a tempting target: the leading ones had a combined capital of $23 million. The big one was Chicago Title and Trust with a capital of $5 million. The previous year it had earned a net profit of $429,000.

By 1900 the cause of the general practitioner was doomed. S. S. Gregory, president of the Chicago Bar Association, said that he knew scores of men who were leaving the profession daily for some more lucrative trade; he doubted whether half the lawyers in Chicago were earning a living. A county judge declared that the best chance to succeed lay in specialization. Federal Judge Peter S. Grosscup said that he could look around his courtroom in the morning, see which lawyers were present, and tell from that fact alone what kind of cases would come up during the day. Clarence Darrow scoffed at the idea that merit alone could bring success; the would-be lawyer, he said, also needed "money, pull, and luck."

The trick was to find ways to be useful to the big corporations, or, better yet, to form big corporations. Thus in 1898 the young lawyer Frank O. Lowden and a few other Chicagoans brought 138 bakeries into the organization of the National Biscuit Company, which controlled 90 percent of the commercial biscuit making in the United States. The next year he reorganized the American Radiator Company and merged three competitors into it; the new firm controlled about 75 percent of the national market for its line of products. But

Lowden had special qualifications for these promotions: he was the son-in-law of George M. Pullman and could count on the financial backing of Field and Armour.

While the ordinary lawyer suffered, the big ones thrived. Men like Levy Mayer, attorney for the Illinois Manufacturers Association, who reportedly got $500,000 for negotiating the sale of the Ogden Gas Company in Chicago to the Gas Trust, and split another $250,000 for helping to handle the Whiskey Trust litigation. And like Edwin Walker, the man who had played a leading role in smashing the Pullman strike and picked up $100,000 for his part in the Chicago & Vincennes railroad case. And like Altgeld, Darrow, & Thompson, the partnership created when the ex-governor returned to private practice. Darrow incorporated the Hearst papers in Chicago and became their general counsel: the *American* in 1900; the *Examiner* in 1902. He represented the Chicago Title and Trust Company. He acted in specific cases for the city of Chicago, for railroads, for street-car companies.

But Altgeld and Darrow did not become conservatives like most of the other successful lawyers. They even refused to join the Chicago Bar Association on the ground that it was sympathetic to monopoly, and in 1902 they helped set up a new bar association. The new body declared that one of its main purposes was to seek reform legislation: raising the indemnity for a human life in Illinois above the $5,000 maximum, regulating the issuance of injunctions, uplifting the character of the bench and bar.

Many Chicago lawyers were ready for this program. They were eager for legislation that would right the balance, restore equality, protect the public interest and their own personal interests. In order to get the laws they wanted, they were ready to drive the boodlers out of the city council and the state legislature. These discontented lawyers and discontented women were prominent in the leisure-class segment of the progressive phalanx.

II

As Chicago women became concerned about public affairs, their interest flowed in all directions. In 1896 the Fortnightly Club of Evanston was asking Henry Demarest Lloyd to speak about socialism. Four years later the Women's Anti-Imperialist League was denouncing American policy in the Philippines. Four years after that, the philosophy and science department of the Chicago Woman's Club was hearing eight lectures on "Herbert Spencer and Evolution."

But alongside these diverse and momentary interests, upper-class women made a persistent effort to prevent child labor and to improve the conditions of working women. Their lasting achievements were in this area, and the main agency that won them to a social-welfare program was Hull-House. The first problem, as Jane Addams saw, was to tell the upper class how the lower class lived. This she did. Even men like Darrow and Lloyd, who themselves had personal contacts with workingmen and unionists, relied on Hull-House for knowledge of current problems. When the garment workers went on strike in 1896, it was Florence Kelley (the impartial state official) who wrote to Lloyd asking him to speak at a meeting in protest against the sweating system. A month later it was Ellen Gates Starr who told Darrow and Lloyd that the Bohemian strikers seemed "to be getting depressed" and needed a rousing talk to cheer them up.

Hull-House stood between the working class of Chicago and the upper class and had intimate contact with both. In this it was unique, and indispensable. Information about people's needs flowed upward through it; through it, money and encouragement and support passed downward.

Hull-House was more than a message center, it was also a recruiting office. At first Ellen Starr and Jane Addams were alone. Then Florence Kelley came, Julia Lathrop and Sophonisba Breckinridge went east to Wellesley College and persuaded Edith Abbott to come to Chicago. Alice Hamilton came. Each of these enlisted dozens of others. The ranks of reform grew steadily, and at the center of it all was Hull-House, and its net caught many young women of independent means.

Women like Margaret Dreier, who grew up in Brooklyn and joined the Women's Trade Union League in New York. In 1905 she married a young Chicago minister named Raymond Robins and returned with him to his home city to serve the cause of the Social Gospel. They lived first at Hull-House, then in their own tenement. Margaret Dreier Robins investigated shoe factories. She spoke at strike meetings. Soon she was president of the Women's Trade Union League in Chicago. In 1907 she became national president. The next year she was elected to the executive board of the Chicago Federation of Labor. And this was a woman who had inherited, in her words, "a comfortable fortune," who could offer to give Hull-House $20,000 in one sum.

If Robins and his wife descended into the working class, other reformers were content to stay in high society and do their agitating there. Ellen M. Henrotin was the wife of a leading broker, a wealthy clubwoman who, as vice-president of the Woman's Branch of the Auxiliary at the World's Fair of 1893, arranged concerts of working songs by immigrant groups. After Florence Kelley became head of the National Consumers' League, Mrs. Henrotin used her position as national president of the Federation of Women's Clubs in 1899 to boost the new organization.

The idea behind the Consumers' League was simple: It would organize boycotts of companies that exploited women and children. Such companies were legion. At the time Hull-House was founded in 1890, a corset factory employed 750 women; 150 of them earned less than 30 cents a day. Women in shirt factories earned as little as 50 cents a day, and they had to buy from their employers the thread they used—paying 2 cents a spool more than it cost elsewhere. In one shirt factory, earnings were only 40 cents a day, and each woman had to rent her sewing machine as well as buy the thread.

The state labor commissioner went to see Marshall Field to protest against that store's purchases of home-manufactured garments. Field said that he could not deprive worthy widows of the chance of working at home with their children. The commissioner reported: "The only one I have yet found working for him, earned $9.37 *in 13 weeks* and we fed her children meanwhile!"

Most of the working women were widows or young unmarried women, but not all. A married couple could hardly get along on less than $10 a week, but many men in downtown stores and offices earned only $6 or $8 weekly. The wives had to work too. In one restaurant that employed sixty women, fifty of them were married or widowed.

By 1903 there were an estimated 160,000 working women in Chicago, nearly one person in every ten, perhaps one in every four women. Thousands of them were in factories, more than five thousand in the stockyards alone. In the canneries, three workers in every four were women, doing such "kitchen" work as cutting dried beef, stuffing sausage, packing and labeling cans. The canning firms claimed that the proportion of women in the labor force had been stationary for a decade; settlement workers said that it had doubled in five years. But the concentration of women employees continued to be in the department stores: fifteen thousand downtown, another ten thousand in the outlying areas.

And it was here that the Consumers' League focused its efforts, asking consumers to do their Christmas shopping only in the "standard" stores that did not allow any child to work after 6 P.M. and paid each child a minimum weekly wage of $2.25, gave women equal pay with men for doing equal work, paid a $6 weekly minimum to women of six months' experience, provided seats for women clerks, and gave extra pay after 6 P.M. When this boycotting tactic proved inadequate, the reformers turned to publicity. The Woman's Club published a devastating report on its investigation of the big State Street stores in the pre-Christmas rush.

Marshall Field was paying the $6 weekly minimum. But it furnished only one stool for every ten clerks in some departments. Women who worked night after night until 10 P.M. got only their regular pay, plus 50 cents to buy supper. In other stores, conditions were worse. In one, clerks were not allowed to go to the restroom except during their lunch period. Clerks sometimes worked from 8 A.M. until 10:30 P.M. every day for the ten days before Christmas. They got no extra pay and a supper allowance of 35 cents.

Employers interviewed doubted that the wages they paid were sufficient to support a person. They estimated that not more than 65 or 75 percent of their employees lived at home. How the others lived, they had no idea.

Some were helped by the luncheon clubs for working women, which were run on a nonprofit basis by the alumnae associations of women's private schools. They served lunch at about a third the cost for a comparable lunch in a restaurant. But their clientele was almost exclusively white-collar employees from stores and offices: luncheon clubs were not located convenient to the factories, and many factory workers would not leave the plant in their work clothes but lacked the time to change clothes twice during their lunch periods.

Other philanthropists set up working girls' homes which provided room and board to department-store employees for $2.50 or $3.00 a week. But *The Public* protested that such facilities helped to undermine the wage scales of women generally. A few women were permitted to live in comfort at less than cost and thus could get along with lower wages if they had to. Employers counted on this when they wanted to cut pay scales.

Whereas white-collar employees made little effort to combine for self-protection, factory women frequently resorted to unionization and strikes. And the strikes often followed the same pattern as walk-outs of men.

Scene: *Exchange Avenue, Outside the Libby, McNeill & Libby
       cannery*
Time: *5:30 P.M., March 10, 1900*

> Women workers are on strike, but the company is running
> the plant with strikebreakers. Ever since the snow fights and
> hairpin jabbing of two days ago, trouble has been expected.
> Captain Lavin of the Stockyards Station has detailed twenty
> policemen to keep order.
> The workday ends. The nonunion women emerge from the
> plant. Strikers begin parading up and down the street. Over
> two thousand persons cheer them on. The strikers begin hurling
> lunch buckets and empty tea bottles at their enemies.
> Hastily the police form the nonunion women into groups and
> convoy them to the street cars. But one group is found un-
> protected, and its members are pelted with chunks of ice.

The women's unions often cooperated with men's unions or
even struck in sympathy with them. This happened at a nail
company where 120 women made $10 to $12 a week on piece-
work, while the 80 men received only $1.75 per day. The
women went on strike, demanding a 10 percent raise for the
men and nothing for themselves except that ten of their number getting $1.25 per day should have a 25-cent increase. Even
the employer applauded this gesture, and after a strike of only
half a day he agreed to the demands. When he offered the
women strikers a 10 percent increase along with the men, they
refused it.

In other instances the men reciprocated, but often not.
When women in the twine room at International Harvester
struck in 1903, they demanded better restrooms—and measures
to prevent men in the plant from subjecting them to indignities.
Men's unions, such as the Building Trades Materials Council,
demanded that all women employees should be eliminated
from their trade. First the council asked the state factory inspectors to bar women on the ground that the work was un-
healthy. Rebuffed, they went to the employers. That failed
too. A year later, a leader of the male Metal Polishers Union

claimed that they had found the answer: they were marrying off their members to the female competitors.

Although the claim was ridiculed, it did focus attention on the chief handicap of women's unions. Working women were usually young. They wanted to get married and have families, an aim that proved realistic for most of them. So the turnover of women workers in any plant or store was high, and the employees at any time felt themselves to be there temporarily and did not identify their futures with the welfare of the group. They were hard to organize into unions. Once organized, they left, and the job remained to do again.

The Women's Trade Union League, recognizing these facts, sought a solution. Sophonisba Breckinridge said that women's unions could not focus on the same aims as men's unions, because women were chiefly concerned with the effects of their jobs upon marriage. So let the women's unions sponsor dowries which would be paid to any member who quit work to get married. The scheme was realistic and ingenious, and it could have been organized on the same actuarial basis as any kind of insurance—but it never came to much. Nor did the women's unions ever have much effect on the conditions under which the great majority of women worked.

The Chicago *Tribune* was right in saying that responsibility for adjusting the grievances of employed women had to rest chiefly with the employers and the public. The day for sweeping legislation to protect women still lay in the future, but the agitation by the women of Chicago fifty years ago helped to prepare the way.

Their chief tangible achievement at the time was to improve the conditions of children, and women's organizations of all types were drawn into that effort. The Union of Bohemian Women was founded in 1863 as a protective society that paid death and sick benefits. But children of its members went to school and soon knew more than their mothers. Now the Union turned to sponsoring fortnightly education meetings on literature, law as it related to women, the history of women. By

1898 it was the largest women's literary society in Chicago, with 2,300 women. Many of the members still lived in poor wards, or they had memories of poor wards, where boys refused to go to school and got into trouble with the law. The organization already had drafted a bill for parental schools to which truants could be sent when necessary. Here was the sort of protest a ward boss understood and would respond to.

III

Long before leisure-class women swarmed into social-welfare activities after 1890, a few leisure-class men were finding time for civic improvement. The Citizens' Association of Chicago, founded in 1871, was the oldest civic reform organization in the country. In 1893 Darrow, Lloyd, future baseball commissioner Kenesaw Mountain Landis, and a handful of other liberals started the Chicago Civic Centre Club as a nonpartisan group to improve city government. But such efforts were ineffective. The gray wolves continued to run the city council. Mutual animosity between the wage earners and businessmen continued to grow. A hereditary class of workingmen seemed to be forming, in mockery of the ideal that a man should be able to raise his status by his own efforts.

Scene: *Central Music Hall, Chicago*
Time: *November 12, 1893*

The Columbian Exposition is over, and the city is filled with jobless men. They walk the streets looking for work; they throng around police stations and saloons to get soup; they sleep wherever they can keep warm. Tonight they gather around this hall.

A meeting sponsored by the trade unions has been called by W. T. Stead, the English editor and reformer who is visiting the city. A special invitation was sent to every church. The result is amazing. All groups in Chicago are present in force. On the stage businessmen sit by labor leaders, madams by preachers, city officials beside one of the Haymarket defendants just pardoned by Governor Altgeld.

Stead speaks as a Christian appealing to Christians. He speaks of the depression, of police protection of the red-light district, of the city government's indulgence of evils. He meets with some hissing, but more applause.

Tommy Morgan gets up, a veteran local socialist, speaking now for labor. He talks directly to the upper classes. He tells them that when laborers tried to assemble peacefully on the Lake Front to beg for work, police were used to drive them back into the tenement districts so that visitors to the World's Fair would not see their misery. Of the well-dressed and well-fed, he asks:

> Do you believe that under these social conditions here in this free country there are no anarchists, no bombs, no dynamite? Do you not believe some desperate man, under the load which you allow to rest on him, will get uneasy and will revolt? . . . if the pleadings of editor Stead, in the name of Christ and for justice, cannot shake you out, someone may blow you out with dynamite.

At the mention of dynamite, men get to their feet. They gesture violently. The memory of Haymarket is fresh still, seven years later. There are protests against Morgan. And threats too.

But Morgan's words have struck home to many. They nod their heads in agreement. The gap between rich and poor in Chicago has grown too great. Justice and mercy must be shown to the squalid victims of industrial growth. Otherwise they may indeed revolt.

The meeting resolves that a civic federation be formed to combat the evils named by Stead.

Within a few weeks the Civic Federation of Chicago was formed. The Union League Club contributed heavily to its founders. Its president was Lyman J. Gage, president of the First National Bank. Its vice-presidents were Mrs. Potter Palmer and a labor leader. Soon the organization had a branch in each of the city's thirty-four wards. It went to work at once.

That winter it organized the Central Relief Association, which expended $135,000 to succor the homeless. This evolved into the permanent Bureau of Associated Charities, and the Federation met all its expenses the first year.

In June, 1894, the Federation's goal of class conciliation was tested by the Pullman strike. And it proved that it was not simply the type of "citizens' association" that gives an air of impartiality to the employers' viewpoint. An investigating committee that included Jane Addams gave an honest report about conditions in the town of Pullman. The Federation recommended that the dispute be arbitrated, as the strikers and Eugene Debs were asking. Here the Federation met the limitation of being a voluntary organization. Marshall Field was one of its trustees, he was also a leading director of the Pullman Company, but its recommendation went for nothing. When the company twice refused to arbitrate, Mrs. Potter Palmer was shaken in her belief that the Federation could be useful in time of crisis. But it could help to prevent crises. It called a national conference to consider the labor question, which helped carry to success Altgeld's efforts to secure a state arbitration law.

The Federation the next year, enraged at Mayor Hopkins' toleration of vice, hired an army of special constables to raid the gambling houses, seize the equipment and burn it. When one manager asked for their authority the head of the raiders, Matt Pinkerton, roared: "The authority of the Civic Federation!" When the Federation called a mass meeting on the subject in Central Music Hall, the corporation counsel appeared to defend Mayor Hopkins. He declared that the city had never had an administration as hostile as the present one to the criminal classes, "not only to the ordinary criminal classes who commit the everyday offenses of shoplifting and gambling, but to the infinitely more dangerous criminal who will occupy a front pew in a fashionable church on Sunday and on Monday attempt to secure a corrupt franchise ordinance by bribery."

The Federation took that up too. At a mass meeting to protest against boodling by the Gas Trust and the traction companies, the roster of speakers ranked from Marshall Field and William Rainey Harper to Clarence Darrow and Henry Demarest Lloyd. The Federation turned to civil service and organized a committee, made up of representatives of the leading Chicago clubs, that drafted a law and then secured its adoption in a referendum by a majority of more than fifty thousand. When the law was not enforced, the Federation hired detectives to catch the violators, and constantly was instituting cases before the civil service commission or in the courts.

This upper-class group also founded the first vacation school in Chicago in the summer of 1896, taking children on excursions to the country and organizing athletic programs for them instead of leaving them to roam the streets. By 1898 it was able to induce women's clubs to accept this task, and they conducted six schools that summer at an expense of $6,000. The Federation thus demonstrated a major divergence of its views from the philosophy of Jane Addams and her associates. Hull-House was continually organizing a desirable activity, then calling upon the government to take it over. But the Civic Federation insisted that vacation schools, like its relief work during the winter of 1893-1894, should be conducted by private groups out of voluntary donations. To have done otherwise would have violated one of its cardinal aims: economical government and tax reduction.

It sought to realize that aim in many ways. Contracts to clean the streets in downtown Chicago were granted annually to private firms. The Federation decided that too much was being paid for this work. It raised $30,000 by private subscriptions and cleaned the streets at a cost of less than $10 a mile, while the city had been paying $18.50 and getting worse results. The next year the city paid only $10.50 a mile. The Federation also pushed through the legislature a law to reduce discrimination in levying taxes: it provided that assessments should be publicized, and it set up a board to review them.

The chief way to reduce government expenses was to drive the boodlers out of public office. But often there were no honest candidates running, because the ward bosses were able to control the nominating conventions. In January, 1898, the Federation called its second national conference to consider reform of the primary elections. With this impetus, it persuaded the governor to call a special session of the legislature, and representatives of Chicago's leading clubs lobbied into law a measure that divided Chicago into primary-election districts and provided for appointment of election judges and clerks over primaries. For a time there was hope that this law had broken the power of the ward bosses, but it did not.

The third national conference called by the Federation urged the establishment of a court of international arbitration. The fourth, in September, 1899, was to deal with trusts. Chicago's radicals spurned it, even though the Republican governor named several of them as delegates: Darrow and George Schilling, both members of the Civic Federation; Altgeld, who said it would be a "trust love feast." *The Public* charged that the whole thing was a Republican plot to remove the trust issue from the 1900 election by declaring against trusts but offering a weak program to control them. And so it turned out: the conference recommended that the government have the right to inspect the operations of big corporations and to engage in mild supervision.

This soon became the program of that master straddler on the trust question, Theodore Roosevelt, who asked for such legislation in his first annual message to Congress in 1901. When Congress did nothing, the President took his appeal to the country in several speeches. In 1903 the Department of Commerce and Labor was set up, with a Bureau of Corporations empowered to make investigations of big firms.

By that time the Federation had already given birth to a parent. The 1899 Conference on Trusts, in spite of its ineffective recommendations, was hailed as a great success by the press of the country, and primary credit went to Ralph M.

Easley, secretary of the Federation and its administrative head from the beginning. This encouraged Easley to resign from the Chicago organization to organize a national body that would promote the discussion of public questions. He secured the support of Senator Mark Hanna, chairman of the Republican national committee, and of Samuel Gompers, president of the AFL, and the National Civic Federation was launched in June, 1900.

The chief aim of the new association soon became the promotion of class conciliation: its chief method, the settlement of labor disputes. Although its headquarters were in New York, it quickly made itself felt in Chicago. When a strike started at the Allis-Chalmers plant, Ralph Easley was in Chicago and admitted that he was interested in settling the dispute. Then a threatened street-car strike was arbitrated by a member of the National Federation, who ruled that the companies should cease their opposition to the formation of a union on their lines and that they should negotiate with the union about all future grievances. Protection of collective bargaining was the policy of the Civic Federation thirty years before it became the policy of the Federal government.

IV

Ralph Easley was not boasting idly when he declared in 1899: "there is probably no reform organization in the United States which can show more actual accomplishments of practical value than the Civic Federation of Chicago." But on one of its main goals it had long since admitted defeat: as early as 1896 the Federation conceded that it was not the type of organization that could drive the boodlers out of the city council.

That January, before a group of two hundred men from the reputable clubs, Lyman Gage confessed that "for some reason, they had failed." The meeting named a committee of fifteen to find other forms of action. This was one of most significant things the Federation ever did, for the fifteen men decided to strike out on a new tack. Instead of organizing a new party, they would pick one man, let him find eight others, and this small nucleus would then organize a Municipal Voters' League and run it in whatever way they chose. Here was the same sort of centralized authority that the ward bosses wielded so effectively.

The benign, white-haired Judge Murray F. Tuley, one of the most liberal and most respected men in the city, stood on the stage of the Central Music Hall before fifteen hundred people and introduced the man they had chosen, "this little, sawed-off giant of reform, George E. Cole. He is our machine, tireless and fearless." Stationer and printer, Cole had won a reputation the previous year by making an independent race for alderman against one of Yerkes' leaders in the city council. He was also a veteran member of the Union League Club, and he picked six fellow members as the ruling clique of the new Voters' League. Every one of them was a prominent professional man or businessman.

The aldermanic election was just ahead. The League wasted neither time nor words. It stated bluntly that of the sixty-eight aldermen, fifty-seven were "thieves." Of the thirty-four whose terms were expiring, it condemned twenty-six. It set out to beat those twenty-six men. During the campaign the stocky form and pugnacious face of George Cole appeared everywhere, and he showed a willingness to use any tactic to achieve his end. He acted like a politician—like the men he was trying to beat. The League dug up cases of graft and published them. If they were not publishable, it sent for the culprit and advised him to get off the ticket. Blackmail or not, it worked. Of the retiring aldermen, sixteen were not renominated. Now the League went after the other ten. It went into the wards, persuaded the minority party to put up an honest man, and campaigned against the incumbent, with leaflets from door to door, with mass meetings, with parades. It made deals, it dickered with ward bosses, and it beat four of the aldermen.

But Cole suffered for it. In spite of the wealth of most of his close associates, the typical businessman did not like what the League was doing. When Lincoln Steffens investigated reform in Chicago, he reported that because of Cole's political activities, "the big corporations, the railroads, great business houses and their friends, had taken their business away from him." Cole met the boycott by saying: "I have a wife and a boy. I want their respect. The rest can all go to hell."

Now, with twenty-two aldermen, nearly a third of the council, believed to be honest, the League set out to develop an issue that could be used to beat the other boodlers. It looked ahead to 1903, when many vital street-car franchises would expire, and demanded that the city should receive proper remuneration for renewing them. The chief spokesman was John M. Harlan. An alderman and son of a Justice of the United States Supreme Court, Harlan was handsome, forceful, a brilliant orator. He was conservative on economic matters, but he was outraged by the street-car companies' debaucheries. When the Republican bosses put up a hack for mayor in 1897, Harlan bolted to make an independent campaign with the backing of the League. Time after time he got up in the city council to call the names of prominent businessmen and ask what they were doing while laws to benefit them were being boodled through the legislature. He pointed accusingly at the activities in Springfield of Yerkes' agents.

When the campaign ended, Harlan had 70,000 votes, 10,000 more than the regular Republican nominee; his independent candidacy made Carter Harrison the mayor of Chicago. Of the thirty-four outgoing aldermen, the League had blacklisted twenty-seven. Fifteen were not renominated. Nine of the others were beaten.

The next year Yerkes pushed the Allen Law through the legislature, and the ordinances extending his franchises for fifty years were introduced into the city council. The League made an even more furious fight in the aldermanic elections, and it elected forty honest men compared to twenty-eight it thought dishonest. When the vote came on Yerkes' franchises, they were denied. Four months later John Peter Altgeld, in 1899, made his independent race for mayor, and the League increased its majority in the city council and organized that body on a nonpartisan basis for the first time. The gray wolves who remained seemed impregnable: men like "Bathhouse" and "Hinky Dink" in the First Ward, Johnny Powers in the Nineteenth, Billy Loeffler in the Ninth.

But the League cut Loeffler down too. At the head of the League now was Walter L. Fisher, an even tougher politician than George Cole and having the same oligarchic powers. He used his resultant capacity for flexibility against Loeffler, the Democratic boss of a heavily Democratic ward. Loeffler's business partner, "Hot Stove" Brenner, was the Republican candidate for alderman. Loeffler went to Fisher and generously offered to let him name the Democratic candidate against Brenner. Guessing that Loeffler planned to throw his support secretly to Brenner, Fisher accepted the challenge. At his suggestion, the Democrats put up Michael J. Preib. Then, with an eye to the big Jewish vote in the ward, Fisher had Jacob Diamond enter the race as an independent. He told both Preib and Diamond that the League would back whichever of them seemed stronger. Five days before the election, it was clear that this was Preib.

Fisher went back to Loeffler and accused him of not doing enough to help Preib. Fisher dictated a letter from Loeffler to his personal friends asking them to vote for Preib. Loeffler reluctantly signed it. Fisher then rushed to League headquarters and mailed copies of Loeffler's letter to every voter in the Ninth Ward. The election came before Loeffler could undo the damage. Preib won.

The shrewd journalist Lincoln Steffens concluded, after visiting Chicago, that the city was "half free and fighting on." And he gave the credit to the realistic methods of a political machine devoted to reform: the Municipal Voters' League.

CHAPTER 11

The Road Back

Without ideals, he does only what is demanded of him. . . .
Every time Chicago wants to go ahead a foot, it has first to
push its mayor up inch by inch.
  —A judgment of Carter Harrison, Jr., by Lincoln Steffens *

I

DUE LARGELY to the efforts of the Municipal Voters' League,
a majority of the aldermen in early 1902 could be counted on
to deal honestly with the most urgent issue before the city:
What should be done about the street-car companies, now that
many of their key franchises were expiring? The program of
the leisure-class reformers was already known. As early as
1899, a committee of the Civic Federation had made a report
that demanded a proper valuation of the capital of the companies. If that were done, said the report, the companies could
set aside 4 percent depreciation, pay 6 percent dividends, and
would still be able either to pay 20 percent of their gross income to the city or to reduce the fare from a nickel to four
cents. Nowhere did the report suggest that city ownership
might be the best solution. Similarly most of the honest aldermen wanted only to tame the traction companies so that the

* The Shame of the Cities, 1903 (New York: Sagamore Press, 1957), p. 192.

public interest could be protected when their franchises were renewed.

But the companies were recalcitrant. Yerkes was gone, but some of his methods were not: schedules were still unreliable, street cars were still jammed. The voters of Chicago struck back at these abuses. The previous winter the legislature had passed a law giving any city the right to hold an advisory vote on any question at the request of 25 percent of the voters. In Chicago, this meant 104,000 signatures. A Referendum League was hastily formed and began circulating petitions for a vote on city ownership of the street-car lines. The response was galvanic. The street-car workers, engaged in a bitter fight to form a union, supported the petition as the best way to improve their own condition. The Chicago Federation of Labor campaigned for it. Hearst's Chicago *American* joined in. Even citizens who opposed city ownership signed the petition in order to improve the city's bargaining position in negotiating with the private companies for renewal of their franchises.

The petition got 140,000 signatures, and the question went on the ballot for the April election. The sensitive politicians on the city council could now see that it would be wise for them to act, so they passed an ordinance requiring free transfers: to ride from Austin on the West Side to the downtown Loop, a person need pay only one fare. Union Traction, which had taken over Yerkes' lines on the West and North Sides, refused to obey. Passengers who would not pay two fares were ejected from its cars. The city brought more than six hundred suits against the company, seeking a $200 fine for each violation.

At this juncture the election was held. In an off-year with no contest for the mayoralty, city ownership of the street railways was endorsed by 142,826 Yeas to 27,998 Nays. To some, this was merely a threat, a club to beat the companies into line. But to others, it was the only sound program. Altgeld had died three weeks before the election, but thousands of his admirers revered his heritage. They were a minority, but an aggressive one.

On April 20, at a memorial meeting for Altgeld, three thousand persons heard Clarence Darrow give a full-length panegyric. Altgeld would not be properly appreciated, said Darrow, until the world was ready to recognize "some other god than greed"; all that could be done amid the wickedness of 1902 was "to plainly and patiently state the truth." The truth was that Altgeld had been mercilessly attacked for a simple reason: "he was a lover of his fellow man. This has ever been the only unpardonable sin that the rulers of the world cannot forgive."

Weaving headlong eloquence and defiant challenges into his recitation of the facts, Darrow made a detailed examination of the main events of Altgeld's career. First, his action about Haymarket: "the greatest, the bravest and the most important of his life." After describing the bombing, the amnesty movement, the executions, his own visits to an Altgeld thought to be wavering, Darrow asserted: "Few men have ever thoughtfully and candidly read Governor Altgeld's message who were not convinced by its logic and its facts, that this pardon was righteous and just."

Then Darrow talked about the Pullman strike. Again the same meticulous account of the situation: the strike, the arrival of the Federal army in Chicago, Altgeld's protest. Nobody could doubt, said Darrow, that President Cleveland's intervention had been illegal, because the Constitution said that Federal troops could be sent into a state only on request of the legislature or governor. "Under the popular definition of anarchy, which means a disregard for the constitution and law and the substitution of individual government for both, this was the most conspicuous act of anarchism that the history of the United States had recorded up to the time the troops were sent."

Then the fight against government by injunction, for trial by jury, against "the encroachments of the federal judiciary upon the rights and liberties of the people of the United

States." Then, the Chicago Platform of 1896: "a great revolutionary document second only to the Declaration of Independence." Then, equality of treatment for Negroes, for women,
for the Boers and the Filipinos, for everybody. Then, trade
unions, labor arbitration, the eight-hour day, factory and mining laws. "His creed was broad enough to take in every human
being on the earth on equal terms."

Darrow scorned the charge that Altgeld was a demagogue,
ruled by the desire for votes and power. Altgeld was a wise
man, and any wise man knows that you can't get power by
advocating the cause of the poor and the weak. Only those
with power can give it. Look at John Brown: he had thought
the slaves would rise up and follow him, but they did not—
because they were slaves. Workingmen were often the same;
they "may feel the deepest love for those who espouse their
cause but they forget even the day or the place where their
ballot should be cast." Altgeld had no desire for public office.
He knew that the politician must abandon his convictions to
expediency. He knew a greater truth: "Great reform move-
ments are never led by politicians and office-holders, they
come from the common people, and it is only when the tide
rises so high as to sweep away the old evils that the politician
supports the cause to save his miserable and petty life."

But when the tide is ebbing, Darrow asked: What then? A
man will fight then only if he has moral courage, the greatest
kind of courage there is, the kind that Altgeld had. "When
John P. Altgeld died, the poor and weak and defenseless lost
their truest friend. . . . He was a sentinel who never slept, who
always gave the cry regardless of the invincible numbers in
which the enemy approached. . . . It is left for us who knew
him, who loved him, . . . to fight for the principles dear to him,
to uphold as best we can the great cause of human liberty for
which he lived and died."

While Darrow tried to fill the voters with inspiration, the
street-car companies filled them with anger: agents of Union
Traction were convicted of spending money to corrupt the

courts. It was not the first time this had happened. In 1898 a bailiff in the county court was indicted for bribing jurors in a personal-injury case against the West Chicago Street Railway. He fled Chicago and went into hiding. In 1901 he returned to confess that a lawyer for the company had in several cases given him $50 or $100 to pass along to jurors. He also said the lawyer had persuaded him to flee to Canada. The lawyer was indicted for conspiracy to help the bailiff evade justice and convicted. But in that instance, after all, the contestant against the company had been a single individual who claimed to have been injured. Now the city government, and thousands of street-car riders, had a direct stake.

The first suit against Union Traction in the transfer cases came to trial on April 14. It took the six-man jury only three minutes to return with an acquittal. A week later the second suit went the same way. It looked peculiar. And within the month, seven men had been indicted for bribing jurors. They were Patrick O'Donnell, prominent Republican and the Public Administrator of Cook County; his brother John; another of his law partners, James T. Brady; Cyrus Simon, trial attorney for Union Traction; two members of the jury in the first transfer case, and one W. J. Gallagher.

When they were brought to trial, the chief problem was impaneling the jury. Almost nobody was impartial; 700 veniremen were examined before the twelve jurors were picked. Witnesses told in detail how the jury bribing had worked. Gallagher went to the O'Donnell-Brady offices. There he got money and instructions from Simon, the Union Traction lawyer. Gallagher went to the constable who was to choose the jurors in the transfer case and gave him $15. Then Gallagher went out and recruited his jurors. Each got $5, and was sent to the lobby of a hotel. The constable recognized them by the pins they wore in their coat lapels. He took them to the justice court, where they were put on the jury. They returned their verdict—bought and paid for.

All seven defendants were convicted, but only Gallagher

was sentenced to prison; the others were fined. The convictions of Brady and Patrick O'Donnell were later reversed on appeal, but this did Union Traction little good. The business element in Chicago, which would have supported the company on grounds of public policy, now had to admit that one of its lawyers had tried to buy the city government. Union Traction, which needed friends badly, was driving them away. Increasingly it would have to buy what support it received.

Not that money was powerless. When the O'Donnells and Brady appeared in court for trial, their chief attorney was Clarence Darrow. At the same time Darrow was chairman of the executive committee of the Public Ownership League, the spearhead of the drive for city ownership. As if to emphasize his indifference to the charge of jury bribing, Darrow soon gave Cyrus Simon himself a job in his office. Even Edgar Lee Masters, Darrow's partner, balked when Darrow wanted to put Simon's name on the door.

Some reformers had long looked skeptically at Darrow's professional activities. They thought he charged exorbitant fees when he represented trade unions. They were willing to tolerate his service as counsel to the Chicago *American,* but what of his willingness to speak for any rascal who could meet his price?

Darrow could have explained that Anglo-American law is rooted in the adversary principle, that each party in a legal action is entitled to have his case presented as forcefully as possible, that justice is presumed to arise from this contest. But he abjured this ground. Years later he could write to Jane Addams: "I have been so long striving for realities—and seeking to look life in the face, that I cannot do otherwise. . . ." And the last person he tried to dupe was himself.

Actually in his memorial address to Altgeld he referred to his own inconsistency. Every man, he said, is rent by a perpetual struggle between his conscience and his desire for prestige and comfort. "A typical politician puts his conscience entirely aside and considers only the conduct which will serve his selfish end. The devoted fanatical zealot, who sees nothing but his duty to his fellow men, wholly forgets himself and lives only for the principles and convictions that take possession of his life. . . . Probably no great statesman ever lived who was wholly true." But many of Darrow's acquaintances were not satisfied with such a general statement. Most of the queries he ignored. But he did not ignore Ellen Gates Starr, Jane Addams' most intimate associate since the founding of Hull-House, when she asked why he had taken the job of getting favorable amendments to the franchise of a street-car company.

I did it, said Darrow, for the money they paid me. He wrote to Ellen Starr that, judged by "the ordinary commercial and legal standard of ethics," he had been right to represent the street-car company. But "judged by the higher law, in which we both believe, I am practically a thief," he admitted. "I am taking money that I did not earn, which comes to me from men who did not earn it, but who get it because they have a chance to get it. I take it without performing any useful service to the world, and I take a thousand times as much as my services are worth even assuming they are useful and honest."

Years earlier, Darrow explained, he had discussed these matters with a friend named Swift, whose father owned a drug store. When the father died, Swift took all the patent medicines out in the yard and broke the bottles. He renounced his inheritance, left town penniless, lived straitly by his own code. During the 1893 depression he raised a Coxey's army and marched to Washington. Swift, wrote Darrow, was a man who "has perhaps done some good in his way by refusing to compromise with evil." But was there some other way to do good? Was it essential that a good man should wear a hair shirt?

Darrow chose another way, deliberately. "I came to Chicago," he wrote. "I determined to take my chance with the rest, to get what I could out of the system and use it to destroy the system. I came without friends or money. Society provides no fund out of which such people can live while preaching heresy. It compels us to get our living out of society as it is or die." He explained that, if he were to refuse the business of tarnished clients, he would be prompted not by principle but by fear of public reproach. He cared very much what his friends thought of him, but he would not let it influence his actions. The vital thing, he emphasized, was not to allow professional interests "to influence me as a citizen to the support of measures in which I do not believe. . . ."

In short, he would continue to represent the street-car companies or anybody else, for a fee; at the same time he thought the street-car lines should be owned and operated by the city of Chicago. This sort of compromise, he thought, was forced on the honest man at a time when "society is organized injustice." The country, wrote Darrow, was ruled by business, and "business is legal fraud." There were only two classes: "the despoiler and the despoiled." The only place to get money was from the despoilers; the despoiled had none.

II

For use in the autumn election of 1902 the Democratic Party of Cook County issued a very forward-looking Campaign Book. Reform principles were in every line of it. It urged that the legislature should immediately pass an enabling act giving cities the power to own and operate public utilities. Even if this power was not exercised at once by the cities, it would arm them to negotiate better terms with the private firms. Public ownership would result in better service, lower cost to the consumers, and higher wages for the employees. To those who said that city ownership would create a vast fountain of political patronage, the Campaign Book said this could be prevented by "a good civil service system." In fact, it went on, the street-car lines in private hands were a vast fountain of political patronage; much of the influence of the ward bosses had arisen from their ability to get jobs for their supporters from Yerkes' companies. "Without question the greatest corrupting influences in American city life today are the private corporations engaged in carrying on public business under franchise grants. The strongest argument for municipal ownership, therefore, is the moral and governmental argument."

The politicians who issued this militant document at once took steps to ensure that they would not have to enact it into law. The tradition in Chicago had been for the two major parties to divide up the offices available in any election. This was especially easy to do in the lower house of the legislature, since three members of it were chosen at large from each senatorial district. Where the Democrats had a safe majority in a district, they would nominate only two candidates; the third vacancy went to a Republican. And so on. Cut and dried. In 1902 they went further yet. In the lower house it would take seventy-seven Democrats to make a majority. But in the entire state they put up only seventy-nine candidates.

The whole deal, screamed the reformers, had been cooked up in the interests of the Gas Trust and the traction companies. The Republicans had not promised municipal ownership; the Democrats had. Now they would throw the election and claim they were powerless to carry out their pledges. Look at the Seventeenth district in Chicago, where John Powers, having done his apprenticeship in the city council, was preparing to move up to the state senate. Powers had the district in his side pocket, but the Democrats had nominated only one man for the lower house.

But before they started this shell game, they should have changed the election laws, which permitted a voter to plunk for only one of the three candidates in a district. If he did so, it counted as three votes for the man designated. The situation was perfect for organized minorities to move in. And they did. The Public Ownership League began petition campaigns to run several men for the lower house, including Clarence Darrow in Powers' own district.

Darrow got on the ballot. Other events helped to project

him into the spotlight. First came a persisting labor dispute on the street-car lines, where the workers were trying to organize into the Association of Street Railway Employees, an AFL affiliate. In June the National Civic Federation had secured agreement of the companies to stop interfering with the unionizing drive. But the union charged Union Traction with breaking this agreement. The union also made wage demands. Things were tense. When arbitration was agreed to, Darrow was named as the union's member of the three-man board.

Before that arbitration ended, Darrow got into a much bigger one that held the headlines from coast to coast. On May 12, 1902, the entire anthracite industry had been shut down by a strike of 142,000 miners. As cold weather approached the situation became desperate, because anthracite was the fuel most used to heat residences in Eastern cities. The owners refused to arbitrate or to concede anything. President Roosevelt moved in, appointing a commission to hear testimony and make recommendations to settle the dispute. J. P. Morgan brought pressure on the company officials to accede to Roosevelt's action. They did so. And in late October, Clarence Darrow was named as chief attorney to present the strikers' case to the commission, with Henry Lloyd as one of his associates.

A few days later Darrow scored a stunning victory in the election in Chicago. His 11,000 votes were nearly double the vote of the other two successful candidates in his district. Johnny Powers was elected to the senate, but he had been unable to stop Darrow.

Right after the election, the arbitration award of Darrow and his colleagues in the Union Traction case was announced. It gave the workers a substantial pay increase, aggregating some $350,000 a year, more than $100 a man. It also ordered Union Traction to dissolve a so-called "benevolent organization" or company union. Darrow's popularity with the laboring men of Chicago soared. Plans were made to organize a union labor party for the Chicago elections in April, 1903, with Darrow as the nominee for mayor, and public ownership of public utilities as the platform.

All through the winter, Darrow's activities before the Anthracite Commission in Scranton and Philadelphia were reported on the front pages of the Chicago newspapers. The legislature organized at Springfield on January 6, but Darrow was not there to be sworn in. Rumors were rife in Chicago that he had written so-and-so that he would run for mayor, had written so-and-so that he would not run for mayor. Darrow himself did not know what he meant to do. Since he was busy twelve or fifteen hours a day with the anthracite hearings, he had little time to think about it. He stalled.

Mayor Harrison and his Democratic henchmen became worried. Even if Darrow could not win, he might draw enough votes to throw the election to the Republicans. The Democratic candidate for mayor had to be named at a primary election, and perhaps Darrow could even win that. Mayor Harrison moved fast. The county committee endorsed him for reelection. He in turn endorsed the Mueller bill in the legislature, which would authorize cities to own and operate public utilities. He also pledged that he would veto any renewal of any traction franchise until the legislature had passed the Mueller bill. This ultimatum was a way of bringing pressure on the street-car companies and their hirelings in the legislature not to block the Mueller bill.

In mid-February the anthracite hearings ended. Darrow returned to Chicago, spoke about the anthracite strike to an uproarious crowd of 4,500 union men in the Auditorium, held hurried sessions in smoke-filled rooms about the mayoralty race, and then went to Springfield to take his seat in the legislature. He left the Democratic leaders sweating: he had said that he would not enter their primary, but he had refused to commit himself about an independent nomination. Darrow was their only worry; even Daniel Cruice, head of the Referendum League, had announced that Darrow was the only man capable of pulling together the old Altgeld coalition behind a public-ownership platform.

Darrow had consulted many people about the decision to be made. Samuel Gompers urged him not to run, writing that any executive official, even the President, had to "carry out the laws as you find them upon the statute books." The trouble was in the laws; the problem was to change the laws. John Mitchell, president of the United Mine Workers, and Henry Lloyd also advised Darrow not to run. Darrow himself wrote to Daniel Cruice that an independent candidate could not count on the support of the Chicago *American*. Its owner, William Randolph Hearst, pretended to be for public ownership, but what he really wanted was the Democratic nomination for the Presidency in 1904. If it looked as though Mayor Harrison would control the Chicago delegation to the Democratic national convention in 1904, Hearst would support Harrison for reelection in 1903.

On February 23, Darrow announced in Springfield that he would not make the race. He did not see what he could do as mayor. What the people of Chicago wanted was public ownership. That could not be secured until the Mueller bill was passed. Therefore the important thing to do was to get the law enacted, and the place to achieve that end was in the legislature, where he already sat.

With Darrow out of it, the Union Labor party put up Daniel Cruice for mayor. And Darrow set about fighting for the Mueller bill. The legislative session in Springfield, after two months, seemed to have done almost nothing. In the lower house the Mueller bill was bottled up in the committee on municipal corporations, manned solely by rural representatives who knew nothing about such corporations and who would do what the Republican leadership told them to do (and those practical men would do whatever seemed likely to get them the biggest campaign contributions from the Chicago street-car companies). The situation called for vigorous pressure. But what?

In Chicago, feeling against the traction companies ran so high that even Graeme Stewart, Republican candidate for mayor, had to call for passage of the Mueller bill. A nonpartisan committee, half its members named by Stewart and half by Mayor Harrison, went from Chicago to Springfield to lobby for the bill. They achieved nothing.

Now Darrow got worried. Looking at the political set-up in the lower house—eighty-eight Republicans to sixty-two Democrats and two Public Ownership men—he began to doubt that they could pass the Mueller bill. If Daniel Cruice drew enough votes away from Harrison, Stewart would become mayor of Chicago. In that case, the franchises of the private street-car companies might be extended another twenty years with Stewart's approval, and all of the agitation for city ownership would be wasted. Harrison had pledged himself to veto any extension of the franchises until the Mueller bill was law. Would Stewart make the same pledge?

Down from Chicago to Springfield went Judge Edward F. Dunne to urge Darrow to come out for Mayor Harrison's re-election. I will, said Darrow, if Stewart does not make the pledge we want. Stewart did not. And it was announced that Darrow would give a campaign speech for Harrison on April 3, four days before the election.

Bitterness against Darrow in the ranks of the Union Labor party was intense. Eight union officials charged in an open letter that Darrow had never done anything for labor unless he was paid an inflated fee. William E. Burns, who was one of Eugene Debs's chief lieutenants in the Pullman boycott, thundered: "When Clarence S. Darrow was defending men who had bribed juries in cases where crippled children were asking for justice from the traction companies which had injured them, it was explained in extenuation that he was acting as 'a lawyer.' I suppose it will be explained that he is acting as 'a lawyer' now."

Cruice was equally bitter, charging that Darrow was guilty of "a breach of trust."

Darrow admitted that he had promised to support Cruice. But to keep that promise now, he wrote Cruice, "could not do you any good and could only result, from my standpoint, in serious injury to the people of Chicago." Darrow conceded that he had never liked Mayor Harrison. But that was not the point now. "I believe that your prejudice against him," he wrote, "has absolutely destroyed your judgment as to what is best in this crisis."

And Darrow went back to Chicago and gave his speeches for Harrison and ignored the names he was called. To do otherwise, he said, would be to abandon "all the work done in the fifteen years I have advocated municipal ownership, and to see the streets of the city lugged off under my nose. I could not do it and would not do it. A man has to do what seems to him to be his duty."

At the election, Mayor Harrison squeaked through. He had less than half the total vote. His margin over the Republican was only 8,000. The Socialist candidate had 11,000. Cruice had 10,000. Everybody knew that Darrow's influence with the workingmen had given Harrison the victory. Cruice complained bitterly of Darrow: "He held over 18,000 votes in his vest pocket and he threw them as he wished." Darrow had done it for principle, but he saw no reason to be content with principle. His friend George Schilling was named by Mayor Harrison to the board of local improvements, his friend Joseph Errant, to the civil service commission.

III

Darrow again went to Springfield, where the Mueller bill, having passed the senate, was about to come up in the house. An immensely complicated measure, it provided that any city could own and operate street railways. It could build the lines itself or buy them. To raise the necessary funds, it could issue bonds if two thirds of the voters approved the bond issue, or the city could issue "Mueller certificates" on approval of a majority of the voters. These last could be paid solely from the income of the street-car company. In other connections, the bill provided (in memory of the Allen law of 1897) that consent of the landowners along a right-of-way was not required before the city could grant a franchise for a street railway; and it made possible a referendum on any franchise of five years or more granted by the city council to a private company.

Finally the committee on municipal corporations reported the Mueller bill onto the floor of the lower house, with a recommendation that it should not pass.

Scene: *Chamber of the Lower House, Springfield*
Time: *April 23, 1903*

The galleries are filled with spectators, who have come to hear the opening of debate on the Mueller bill and the Lindly bill, hastily drawn by Cicero J. Lindly for no purpose except to block the Mueller bill. Each bill is now up for second reading —the crucial one, since it is the occasion when a measure is debated and amended. Any bill that passes at second reading is printed in final form and advanced to third reading, when members have to vote yes or no on the proposal as a whole.

In the chair is John H. Miller, Republican, machine hack, hand-picked for the job by the Republican boss of the state, Congressman William Lorimer of Chicago. Early in January when the Republican members had caucused to choose their candidate for speaker, Miller was picked by the narrow vote of 49 to 30 over Lawrence Y. Sherman. Today the chamber is so crowded that several elegant ladies are sitting directly behind Miller on the speaker's platform.

Miller orders several amendments to the Lindly bill to be read. The clerk reads the first of them. Miller puts it to a voice vote. Instantly several members leap to their feet and demand a roll call. Miller ignores them. He raps his gavel, declares the amendment adopted, and orders the clerk to read the next.

Chaos. Lawrence Sherman leaps onto his desk, swings his chair over his head, and screams at Miller. Voices shout:

"Mr. Speaker! Roll call! Roll call!"

The clerk's lips continue to shape words that nobody can

hear. Miller's gavel raps, showing that the second amendment has passed. The clerk begins reading the third. Fights break out between the rival factions. Clarence Darrow gets into a ruckus, finally knocks his opponent down and wedges a waste basket over his head. (One of Darrow's friends nearly bursts with delight; lately Darrow has been going around Chicago giving lectures in favor of Tolstoi's doctrine of nonresistance.)

Members begin shouting at the speaker to clear the women off the platform. Miller, seeing their protective value, assures them that nothing serious will happen. They remain.

Many of the representatives are banging incessantly on their desks. Some are using the huge bound volumes of bills submitted to them for their quiet and public-spirited consideration. Others have torn rungs out of their chairs, and use those.

Capital police march into the chamber, stars on their jackets. They form a cordon around the speaker. The clerk's lips continue to move. Occasionally Miller's lips move. His gavel raps. At last Cicero J. Lindly rises, and his lips move. Miller raps his gavel. The Lindly bill, as amended, has been advanced to third reading. The speaker with his police guard makes his dignified exit. His supporters follow him.

A majority of the members remain. A representative shouts: "Gentlemen of the house, I notice that we are without a speaker." Representative Allen is elected speaker pro tem. A roll call shows that 97 members are present, a liberal quorum of the membership of 153. Allen rules that the house is still in session. He also announces that a hundred lunches have been ordered. The members sit munching their sandwiches, while they substitute the Mueller bill for the Lindly bill, section by section. To sew matters up, a motion to reconsider the question is formally made. It is defeated. Another resolution is adopted declaring that, since Speaker Miller has used the "revolutionary and unconstitutional methods" of gavel rule to deny a roll call, the house should be permanently reorganized, that is, a new speaker should be chosen.

John H. Miller resumes the chair at 2:30 P.M. and is confronted with this motion. Clearly he has gone too far. The house adjourns until 5 P.M.

When it reconvenes, Miller says that he wants to explain his conduct in the morning. The clerk reads Miller's statement saying that he refused the roll call because he had been approached by parties who hinted that he could "make money" by permitting the Mueller bill to pass.

Outraged members are on their feet.

"Names! Names!" they shout.

Miller declines to give them.

A motion is made that the speaker appoint a five-member committee to investigate all charges of bribery in connection with the Mueller bill. The motion is adopted. The house adjourns until morning.

April 23, 1903, said the Chicago *Tribune,* was "the most exciting day the Illinois legislature has ever known." The day following was hardly tranquil. The session opened quietly and continued so while Cicero Lindly asked and received unanimous consent to have his bill recalled to order of second reading for amendment. But when he switched to an attack on the Mueller bill, a member objected to any discussion of that topic so long as Miller's allegations of bribery had not been investigated. A motion was made and carried unanimously.

Miller named the five members of the investigating committee. He scandalized everybody by naming five of his own henchmen. Darrow at once moved that six specified representatives be added to the committee. The motion carried, 72 to 60. But the opposition to Darrow's motion was spearheaded by the Democratic leader of the house; at last the Democratic machine in the state had exposed its real desires.

When John Miller appeared before the investigating committee, he said that he could not identify the men who had approached him with offers of bribes, but that their faces were familiar to him. He also said that he had received a letter, unsigned, hinting that he could get $10,000 by promoting passage of the Mueller bill. If this was vague, Miller's testimony suggested what had really happened. After the house rebelled against his gavel rule at the morning session on April 23, he hurried to Governor Yates' office for a strategy conference.

Also present were the lieutenant governor, boss Lorimer, and Cicero Lindly. The others were desperate for some way to head off the Mueller bill. Miller mentioned the vague offers of bribes, to which he attached little significance. But his colleagues caught a glimmer of hope. Miller must reveal these "facts" to the house. He did so, with fatal results.

The committee heard seventeen witnesses, and on April 30 it reported that it had no evidence of corruption. Miller's five adherents on the committee signed the report. The house adopted it unanimously. Even though the time was 8:30 P.M., the Mueller bill was called up at once. Clarence Darrow led the defense of the bill. He made statements, answered questions, grinned at the badgering and the heckling. This was his favored role, and he held the floor for more than an hour.

The next morning the bill's opponents tried all sorts of delays to sidetrack the bill from third reading. But it became obvious that a majority for the bill was present in the chamber and would remain until they had a chance to vote on it. The roadblock collapsed, the vote was taken. The bill passed 93 to 20, but forty-three members were absent and not voting. Only one Democrat dared to vote in the negative.

On May 5 the senate concurred in the house amendments. Governor Yates waited two weeks before signing the bill; even then he said that he thought it faulty but would sign it because he was confident that the Chicago city council and the people of Chicago would not misuse the authority it granted. The job in Springfield was done.

Not in Chicago. Mayor Harrison and the city council now insisted that immediate municipal ownership, always called IMO, was not possible. They refused to submit the Mueller Act to a referendum. The council's committee on local transportation actually began negotiations with the Chicago City Railway about the terms for renewing its franchise. All summer and autumn the IMO forces held rallies to force the city officials to act. Darrow and other lawyers explained in detail the practical steps that should be taken. But none were taken.

Then the reformers got an issue they could really agitate. On November 12 a strike started against the Chicago City Railway, which operated all the lines on the South Side. When the 2,200 employees quit work, the company was prepared. It had already hired motormen and conductors in other cities to serve as strikebreakers. To serve as boss strikebreaker it imported one James Farley, who had recently smashed strikes by force on the traction lines of Cleveland, St. Louis, and other cities. The first day there was much rioting. At least thirty persons were arrested. Any street-car that moved was stoned, its windows broken, its crew mauled. The next day every street-car carried a heavy contingent of police. The rest of the city was left almost unprotected, while street-car service continued sporadic and hazardous. The union consistently offered to arbitrate; the company consistently refused. And the Chicago Federation of Labor hardened in its demand for immediate municipal ownership.

A series of conferences began and ran almost without interruption, with Darrow serving as representative of the union. Mayor Harrison took a hand. The parties called each other names, made offers, which led to counter-offers but not to settlement. Ten days after the strike began, five thousand strike sympathizers paraded to a meeting, where the crowd was estimated at fifteen thousand. A chant went up for Darrow, who was not scheduled to speak. He came forward: "This strike was brought about by those persons who believe the class which holds property has all the rights, and that which does not has none; by those who believe that a business belongs absolutely to the employer and not to the employes who give their lives to it." The strike, he said, would have been settled easily if the company had not thought it was about to get a new franchise from a city council elected by the votes of workingmen.

Dusk had crept into the huge, bare hall. The audience was

a faceless mass that shifted, swayed, cheered every mention of the strikers, hooted any reference to the company. Darrow demanded that the mayor and council break off negotiations with the company for extension of its franchise. The meeting adopted a resolution to that effect, and also called on the city council "to institute proceedings at once to take over the lines operated by this company, and place them immediately under municipal ownership and operation." Three days later the strike was settled.

More meetings, more agitation, and just after Christmas the council's committee on local transportation at last agreed to hear testimony against its extension franchise to the Chicago City Railway. At the hearings Darrow charged that the ordinance would be "a graft of $200,000,000." Analyzing the report on which it was based, he said it was filled with false estimates: of the value of the property, of what it would cost to improve the property to meet the standards set by the ordinance, of the income of the company. The company, he said, had earned 42 percent annually on its investment for the previous twenty years; it would earn more than that if this ordinance were passed. He jeered at the provision that if the city wanted to buy the property its value should be appraised by a Federal court; any child knew that Federal judges would favor the company against the city. Lastly he turned to a clause providing that the city should be paid cash compensation for permitting the company to use its streets. This was pure class legislation, a way to support the city government out of the pockets of workingmen and shopgirls who rode the street-cars rather than by taxing the property owners. The proper course, he insisted, was to force the company to lower its fares.

But the best course was for the city to take over the street-car lines altogether. And the city officials, whatever their wishes, could not prevent a referendum on the Mueller Act at the spring, 1904, elections in Chicago. On April 5, by a margin of 5 to 1, the voters approved the Mueller Act. By narrower but substantial majorities they urged that the city should not grant any more franchises, and that it should proceed without delay to acquire ownership of the street railways.

The voters could recommend; only the city council had power to act.

CHAPTER 12

Mottled Victory

I am fully convinced that the trade-union movement is on the
eve of a great betrayal by its leaders. They have been se-
duced by the capitalists into the belief that the two great
trusts,—the Labor Trust and the Trust of Capital—can unite
in a common depredation on the public.

—Henry Demarest Lloyd to Herbert N. Casson,
December 19, 1901 *

I

EVEN BEFORE the spring elections of 1904, the traction companies of Chicago could see that they might have to compromise. But they did not like it. When Lincoln Steffens
investigated the city in 1903, he spent a morning talking to
prominent bankers and to financiers concerned with public
utilities. All but one of them became furious in talking about
the moderate reform typified by the Municipal Voters' League.
They said it had hurt the city; they told him about companies
that had moved away, about others that had planned to come
to Chicago but had decided to go elsewhere. He did find some
businessmen who believed in civic honesty and were ready to
pay what it cost financially; he even found a promoter who
expected to enjoy negotiating with the city council for a new

* Lloyd Mss., Wisconsin Historical Society.

franchise. "Those reform aldermen are slow, but they are fair," he told Steffens. But the diehards were bitter.

"Isn't the reform council honest?" Steffens asked them.

"Honest! Yes, but—oh, hell!"

He asked if they were saying that they wanted the gray wolves back again. Their answer, he reported, was "a curse, or a shrewd smile, or a cynical laugh."

Faced with this sort of opposition, the advocates of immediate city ownership seemed dreadfully weak. They did not control the machinery of either major party. In most of Chicago, Lorimer ruled the Republican machine; in the rest of the state, even the factions hostile to him were hostile to municipal ownership. The situation in the Democratic organization was no better. John P. Hopkins, boodler and Gold Democrat, controlled the state committee. Mayor Harrison was spokesman for a gang of genial vagrants who ran the ward clubs of Chicago. The third major faction had small place in the official councils of the party, but by means of Hearst's two Chicago dailies it could sway public opinion and influence votes. Hearst's papers stood momentarily for city ownership, but might desert it to gratify his ambitions.

One difficulty confronts any radical movement: a man cannot do anything decisive for city ownership, say, until he attains a position of power, but any individual who gets power is likely to lose his radical ideas. Often the conversion is sincere; a man cannot easily see serious defects in a system that has let him move to the top. Besides, power gives a man new chances to gain personally by trading favors with the wealthy. The movement for immediate municipal ownership faced this dilemma—which the more radical Socialists had been unable to solve. In the spring of 1903 a Socialist alderman was elected in Chicago. A year later the city committee voted to expel him from the party. His alleged offenses? Introducing "graft" measures in the city council, accepting annual passes from railroads, repudiating Socialist principles, introducing an ordinance to allow aldermen to ride the street-cars free.

Trade unions were suffering a similar erosion. Since 1896 the American economy had been climbing steadily. Prices were rising; the injustice to debtors and farmers that had spawned the demand for free silver seemed a thing of the past. Profits were rising too, especially for many of the new corporations, who had gained the financial slack that allows compromise. And from the knockdown battles of the previous decade, some businessmen had learned that it is not always wise to press a labor dispute to the point of total victory. It was J. P. Morgan, as much as President Roosevelt, who forced the anthracite barons to arbitrate the violent strike of 1902. In similar fashion, Lyman Gage repeatedly tried to moderate social conflicts in Chicago.

Bankers such as Morgan and Gage sometimes sought class conciliation because of their values as individuals, or because bankers more often than industrialists had been born into the cultured upper class and had been taught a type of aristocratic responsibility. But bankers had good business reasons for moderation. Income came to them, not as a maximum rate of profit in the short run, but as a fixed rate of interest over long periods of time. The major consideration for them was stability, routine, an ordered and predictable society in which the safety of investments was unthreatened. It is ironical that bankers were widely regarded as the most reactionary and grasping group of businessmen, when in fact they were content with a limited return, and when many of them were enlightened enough to know that reform is often the truest conservatism.

Conciliation between trade union and company could be carried even further than peaceful settlement of disputes: the two could unite to victimize the consumer. Officials of railroad Brotherhoods argued for increases in railroad fares; leaders of unions in the steel industry went before committees of Congress to plead for increases in the tariff on steel. When the largesse was granted, the company generously gave part of its increased profits to its skilled employees. The American

Way had found a new application, and variants on it operated in dozens of ways.

In Chicago the main exponents were Albert Young and John C. Driscoll. Young in the autumn of 1900 organized the Coal Team Drivers' Union. A few months later, Driscoll brought the employers into the Coal Team Owners' Association. The owners then doubled their previous charges to the coal companies and other large users for hauling coal. The trade association and the union combined to chase off the streets any competitor who tried to undercut the standard charges for hauling coal. Under this arrangement, the wages of union teamsters rose 15 percent the first year, and doubled the second.

Outright racketeering by union officials had appeared in some trades where unions had become strong enough to disrupt production. In Chicago the pioneer was "Skinny" Madden of the Steamfitters. His usual tactic was to threaten a strike on a construction job, and to charge $1,000 for not striking. If the building project were big enough, he might get $10,000 or more. His motto: "Show me an honest man, and I'll show you a damn fool." He cared nothing about the streetcar problem, and he would sell his influence to the highest bidder.

To further splinter the political power of Chicago's unions, Mayor Harrison put many union officials in soft jobs on the city payroll: as building inspectors, bridge inspectors, members of some bureau. In 1903 when the formation of the Union Labor party threatened Harrison's reelection, these men had thrown their weight against the new venture.

Thus the advocates of immediate municipal ownership, however ably they might agitate their cause, had almost none of the organizational apparatus that could change the institutional arrangements. And they faced three intertwined barricades: the street-car companies, the people of Chicago, and the courts. It was certain that the traction firms would not wait passively to be dispossessed. The first move by the city toward taking over any part of the traction system would provoke a drastic response. The private managements could deliberately disrupt service on their lines, thus inconveniencing any annoying passengers. Nobody knew how the passengers would react. They might be moved to wrath that would harden their desire for public ownership of the street-car system. But they might not. The average citizen of Chicago cared little for public ownership as an abstract principle of government. He wanted chiefly to pay less for better service. If the private companies chose to disrupt operations, the voters might seek a compromise, even one weighted for the corporations. George Schilling forecast this outcome; he said the people wanted city ownership, but not enough to tolerate the hardship that would have to be endured to get it.

A more immediate problem was the courts. On April 21, 1904, just after the smashing referendum in favor of the Mueller Act, some franchises of the Chicago City Railway expired. The city at once filed notice on the company to vacate the tracks. The company went into Federal court and asked for an order restraining the city from any interference with its property. The injunction was granted by Judge Grosscup. It was shortly revealed that the judge was a large stockholder in a street-car company operating under a fifty-year franchise in Charleston, West Virginia, but his decisions in Chicago were not invalidated on that account.

II

The Presidential election of 1904 showed how effectively the Altgeld Democrats had been ousted from power in their own party. Twice Bryan and the Chicago Platform had gone down to defeat. The professional politicians in the party were hungry for victory. City bosses like Harrison in Chicago and Croker of Tammany Hall wanted to get their hands on national as well as local patronage. Southern Congressmen and governors wanted the same thing. When Bryan commented that nobody would get the Presidential nomination who had supported the Gold Democrats in 1896, his statement was endorsed by only four of ninety-nine Democratic Congressmen who were polled. Dominant thought in the top circles of the party was to put up exactly such a man, Alton J. Parker, a Wall Street lawyer, and to make the campaign into one long effort to conciliate the business interests of the country.

The only person whom the Altgeld Democrats could offer against this trend was William Randolph Hearst, who for the moment was urging major reforms: public ownership of public franchises, no governmental protection of monopolies, a graduated income tax, a better system of public schools. But all this was uncertain: an Altgeld might find it hard to rise above principle, but Hearst was a different sort. And the Democratic national committee moved fast to block Hearst; fearing that he might use his two Chicago dailies to stampede the national convention, they scheduled it for St. Louis even though Chicago was the favored site.

The Chicago radicals were apathetic. Clarence Darrow was typical. In March he went to Terre Haute to give a speech for Hearst, but instead he talked mainly about trade unions. He was slated to go on to Evansville to give another speech for Hearst, but the route there crossed flooded rivers that were delaying trains. So he stayed in Terre Haute where he shunned Hearst's supporters and spent his time with a lifelong resident there, Eugene Debs.

On May Day, Debs turned up in Chicago as a delegate to the Socialist national convention. In opening the sessions, he claimed that the Socialists were the legal heirs to the anti-monopoly tradition. "Thomas Jefferson would scorn to enter a modern Democratic convention," Debs shouted. "He would have as little business there as Abraham Lincoln would have in a modern Republican convention. If they were living today, they would be delegates to this convention."

Debs made the claim, but Darrow and other Altgeld Democrats were almost willing to accept it—an indication of the varied and contradictory meanings that the idea of anti-monopoly had come to have. If it referred only to an economic program, it could include those, like Louis D. Brandeis, who wanted to break up the great private corporations and restore competition in all industries; it could include Theodore Roosevelt and many members of the Chicago Civic Federation who wanted to use public power to regulate the private monopolies; but it could hardly include Eugene Debs, who wanted a single monopoly, the government, to control all of basic industry. When the Socialists, who sought to expand the power of the state, claimed descent from Jefferson, who had usually tried to restrict it, they were thinking more of a way of life than of a type of economy. They were emphasizing the basic goal they shared with Jefferson—of opening up to all individuals the maximum opportunities for development.

From this broader perspective, the anti-monopoly movement was concerned with all human activities. It dealt with men's values, as Veblen had done, with their education, as Dewey had done, with their sympathy for others, as Dreiser had done, with their physical surroundings, as Sullivan and Wright had done, with justice in the courts, as Darrow had done, with honest elections, as the Municipal Voters' League had done. Anti-monopoly meant the same thing as freedom and equality, and its advocates aimed at removing all obstacles from the individual's striving toward self-fulfilment. It was this broad perspective, the heritage of Jefferson and Lincoln, that Debs claimed to share with Darrow and other Democrats.

But Altgeld's followers were not ready to resign finally from the Democratic party. When Debs gave his speech in Chicago, it was nearly time for the Democratic primaries to choose delegates to the state convention, which would elect (and could instruct) the delegates to the national convention. In New York the state convention put up Parker as its favorite son, on a platform that straddled the trust issue, said nothing of the eight-hour day, said nothing of the monetary issue. When William Jennings Bryan spoke in Chicago on April 24, he called it "a dishonest platform, fit only for a dishonest party." Mayor Harrison refused to comment on Bryan's remarks. In the primaries his henchmen fought an alliance of Hearst and Hopkins, but even so they did well in Cook County.

They would need all the strength they could muster at the state convention in Springfield. It was common knowledge that Hopkins planned to use his control of the state committee to name the temporary chairman of the convention, and to control things thereafter by gavel rule.

The Republicans put up their strongest man for governor. For seventy-nine ballots their state convention was torn three ways, but in the end they deserted both Governor Yates and Frank O. Lowden, the pick of Lorimer and "Uncle Joe" Cannon, to nominate Charles S. Deneen, who had been an effective state's attorney of Cook County.

Springfield in mid-June was bedlam. All of the Democratic factions in Chicago had brought small armies of muscle men with them for the convention: the "stockyards Indians" of Alderman Thomas Carey, the Black Rabbits of Billy Loeffler. Mayor Harrison sedately walked the streets arm in arm with Loeffler while at least fifteen hundred visiting thugs raided barrooms, shouted, paraded, fought with each other, and insulted the local citizenry.

When the convention opened on June 14, Darrow and the other Hearst delegates had been assigned seats together at the rear of the hall where they could easily be reached by the burly red-badged sergeants-at-arms who patrolled the aisles. The chief of police of Springfield sat on the platform and took his orders from Hopkins, as did Frank Quinn, the temporary chairman, who was using a bung-starter as a gavel. The first business was to hear the reports on the contested delegations. Quinn decided every contest favorably to the Hopkins claimants, without asking for any roll calls and without pretending to care whether they had actually gotten a majority vote in the primary. Thus, enough Harrison and Hearst delegates were denied seats in the convention to insure Hopkins' control.

In the afternoon, the same process continued. A solid wall of strong-arm men stood shoulder to shoulder between the chairman's platform and the mass of delegates in the hall, while Quinn with his bung-starter gaveled through one motion after another. Quinn, young, handsome, genial, a criminal lawyer, smirked continuously until two contenders for the gubernatorial nomination withdrew their names from consideration and denounced the methods being used to run the session. Then he became fearful. The storm from the floor grew in volume. Shouts came: "Endorse Deneen and have the farce over." Somebody suggested that the Hopkins clique should steal the hall, since it was taking everything else.

Repeated demands were made for a resolution instructing the delegates to the national convention. Finally the chairman of the committee read one—which the committee did not endorse—instructing the delegation to support Hearst for the Presidential nomination. Instantly Clarence Darrow jumped to his feet and moved a substitute, ordering the delegation to hold for Hearst as long as his name was before the convention. Quinn started to gavel it down, but the temper of the delegates was too threatening, and he allowed a roll call, the only one of the day. Darrow's substitute was adopted by 932 to 382. The irony of the situation was underlined later: of the fifty-four delegates from Illinois to the national convention, not more than seven were personally in favor of Hearst. One of those was Darrow. Several of the delegates had been Gold Democrats in 1896.

The St. Louis convention, if less brazen than the one in Springfield, was no more principled. The contesting Hearst and Harrison delegates were again denied their seats, even though the credentials committee admitted that "questionable methods" had been used in choosing some Hopkins delegates, even though wholesale fraud was proven, even though the cause of the ousted delegates was pleaded by William Jennings Bryan, who charged on the floor of the convention that the Illinois state convention had been "gag-ruled and gang-run."

Bryan or no, the Hopkins delegates were seated by a vote of 647 to 299, with the overwhelming support of the East and South. Then the platform for the campaign, a meaningless morass, was adopted without any debate at all.

(The year 1904, predicted the Chicago *Record-Herald,* was going to be "a black year for the radicals in American politics." The Good Old Party offered "nothing but conservatism," while the handful of professionals who controlled the St. Louis convention "represent exactly the same element that dominates Republican politics.")

Clarence Darrow could hardly have been less interested in the proceedings. He did not even bother to go to the caucus of the Illinois delegation which picked the national committeeman from the state. He was absent again when, early in the evening of July 8, the delegation was polled. A majority wanted to violate their instructions and vote for Alton J. Parker. But Hopkins, as chairman of the delegation, said that wouldn't do; they must do as they had been ordered to do. Free P. Morris was picked to speak for Illinois when it came the state's turn to make a Presidential nomination.

Scene: *Floor of Democratic convention, St. Louis*
Time: *Evening of July 8, 1904*

> Clarence Darrow goes up to John P. Hopkins and announces his intention of making a speech seconding Hearst's nomination.
>
> "For what state?" Hopkins asks sardonically.
>
> "Why, Illinois, of course," Darrow exclaims.
>
> Hopkins says that Free Morris has been chosen to speak for Illinois. Darrow pleads. Hopkins is obdurate. Darrow turns to the other delegates. They offer no sympathy, except for the editor of Hearst's Chicago *American,* who tries to intercede.
>
> Hopkins tells the editor angrily: "You come down here as an Illinois delegate, and when you get here you assume that you are a delegate from the whole United States. You had better get back to your stall with the rest of us."
>
> Darrow, with tears in his eyes and his voice trembling (two resources that were usually available to him) appeals to Free

Morris. Finally Morris swells out his chest, waves his hand grandly, and agrees to yield.

During the early nominating speeches, John P. Hopkins sits, saturnine and amused. He wears a tuxedo with a red carnation in his lapel. When he smiles, his dark mustache ripples. Illinois is called. Hopkins announces that Morris will speak, Morris announces that Darrow will speak. Darrow starts for the stage. Men acquainted with him come alert: they hope for the first excitement in what has been a stifling and dreary day.

Darrow nominates Hearst perfunctorily. Then he says: "It seems to have been decreed by fate that the men who scuttled the Democratic ship shall be once more placed in charge." This assault on the Gold Democrats is applauded from the gallery, but it provokes so many hisses, catcalls, and protests from the delegates that Darrow is forced to stop. The chairman says he assumes the delegates "will not insult a speaker."

Darrow ridicules the effort to conduct a "safe and sane" campaign with a safe and sane candidate. If that is the aim, why not endorse Theodore Roosevelt, "a President who is at least safe if not sane." (Laughter) The Democratic party can win only by holding to "the glorious traditions" of Jefferson, Altgeld, and Bryan. (Many delegates give three cheers for Bryan.) The party must not forget that the United States is far more than "the narrow, crooked lane which men call Wall Street." The party must rely on the true Democratic voters, "who believe and understand that there can be no victory which sacrifices principle, and no lasting defeat where honor is maintained."

"The Democratic party is the party of the common people. It has never ridden into power by either the votes or the gold of the banker or the monopolist, and it never will. Remove from the Democratic party the toiling masses who eat their bread in the sweat of their face, and no Democratic party will be left."

But indeed fate had decreed. The next day the convention nominated Parker on the first ballot. Darrow resigned from activity. He went from St. Louis to Estes Park, Colorado, where he spent the rest of the summer writing a novel about crime and punishment. Thus he was not present in Chicago when the traction situation there moved toward a new crisis. On August 24 the city council's committee on local transportation reported to the council a proposed extension of the Chicago City Railway franchise. This franchise, which came to be universally called the tentative ordinance, would run for twenty years. Although it provided for complete reconstruction of the system, its other features were anathema to the radicals. Worst of all, it barred the city from taking over any of the properties for a thirteen-year period. The ordinance had the support of Mayor Harrison, but it was vehemently denounced in a public letter by two prominent Democrats, Judges Tuley and Dunne.

Darrow, on his return to Chicago, left no doubt as to how he felt. In early October he presided at a campaign meeting where the main speaker was Senator Tom Watson of Georgia, the nominee for President of the now emaciated People's party. Darrow lauded Watson's bolt of the Democratic party after the St. Louis convention. Bryan's endorsement of Parker and the Democratic platform said Darrow, would not "gain him the support of Wall street," and it would alienate those who had supported him in 1896 and 1900. Watson was even more caustic, saying that while Roosevelt was a fighter, Parker was not even that. "Roosevelt," Watson declared, "could tie both hands behind his back and run Parker clear out of the ring just by shining his teeth at him."

Was Darrow supporting Watson? Perhaps. At the end of the month it was rumored that Darrow would vote for Debs, the Socialist. Then he gave two speeches for the Republican who was running for Congress against Mayor Harrison's brother. Preston Harrison replied that at least he was a loyal Democrat. "Meantime Darrow has dodged into and out of the Republican party, into and out of the Populist party, into and out of the Socialist party, and into and out of the Democratic party. He now is reported as making speeches for Watson and promises to vote for Debs."

Actually Darrow was not for any party, because there was

no party that stood for what he wanted. He was only against something—control of the Democratic party by machine politicians or Gold Democrats, by anybody except men of anti-monopoly convictions. That had been the lodestar of the Altgeld forces in Chicago since 1896. Darrow was doing whatever seemed most likely to achieve this aim. But he and his associates were far from achieving their goal in 1904. They could sometimes rally a majority of the Chicago voters on a specific issue, but the party was in the hands of their enemies.

III

Then came the election of 1904. Probably no Democratic strategy could have prevailed, but nobody knew that—they knew only that the unprincipled tactics of the conservative wing had lost, had been routed. Preston Harrison, in a congressional district he had been expected to win, was defeated by more than 6,500 votes. President Roosevelt's majority in Chicago exceeded 100,000. Nobody could say what part local issues had played in the result; the fact remained that it was a stunning rebuke to Mayor Harrison. A week later, he announced that he would not be a candidate for reelection in 1905.

By mid-January it became clear that the Republicans would run John M. Harlan. He would be a hard man to beat, and now Harrison was out of the running. Judge Tuley took a hand again, as he had done in August by denouncing the tentative ordinance. Now he issued an "Emergent Address on the Traction Crisis on Chicago." Declaring that the capitalists in control of the private companies were "stock jobbers," he said that traction was the major issue of the mayoralty race. An independent party for city ownership was an impractical dream; the only organization that could carry that demand was the Democratic party. And Edward F. Dunne was the only man who could be elected mayor who would "throttle the Wall

Street conspiracy to rob the people of their rights in the streets of our city."

Dunne was a genial Irishman who had been in politics nearly all of his fifty-one years. His father, a Peoria businessman, had been an alderman several terms, then a state legislator. Dunne had practiced law in Chicago for fifteen years, in partnership with a Congressman and a former judge on the state supreme court. Then, in 1892, Dunne had been elected to the county bench, where he still sat. He liked almost everybody, even the gray wolves and the leaders of the Harrison machine; yet on policy questions he was usually in the radical element of his party. He was a prominent advocate of city ownership and operation of the street-car lines. A Roman Catholic with ten children, he sent them to the public schools. He was, in short, a man who might paste together the warring Democratic factions.

Nearly every Democratic ward club in the city called for his nomination, and Dunne announced on February 11 that he was willing to make the race. Immediate steps should be taken, he urged, aimed at city ownership of the street-car lines, and they would lead to "early success." He also favored operation of the lines by the city "under a rigidly enforced civil service law," but that issue would have to be resolved later by a referendum under the provisions of the Mueller Act.

Mayor Harrison refused to comment directly on the statement. But five days later he asked the city council to request bids for the construction of a city-owned traction line on streets where the franchises of the private companies had expired. This move was tactical: the mayor still set his hopes on the tentative ordinances. But the Chicago City Railway still had not stated whether it would accept the tentative ordinance that had been offered it, and this new threat was a way to bring pressure on the corporation for a quick and favorable decision. Harrison also hoped by his action, as he wrote later, "in some measure to quiet the municipal ownership demands."

The Republican candidate began a free-swinging campaign

against IMO. The Dunne program, Harlan declared, meant a decade of litigation to clarify the city's legal rights. Even if Chicago won the legal battles, it still would not have the money to put the plan into operation. But Dunne insisted that the city had authority to buy the existing lines of the private companies, at fair valuations, by means of condemnation proceedings. And the funds required could be raised by the issuance of Mueller certificates. So Harlan and Dunne agreed that the traction situation was the main issue of the campaign. But many of the Democratic ward bosses had other concerns. As always, they wanted office, and the spoils of office. Dunne was nominated by the city convention, all right, but his preference for city treasurer was sidetracked in favor of a man whose conduct as commissioner of public works might prove highly embarrassing to the whole ticket. The gray wolves were not ready to become sheep.

Dunne got some good breaks. The independent candidate of the Municipal Ownership and Referendum Association withdrew from the race and urged unity behind Dunne, "not because he is the Democratic nominee, but because . . . through his election alone can the streets of Chicago be saved to the people." Mayor Harrison announced that, although he would not campaign for Dunne because of their disagreement about the traction program, yet he would vote for the entire ticket. It was the Republican camp that was divided: Harlan had many personal enemies, he was the candidate of the bluestockings, and many Republican ward bosses refused to help him because he had bolted the party in 1897.

Dunne seemed to have forgotten everything except the street-car problem. If a man promised to support city ownership, Dunne asked nothing more. On that ground he even endorsed a Republican for reelection to the city council, in spite of the man's foul record. On the same ground he urged a First Ward meeting to vote for Hinky Dink Kenna—a deed that caused consternation; Carter Harrison himself had never made a direct appeal for either Kenna or Coughlin. Clarence

Darrow was asked if he thought it proper for Dunne to endorse a man like Kenna. Darrow hesitated, then said: "Personally I am not in favor of endorsing any man whose record has not been for the public good." He wanted Dunne to use his full influence to elect the right sort of men to the council. Thus Darrow went into the Nineteenth Ward to speak for an independent candidate against Johnny Powers, charging that Powers had been one of the worst aldermanic boodlers.

At first glance the election seemed a straight victory for the radicals. Dunne was elected—the anti-monopolists had carried their man into city hall. And on a referendum, the voters by 150,000 to 60,000 rejected Harrison's tentative ordinance and declared that no franchise should be granted to any private street-car company. But there were dangerous signs: Powers went back to the council by the narrow margin of 419 votes; Kenna and Coughlin delivered a whopping 4,000 plurality for Dunne in the First Ward; on the new city council, the majority for Dunne's traction program was only 39 to 31, even with six Republicans saying they would support it.

The Dunne administration faced some hard problems. If the private companies refused to sell out to the city, some way was needed to force them to do so. But was condemnation of private property legal in cases such as this—when the objective was merely to change the ownership of the property without changing its use? If condemnation was not legal, the city would have to build and operate a competing system. Could funds for this purpose be raised by issuing Mueller certificates? Chicago could go in debt only up to a legal maximum, and that limit had been reached two generations earlier. Mueller certificates were patently a device to evade the constitutional limit on indebtedness, and the courts might invalidate them on that score. Even if the certificates were valid, would anybody be willing to buy them?

But the mayor was optimistic, airily so. When a reporter asked if he did not anticipate "a long, stiff fight in the courts," Dunne replied: "A stiff fight, perhaps, but I should not say a long one." He actually thought that the private companies would cooperate, that they would yield their 720 miles of track without a struggle—and at a reasonable price. If it was necessary to go ahead with condemnation proceedings, he predicted that within six months a county court would set the valuation of the properties; after that, the funds could be raised by Mueller certificates. For guidance in these efforts, the mayor seemed to turn to an old friend. Eight days after taking office, he announced: "I have taken today the most important step of my life"—appointing Darrow as special corporation counsel "to have absolute charge of all traction litigation. . . ."

The same day the city officials became embroiled in one of the ugliest strikes ever to occur in Chicago. Since November, 1904, the garment workers at twenty-eight large inside shops had been on strike in protest against the effort of the companies to farm out increasing quantities of work to the sweaters. This strike reached desperate proportions, and the garment workers appealed to the Chicago Federation of Labor for help. The Federation turned to the teamsters: Would they refuse to carry goods to and from the struck companies? The teamsters responded by calling a sympathy strike against Montgomery Ward only, which employed only nineteen cutters and thus was the least important—to the garment workers—of all the twenty-eight firms. But it was the most important to the teamsters, who wanted a cover behind which they could force Montgomery Ward to stop hiring nonunion teamsters.

Soon the teamsters called off their sympathy strike. Then the big State Street stores, including Marshall Field, fired three teamsters who had refused to deliver goods to Montgomery Ward. The teamsters promptly called a strike against the stores. Meanwhile the companies had started the Employers' Teaming Company to haul their goods, and a Federal judge enjoined any interference with the workers of this company. A Cook County grand jury indicted twelve strike leaders for conspiracy to prevent Montgomery Ward from hiring nonunion teamsters. When the unionists showed up in court to answer the charges, their lawyer was Clarence Darrow, who had announced barely two weeks earlier that he would devote all of his time to the traction situation. To further confuse things, Darrow had been and continued to be the mayor's most prominent adviser in coping with the strike, and his dual role was now used by the employers to discredit Dunne's efforts at mediation.

The strike spread, and bitterness grew. The employers fomented racial tensions by importing hundreds of Negro strikebreakers from St. Louis and the river towns farther south. Civil war raged in the streets of Chicago. Rocks were hurled, pistols were fired, howling mobs hauled Negro teamsters off wagons and beat them into insensibility. Mayor Dunne exclaimed half in jest, half in despair: "It seems as though I had bought nine parts strike and one part municipal ownership." His efforts at peace brought no peace. The strike did not end until July 20, when the teamsters called it off unconditionally. Eighteen men had been killed, four hundred injured, nine hundred arrested for rioting.

IV

Meanwhile Dunne and his advisers had made fumbling efforts to do something about traction. They did many things—things often not consistent with each other. They went off to New York and Cleveland to give victory speeches, ignoring the urgency of the traction situation and the teamsters strike. They moved on several legal fronts, instead of putting all their efforts behind the approach that seemed most likely to succeed. They conferred about the sort of agency Chicago should create to control a publicly owned transportation system, about whether the commission should have one or three members, even though this question could safely have been pushed aside until the city was nearer to actually owning a transportation system. They consulted with Tom L. Johnson, a wealthy erstwhile street-car magnate who had become mayor of Cleveland and was striving for city ownership there. Johnson warned that the private companies would never sell out for a reasonable price, that it would be necessary to build a competing system in order to bring pressure on them. Darrow agreed. But Mayor Dunne continued to make optimistic predictions.

It became increasingly clear that the administration had no program. Worse, it was not a smooth-working team. Each man had his own ideas, and each went his own way. Dunne lacked the steadiness of will and the clarity of idea that could have achieved some sort of coordination. He had retained as corporation counsel the man who had held the job under Carter Harrison and had helped to draw up the tentative ordinances. Then he named Darrow as special counsel, without clearly marking out the authority of each man.

In May, the mayor announced that the city would seek an immediate test of the validity of Mueller certificates, probably by means of a taxpayer's suit. But no suit was filed. Instead they undid one of the few concrete things that had been done. In April, in line with Mayor Harrison's earlier request, the city council had asked for bids to install ten miles of publicly owned street-car lines on streets where private franchises had expired. The bids were due on July 1. But on June 17 the mayor asked to have the request for bids withdrawn, saying that streets were or soon would be available for one hundred miles of track. Where the money would come from, he did not say.

Dunne wanted to hire the manager of the street-car system in Detroit to report on the feasibility, and the financial soundness, of this city-owned system in Chicago. The city council promptly objected, on the ground that they had long since hired another engineer who was familiar with the Chicago situation. Dunne hesitated to do anything decisive. By June 19, Clarence Darrow was fed up with the muddle. He wrote the mayor a letter of resignation, making clear their differences. The basic one, said Darrow, was in estimating the obstacles to be overcome. Getting city ownership would not be easy. On the present city council, Mayor Dunne could count on only a minority—"and probably a small one." His program could not go far "without an appeal to the people, for new aldermen who are true to the cause."

"In my opinion," Darrow explained, "municipal ownership can never be achieved through politicians, men whose sole interest in political life and action is to make a living out of politics. It can only come through men who have convictions, and who are in politics to carry out their convictions."

Now the mayor acted. He persuaded Darrow to withdraw the resignation, and on July 5 he presented alternative plans to the city council. The first provided for the issue of not more than $75 million in Mueller certificates, to buy or build street-car lines that would be operated by the city.

This plan raised many legal and practical difficulties that would have to be resolved. The second, which Dunne preferred, came to be known as the contract plan. Under it, five or more citizens would be granted a charter to construct a "modern electric system covering the entire city." They would issue 5 percent bonds in their private company to raise the funds. All net receipts from the system would go into a sinking fund to the credit of the city. This sinking fund would eventually be used by the city to buy the system, after the legal obstacles had been removed.

The contract plan was more than ingenious, it was realistic. It had been proposed by John J. Cummings, president of the McGuire-Cummings Manufacturing Company, who had offered ten weeks earlier to build all the street cars for a municipally owned system and to accept Mueller certificates in payment. Cummings' incentive was obvious: he was seeking an enormous order for his car-building shops. When the order was not forthcoming, he substituted the offer to build the new system on the basis of the contract plan. Lyman Gage and other capitalists also supported this expedient and could bring to it immense financial resources. The plan evaded momentarily all problems of the constitutionality of the Mueller certificates, and its sinking-fund provision offered a way to finance acquisition by the city of a street-car system even if the Mueller certificates proved invalid.

But the plan was slow compared to the promises that Mayor Dunne had made. Carter Harrison snorted that if this scheme was municipal ownership, "then the tentative ordinance was municipal ownership." It was, he said, "a weak-kneed, ramshackle device." Even worse, Dunne gave the opposition a perfect chance to divert attention from his contract plan altogether.

When Dunne was first elected mayor, he knew that the traction system in Glasgow, Scotland, was city-owned and city-operated. The founder and longtime manager of this system seemed like an ideal man to ask advice. So Dunne asked him to come to Chicago and give his recommendations—not knowing that the longtime manager of the Glasgow system had retired. His successor, the wrong man, one James Dalrymple, talked to Marshall Field in London before sailing for the United States. Dalrymple was in Chicago for ten days in early June. He was much feted by the advocates of city ownership. But he was much influenced by the managers of the traction companies. He went back to Scotland and sent Mayor Dunne his report, recommending that the private franchises be extended if the companies would come to reasonable terms. Since Dalrymple had come to Chicago as his personal guest, Dunne was unwilling to release the report and then attack it. So he sat on it, giving his opponents a chance to taunt him as afraid of the report of his own expert. Day by day the newspapers ran editorial liners: "Possibly Mayor Dunne intends to keep the Dalrymple report as an heirloom, to be handed down from one generation to another in his family."

Mayor Dunne's other expert, the manager of the street-car system of Detroit, made his report in August. Using only those desirable streets on which the private franchises had expired, the report said, a city-owned system of 264 miles of track— serving half of Chicago's population—could be put in operation by January 1, 1908. The total cost would be $25 million. Estimated annual gross receipts were $12 million. Total expenses of operating and maintaining the system, plus paying 5 percent dividends on the $25 million stock, would be less than $8 million annually. If these estimates were accurate, the entire system would pay for itself in six years. This made the contract plan seem not only feasible, but startlingly expeditious.

More delays. The city council's committee on local transportation asked the Chicago City Railway to name a price at which it would sell its properties. Even though the company refused to do so, Dunne used the request as a reason not to press the council to a decision on the contract plan, saying that new negotiations were in progress with the companies. It was rumored that only five Democrats on this crucial committee would now support the mayor, while two Democrats and six Republicans favored the old tentative ordinance as a basis for settlement. The committee went on stalling. Darrow, declaring publicly that the contract plan was perfectly legal, urged the mayor to act.

On September 21 they spoke together at a public meeting. Mayor Dunne said guardedly that he still hoped to get approval of his contract plan from the city council. Then Darrow got up. He said that the council was deliberately blocking city ownership. Mayor Dunne thought that he could carry a majority of the aldermen, but Darrow did not agree. He said that the only hope was to elect new aldermen in the spring of 1906, "men who are honestly in favor of municipal ownership. . . . Then we will be able to pass an ordinance which speedily will give the people what they have asked." A week later Darrow extended this strategy. Reasoning that it would be easier to defeat the incumbent aldermen if the policy question were also on the ballot, he proposed a three-way referendum at the spring election: on the contract plan, the city plan, and a new proposal by the private companies for a renewal of their franchises.

Mayor Dunne could not wait. When the council rejected

his contract plan and continued negotiations with the private companies, he asked Darrow to draft yet another ordinance for submission to the council. This one, embodying the city plan, called for the issuance of $75 million in Mueller certificates to construct or buy a traction system. Darrow drafted it, but he opposed it. The contract plan seemed faster, more certain, less subject to legal delays and possible legal destruction. When it became clear that Dunne intended to send the new ordinance to the council, Darrow resigned—for good—saying that nothing could be done until after the spring election.

The city plan was submitted to the council. It met the same fate as its predecessor; they sat on it, for two months. Suddenly, miraculously, on January 18, 1906, it was passed. This result was engineered by the remaining pack of gray wolves, who piously announced that they could no longer stand against the popular will. A more popular guess was that they had asked to be paid for blocking the ordinance and that the companies had refused to meet their price.

The jubilation was increased by the spring elections, when the voters approved the issuance of $75 million in Mueller certificates. The majority was there, but it had declined ominously—now only 110,000 to 106,669—showing that many voters had become disenchanted by the confusion, the lack of progress, and the continuation of miserable service on the street-car lines. Mayor Dunne at once started a case to test the legal validity of the Mueller certificates, which was upheld by a country judge on September 16. One by one, the legal barriers were falling. But what would the state supreme court do?

And what did the voters want? Eighteen months earlier, just as he took office, Clarence Darrow had commented: "Our battle will be to keep the people behind us, and in a cosmopolitan city like Chicago that is no light matter." The fight for public opinion had needed a quick improvement of street-car service, which had not happened. The new city council picked up two cues. One was the narrow majority for the Mueller certificates in the spring elections. The other, ironically, was a letter from Mayor Dunne to the chairman of the council's committee on local transportation. In this letter the mayor suggested what he regarded as a variant on the contract plan. Let the private companies and the city at once agree on a fair price for the tangible and intangible properties (that is, the unexpired franchises). The city could then at any time buy the companies at that price plus the actual cost of any physical improvements that might be made. Pending purchase by the city, the street-car lines would continue to be operated by the companies "so as to provide for a sinking fund out of the proceeds to apply on the purchase price."

The city council promptly asked the two companies to submit their prices. The companies did so: a total of more than $73 million. An expert commission set up by the council fixed a valuation of only $46 million. Agreement was finally reached at about $57 million. The council quickly prepared "settlement ordinances" on that basis. The companies were to receive twenty-year franchises, which could be canceled by the city for any reason, including purchase under the city plan or the contract plan, on six months' notice. They would receive 5 percent income on their agreed values. Any net income above that would be divided 45 percent to the company, and 55 percent to the city. The companies agreed to improve service promptly.

This was the contract plan, but with a difference. Under one plan, all net earnings above 5 percent would go into a sinking fund; under the other, the companies got nearly half of the net earnings above that figure. The settlement ordinances went on a referendum in the spring elections, 1907. Mayor Dunne, up for reelection himself, campaigned against them. But he was betrayed by leaders of his own party. John P. Hopkins and the Democratic national committeeman, thinking that the Republican candidate would be a compliant mayor, supported him. Equally bad was the desertion of the two Hearst dailies. Hearst wanted to capture the Democratic party so that he would have the state's votes for the Presidential nomination at the 1908 national convention. With that in mind, his agents in Chicago had demanded control of the police department after the 1905 election. Dunne had refused. Hearst got his revenge in 1907; his papers ignored the election, the issues, and Mayor Dunne. The Republican was elected, and the settlement ordinances were passed. "Immediate seats in the cars rather than immediate municipal ownership," commented *Collier's* "proved the winning battle cry. . . ."

Two weeks later, the state supreme court ruled that the issuance of Mueller certificates would be unconstitutional because they would be indebtedness in excess of the city's legal limit. It was the result that Darrow had foreseen when he threw his weight behind the contract plan.

The campaign for city ownership was over. It had not succeeded, but it was not a failure. Service on the street-car lines was substantially improved. For the year ending February 1, 1908, the private companies paid the city more than a million and a half dollars as its share of their net earnings. The companies were now required to make exhaustive records available to the public. Nor were the indirect benefits negligible. Public officials could still be corrupt, but not so openly. No longer could a street-car magnate go to the city hall or to Springfield, his valise stuffed with paper money, and buy himself a franchise. Yerkes was dead, and so was his day.

In the drive toward municipal ownership, the obstacles were too many and too great. When it began, the city council was dominated by gray wolves; where they were replaced, the new aldermen were usually conservative businessmen. Beyond the city council stood the legislature, for the city had no power except what the state chose to give it, and in the legislature the city never had representation in anything like proper proportion to its population. Beyond the legislature stood the state courts, filled with former rural judges and former corporation lawyers. Beyond the state judiciary stood the Federal courts.

This governmental maze offered endless chances for delay, and the companies knew how to improve their opportunities.

The chief obstacle in the road to municipal ownership was the sheer profitability of the private corporations. Their financial resources were immense. They could hire the best lawyers, buy the most newspapers, contribute the most to the campaign funds of the parties. When Yerkes offered a rural lawmaker $10,000 to vote for a franchise, he was offering the man several years' wages for a few minutes' work. And when a new franchise would increase the value of Yerkes' stock by millions of dollars, $10,000 was a modest slice.

Against this, the advocates of reform could not even find a common program. The reform movement in Chicago was dozens of small currents, and no formula could merge those currents into one. "Every one is heartily in favor of reform—ing the other fellow," admitted a liberal. "A really popular measure of reform would be one that would make the poor rich and the rich immensely wealthy. Any leveling up and down measure will meet condemnation from the top and bottom and be given the cold hand by the middle class."

A more forceful leader than Edward F. Dunne—an Altgeld, say—might have been able to achieve more, but probably not. Even Tom L. Johnson in Cleveland, a vigorous mayor who called the signals for capable associates, could not achieve city ownership of the street-car system. That goal would be reached later, when the street-car companies were no longer so prosperous.

But in 1905 they were prosperous. They had leeway—financial leeway—to compromise. They could buy whoever they needed to buy: lawyers, lawmakers, party bosses. In Chicago, because of the campaign for city ownership, they needed to buy the people. And they did, simply by improving service on their lines. The "traction crisis" was dissolved in the prosperity of the American economy. But, because of the reformers, not all of that prosperity would continue to flow into a few pockets. The outcome was no empty victory.

CHAPTER 13

Conquest by Imagination

The true artist . . . must bring the world before our eyes and
make us read and learn. As he loves the true and noble, he
must show the false and bad.

—Clarence S. Darrow *

I

IN CONTRAST to Charles Tyson Yerkes, whose $769,000 art col-
lection was solely for his own enjoyment, some Chicago businessmen used part of their wealth to raise the cultural
standards of the entire city. Charles L. Hutchinson, president
of the Corn Exchange Bank and the Chicago Board of Trade,
also served as president of the Chicago Art Institute from 1882
until his death in 1924. By that time he and Martin A. Ryerson, millionaire lumberman, had built the Institute into a great
museum. First they commissioned John Wellborn Root to design a new building, and he did, in the Romanesque style.

Then they set out to fill it, showing the same aggressiveness
that had made their fortunes in business. When they heard
that Prince Demidoff was offering Dutch masters for sale, they
hurried away to Italy and, at his villa at Pratalino, they bought
the best of his holdings for $200,000, including Rembrandt's
"Young Girl at an Open Half-Door." They snapped up works

* *A Persian Pearl and Other Essays* (Chicago: C. L. Ricketts, 1899), p. 134.

by Rubens, Frans Hals, Holbein, Jan Steen. Ryerson went to
Spain and bought a painting by a man then unrecognized in
the United States, El Greco's "Assumption of the Virgin." And
to France, where he became an early collector of Renoirs.

Just as Ryerson brought great art to Chicago, Theodore
Thomas brought great music, and other philanthropists financed his efforts. Ferdinand W. Peck, millionaire merchant
and real estate man, promoted the Chicago Auditorium Association, which in 1886 engaged Adler and Sullivan to design
the building. Finished four years later, the huge mass of ma-
sonry was the best articulated structure that the partnership
produced. Almost devoid of ornament, the stone exterior
gained its interest from superb proportions and the rhythm of
its windows (some rectangles of varying sizes, some arched).
To grace the interior, Sullivan and Frank Lloyd Wright worked
with deftness and freedom in many different materials. The
engineering by Adler was based on the laws of acoustics, and
created what Wright still calls "the greatest room for opera in
the world."

In 1890 the utility magnate Charles Norman Fay, Cyrus H.
McCormick, Armour, and Pullman were among the founders of
the Orchestral Association, and the next year Theodore Thomas
made his first appearance in the Auditorium as conductor of
the new Chicago Symphony Orchestra. Born in Germany in
1835, Thomas had moved to New York ten years later with his
family. He was a violinist who became concert-master of the
New York Philharmonic, then formed his own orchestra and
toured the country playing popular and classical music. Nearly
every year for two decades he met engagements in Chicago,
until at last he was asked to come permanently. "I would go
to hell," he answered, "if they would give me a permanent orchestra."

His first year in Chicago, he may have thought he was in
hell. Shortly before his arrival, a local music critic had written
that Chicagoans went to hear touring opera troupes "a little
to hear the music, a trifle more to hear the artists (if their

names be sufficiently famous)—but mostly because it is the thing to do." Thomas played a great deal of light music as well as symphonies during his first season, only to find his audiences objecting that any symphony was too austere. But he would not abandon his belief that music should restore men's sanity: "One reason I came to Chicago," he explained later, "was that I understood the excitement and nervous strain that everyone, more or less, suffered who lived there. . . ." He thought that music could ease the strain by giving men a perspective and proper values, but music could do this only if it were the sort that moves men's deepest emotions. "The man who has not come under his spell," he said of Beethoven, "has not lived half his life."

So he began an unrelenting campaign to raise the musical tastes of Chicago. The second year, many of his programs were without a symphony. Gradually he stiffened his offerings, until Chicagoans would accept the best of classical music. More than any of his contemporaries in the United States, he introduced Americans to the great continental composers. He also fought to give American composers a chance. For the musical program at the Columbian Exposition, he commissioned new works by established men and women and urged unknowns to submit their compositions to a committee of judges. What he cared about, all he cared about, was the quality of the music.

He labored constantly to broaden his audience. In order to reach "the class employed in mills, factories and at all kinds of manual labor," he gave a special series of concerts for workingmen. He planned, at the end of a benefit concert, to conduct the symphony orchestra for dancing. The musicians were loath to do anything so undignified. Thomas said that if they would not play, he would go on the podium and conduct the rows of empty chairs. They played.

He recruited his musicians from all over the world, and from the foreign-born neighborhoods in Chicago. He fought off ignorant and venomous attacks from music critics of Chicago's newspapers. But he nearly foundered for lack of money. After ten years in Chicago, he was ready to quit. What he needed most was a new concert hall; because the Auditorium was so large, Chicagoans knew that seats would always be available and they would not buy season tickets. A solution of this problem came from Daniel Burnham, Frank Lowden, Harold F. McCormick, and others, who bought land on Michigan Avenue to build a home for the Chicago Symphony Orchestra. In 1904 Thomas conducted his first concert in it while the plaster was still wet on the walls. His triumphs there were few: within a few months he was dead, and Frederick Stock took his place on the podium.

The Symphony Orchestra and the Art Institute depended on private donations, and the Chicago Public Library got its start the same way. After the Great Fire of 1871, citizens of England contributed seven thousand volumes to Chicago. This spurred action by the city, and a tax-supported library was opened in 1873. Two decades later it had nearly 200,000 volumes and six branches. It was supplemented by the Newberry Library, founded in 1885 by a bequest of $2 million from an early real-estate man. Under the direction of William F. Poole, who quit as librarian of the Chicago Public Library to head the new venture, it built up superb collections in the humanities. A second free research library was started in 1897 under a bequest from John Crerar of the Joliet Steel Company. Crerar's will explicitly banned "dirty French novels" and "works of questionable moral tone." The provision ruled out any effort to build solid holdings in literature or art, and the Crerar Library specialized in the natural and social sciences.

II

Thomas W. Goodspeed, financial secretary of the Baptist Theological Seminary and early leader in the efforts to found a Baptist university in Chicago, complained bitterly that Marshall Field "held back both money and service." Perhaps the complaint was valid if the merchant's philanthropies were compared to the size of his fortune or to the donations of some of his peers, but in absolute terms his gifts were sizable. He gave the first million dollars to establish a museum of natural history, the Field Columbian Museum. He helped to underwrite Theodore Thomas and the Symphony Orchestra. And whereas John D. Rockefeller gave the initial $600,000 to found the University of Chicago, Field donated its site, a ten-acre plot valued at $125,000. Thus he helped found the institution that, more than any other, made local residents conscious of the cultural heritage available for conquest by anybody who had the time, the ability, and the will.

From the day its doors opened in 1892, the new University was expanding that heritage. William Rainey Harper, chief promoter and first president, had determined that the graduate schools should not be neglected in favor of the college, and he recruited for the faculty several of the greatest scholars in the world. Harper's round body, round face, and small genial eyes made him look like a friendly pig. But where talent was concerned, he was a greedy hog. By nature he was an expansionist, an imperialist: when the United States seized the Philippines, he said it was the happiest moment of his life. He was a great scholar of Semitic languages, and a great organizer —as he had already shown by his aggressive leadership of the national Chautauqua.

Now he wanted the best, and he knew well enough to know that scholars, however personal their intellectual interests, are likely to share the common interest in money. If a scholar was indifferent to material comfort and invidious consumption, probably his wife was not. So Harper set forth to outbid his competitors in the market for brains. For the top professors he fixed an annual salary of $7,000—ample, in a time without income taxes, for a man to live in a big house, have two servants, go to the opera, and spend his summers traveling. (In 1896 when Woodrow Wilson, a professor at Princeton, was trying to entice Frederick Jackson Turner there, Mrs. Wilson set up a sample budget for a professor earning $3,500 a year. It included two servants—together getting $29 a month.)

Harper himself chose many of the men in history and the humanities. He got a rich combination of youthful vigor and ripened prestige, of men on the way up and men at the crest. One was Ferdinand Schevill, just out of graduate school at the University of Freiburg, who became a foremost student of the Renaissance. The greatest coup of all, so far as the general public was concerned, was to lure away from the same German university the renowned Hermann Eduard von Holst, whose *Constitutional and Political History of the United States* was enjoying a lively sale in English translation. One of the translators, Paul Shorey, came from Bryn Mawr to Chicago as professor of Greek. From Yale alone came four other men in classics and modern languages.

Harper did well; one of his agents did even better. The president knew little about the natural sciences; as his personnel chief in those fields he borrowed Franklin P. Mall for a year from Johns Hopkins, which had been founded in 1876 as the first graduate school in the United States. Mall turned his eye, not toward his own institution, but toward Clark University in Worcester, Massachusetts, which had been established as a purely graduate school only three years earlier. The president of Clark was an eminent psychologist, G. Stanley Hall, and he had built up a select faculty. Then Harper's agents lured away four outstanding scientists: Henry H. Donaldson, John Ulric Nef, Charles Otis Whitman, and Albert A. Michelson. (President Hall, frustrated by Chicago moneybags and outraged by the raid, called it "an act of wreckage . . . comparable to anything that the worst trust had ever attempted against its competitors." But the departing professors made no complaints. In Chicago, men knew how to get things done: Yerkes bought legislators, Ryerson bought paintings, Harper bought scholars, for cash on the line.)

Donaldson, who became head of the department of neurology, published *The Growth of the Brain* in 1895 and "Physiology of the Central Nervous System" in 1896. In 1903 he supervised the dissertation of John B. Watson, who then took charge of animal psychology. Nef was professor of chemistry until 1896, when he became head of the department. Whitman immediately became chairman of the zoology department, and, even after his move to the Midwest, he continued as director of the great Marine Biological Laboratory at Woods Hole, Massachusetts. He was editor of the *Journal of Morphology*, and in 1897 became editor also of the *Zoological Bulletin*.

Amid all the bright lights from Clark, the brightest was Michelson, the most famous physicist in the United States. Fifteen years earlier, recently graduated from the Naval Academy at Annapolis and teaching there, he had devised a simple method that brought unprecedented precision to the measurement of the speed of light. He was natty in everything—in dress, in speech, in scientific technique. When Maxwell asserted, on the basis of his new electromagnetic theory of light, that light traveled faster in air than in water, Michelson found a way to verify the assertion experimentally. At a time when most physicists claimed that all space was occupied by something they called "ether," Michelson invented a device he called the interferometer, split a beam of light, and proved that no such "ether" existed. One of his findings—that the speed of light is constant regardless of the motion of the observer or of the source of the light—was seized by Albert Einstein and became a major element in the special theory of relativity. In 1907 Michelson was given the Nobel Prize for Physics, the first American to win this honor.

Of comparable stature was Jacques Loeb, a German physiologist who went from Bryn Mawr to Chicago in 1892. In contrast to Michelson, a rigorous specialist who cheerfully confessed his ignorance of all else, Loeb scorned the boundaries between academic disciplines. When asked whether he was a neurologist, a chemist, a physicist, a psychologist, or a philosopher, he replied: "I solve problems." He dumbfounded listeners by the speed with which ideas came to him, so rapidly, indeed, that often he did not know which to investigate. But when he singled one out, he tested it with ruthless vigor. Having identified the machine-like reactions of plants and animals that he called "tropisms," he made countless experiments, doing them carefully, repeating them often, working with such rigor that few of his factual observations had to be modified later. In 1899 he broke open a second major field, artificial parthenogenesis, by causing the *unfertilized* egg of a sea urchin to begin development; he gained this result by subjecting the egg to sea water of a higher salt content than normal.

John Merle Coulter, formerly president of Indiana State University, who came in 1896 to head the botany department, was another sort. He and Loeb were both founders and editors of the main scholarly journals in their fields—the *Journal of General Physiology* and the *Botanical Gazette*—but the resemblance ended there. Loeb was a creative research scientist; Coulter exerted his main influence as administrator, editor, and teacher. He gave his colleague Henry C. Cowles such resources to develop the new field of ecology that it became one of the chief branches of botany. He turned out more students who achieved eminence than any other botanist of his time. Another original scientist and sound administrator was T. C. Chamberlin, who resigned as president of the University of Wisconsin in 1892 to become head of the geology department at Chicago. Already the leading glacial geologist in the country, he founded the *Journal of Geology* in 1893 and later did major work in investigating geological climates and in cosmic geology.

The best known social scientist on the original faculty was J. Laurence Laughlin who came from Cornell to teach political economy, bringing his student and protégé Thorstein Veblen along. Laughlin was the prototype of the classical economists that Veblen flayed so tellingly: he believed in the justice of market decisions and in laissez faire, and he liked to give his lecture on "Political Economy and Christianity" in which he said that Jesus had urged not poverty but thrift (Where saving

occurs, investment must follow; Christianity and free enterprise are at one). Apart from Veblen and Dewey, the social
scientist at Chicago who exerted the most long-term influence
was Albion W. Small, who quit the presidency of Colby University in 1892 to found a sociology department on the Midway.

The Chicago Theological Seminary had started a sociology
department in 1890, but Chicago was the first university to
have one. And Small was the ideal man to head it. A historian
and political scientist, he was immune to the insularism that
constantly threatened to make of the social sciences a random
collection of isolated specialties pursuing unrealistic premises
to sterile conclusions. He insisted that the study of man and
society is a single subject and must result in a single coherent
body of knowledge. Trained as a theologian, he rejected the
demand for an impartial "value-free" sociology; he insisted that
all investigations must relate to the improvement of society and
the enhancement of human life. A man with the common sense
to see that practical efforts at reform must start from the facts,
he subjected studies by the United States Bureau of Labor to
most searching criticism which did much to raise the quality
of statistical analysis. And, like so many of his colleagues at
Chicago, he founded a journal, the *American Journal of Sociology,* which, in the thirty-one years he served as editor, was
hospitable to the best work being done by other sociologists.

Eminent scholars, all of them, but none so famous as Amos
Alonzo Stagg, football coach at the University. Idolized by
the students and by much of the city, he was no hero to his
lowly colleague Thorstein Veblen, who countered claims that
football helped to develop the body by writing, "the relation
of football to physical culture is much the same as that of the
bull-fight to agriculture." To those who claimed that sports
encouraged "self-reliance and good-fellowship," Veblen replied: "From a different point of view the qualities currently
so characterised might be described as truculence and clan-
nishness."

Intercollegiate athletics, while useful and valid evidence for Veblen's *Theory of the Leisure Class,* were a minor blemish on the achievement of William Rainey Harper. For any organization, the first years are crucial. If key positions are filled with incompetents, they will choose as subordinates other incomcompetents, who rise through the ranks to the key positions. Mediocrity becomes the characteristic of the organization, and it breeds itself. The level of quality is especially hard to raise in a university, where entrenched deadheads are protected in their jobs, not only by their power within the organization, but also by the tenure regulations peculiar to academic life. At Chicago, the start was right. The top men at the beginning were good, and they knew how to identify and attract their equals or superiors. (When Robert A. Millikan finished his postdoctoral work at Berlin and Göttingen in 1896, Michelson brought him to Chicago as an assistant in physics. He stayed for twenty-five years. Two years after he left, he won the Nobel Prize.) The University of Chicago started life as a great university: both storehouse and workshop. Harper's vision was sound, and he made it a reality.

III

Until 1900 the new University and the leisure class of Chicago were the breeding grounds of the most important novels about the city. In *The Cliff Dwellers* (1893), Henry Blake Fuller ranges over the tenants of a recent skyscraper. Here are the businessmen, some gross, some seemingly cultured, but all devoting their lives to getting rich. Here are their wives, engaged solely in ostentatious spending of the wealth accumulated by the husbands. On the basis of an inherited New England morality and sense of civilization, Fuller examined his Chicago, and condemned it all. His book had a quiet intensity, but the intensity belonged to the author, not to his characters; for psychological depth *The Cliff Dwellers* could not compare with *The Theory of the Leisure Class.* In 1895 Fuller published a

second realistic novel about Chicago; then he quit trying to
come to terms with the life of his city and turned to writing
fanciful romances.

The theme that Fuller dropped was picked up by Robert
Herrick, who went from Harvard to the University of Chicago
in 1893 to teach English. *The Gospel of Freedom* (1898) has
two male characters who symbolize, respectively, commercial
success and esthetic withdrawal. After the heroine has rejected both alternatives, a civic reformer tells her that the city
must be reshaped "painfully, without regard for self." This
vague affirmation died quickly. In *The Common Lot* (1904),
Herrick tells how a young Chicago architect sets about making
money by sharp methods. Many persons are killed when fire
destroys a hotel the architect has built. He is beaten by guilt
and realizes: "The spirit of greed had eaten him through and
through, the lust for money, the desire for the fat things of the
world, the ambition to ride high among his fellows." Herrick
sounded a new note: to Fuller, Chicago had been the villain
that corrupted men, while Herrick implied that it only encouraged them to express their innate corruption. If this was the
problem, civic reform was not a total solution.

But just as Herrick had seized the theme that Fuller abandoned, so now the solution that Herrick eschewed was elaborated by Upton Sinclair. In 1904, on his twenty-sixth birthday,
Sinclair arrived in Chicago and went to a settlement house in
the stockyards district. For seven weeks he wandered through
packing plants, canneries, saloons, seeing hogs slaughtered and
lard made and people married, taking copious notes all the
time. Then he went back to a shack near Princeton, New Jersey, and wrote *The Jungle*. It was published serially in 1905
in *The Appeal to Reason,* a Socialist weekly with a circulation
of a half-million copies. The next year it came out as a book,
and for six months it was a best-seller in the United States
and England.

Sinclair's novel sold more copies than all the novels written
by Fuller and Herrick together, but it exaggerated many of

their failings. Their novels were like rooms crammed with furniture; *The Jungle* slopped over on all sides. Sinclair could not refrain from including every scrap of scandal he had learned about Chicago: the Illinois Telephone tunnel that became a subway; the railroad crossings "on the level with the sidewalk, a deathtrap for the unwary"; the secret water mains of meat packers through which they stole water from the city; how companies advertised for two hundred men when they wanted twenty, and three thousand applicants appeared. He put in propaganda for vegetarianism and for prohibition (the focus here was not on the characters at all but on the author, who grew up in Baltimore in a home beset by postwar poverty and a father addicted to alcohol), and the increase in the Socialist vote from 1900 to 1904. One passage was a summary of *The Theory of the Leisure Class*, but without Veblen's succulent irony.

Readers of the book, confronted with a bewildering mass of unintegrated data, were diverted away from the plot—and perhaps it was better so. Every calamity that ever befell any immigrant workman was heaped onto Sinclair's protagonist, Jurgis Rudkus, during the first few years of his life in Chicago. He was gulled into thinking a ramshackle second-hand house was new, and bought it. He paid on it for years and lost it. His family nearly starved because he sprained his ankle in a packing house and could not work (he of course got no compensation for the injury). On another job he was injured so badly he had to go to the hospital. He was fired, blacklisted, laid off, and sent to jail twice: once for striking a boss who had virtually raped his wife, Ona, again for striking a bartender who stole $99 that Jurgis had miraculously acquired. Ona died in horribly painful childbirth, attended only by a filthy and avaricious midwife. The unborn baby died too. Ona's cousin Marija was forced into prostitution. Her younger brother became exhausted one day at work, lay down to rest, and rats ate him. Jurgis' son drowned in a huge hole in the street. And lots more.

Such a sea of troubles can be credited in an allegory, as in the Book of Job, but not in a supposedly realistic novel. The book fails, because it has no integrity. Long before it ends, the reader's suspension of disbelief fails him and he can no longer care about the fate of the characters.

Sinclair just did not view experience as a novelist must view it. When a vivid episode was needed, he wrote lifeless abstractions: "the souls of none of them were dead, but only sleeping; and now and then they would waken, and these were cruel times. The gates of memory would roll open—old joys would stretch out their arms to them, old hopes and dreams would call to them, and they would stir beneath the burden that lay upon them, and feel its forever immeasurable weight." The phrasing is worn and pretentious, but the fatal fault is elsewhere. What were the old joys, the old hopes and dreams? How did Ona's differ from Jurgis'? What were the signs that they stirred beneath their burdens? Sinclair did not say. He did not know.

Occasionally he came close to feeling the emotions of his characters and to communicating them, but the best parts of *The Jungle* are reporting or anthropology. He wrote well of the terrors that a Chicago winter brought to the poor. He gave vivid accounts of a Bessemer furnace, of how animals were slaughtered, of how sausage was made. He mixed humor with pathos in describing a garish handbill that advertised houses for sale to immigrants. He had important insights into the disintegration of peasant customs in an urban environment, and the difficulties of immigrants who clung to customs that their fellows were abandoning. He told in nauseous detail how the packers dressed up rotten meat or made it into sausage, and how men fell into the rendering tanks and were sold as lard—but he could not forbear repeating the allegation, and he told it in a way that almost made it seem a joke.

While Sinclair was in Chicago, he went to Hull-House for dinner and sat next to Jane Addams. He made ardent socialist comments of the sort he put into *The Jungle*. Later he was told that Jane Addams had commented: "That young man has a great deal to learn." He did indeed. He had yet to learn that art is not life but a selection and organization from life: the fact that episodes have really happened is not enough to make them convincing, let alone moving. He had yet to learn that a novelist must know the inner life of his characters, and that seven weeks is not long enough to learn the inner life of Lithuanian immigrants. *The Jungle* was an amazingly successful instrument of reform, but hardly a novel at all.

Herrick, Fuller, Sinclair—all had stumbled over their inability to solve problems that required solution if the realities of Chicago were to be subdued by fiction. Fuller had resigned at the start by his basic conception: "Instead of a searching and indelicate analysis of the individual, I . . . favor the study of a group of individuals in their relation to the community." The good novelist is not forced to this choice; he does both. He also realizes that a novel holds its readers only if it focuses on changes of self in the characters. He builds his plot on that realization and makes a disciplined selection of episodes that carry the plot forward. In the novel, character and plot become one, and everything that is not essential is excessive. The good novelist has enough mental complexity to give his book some intellectual sinew, in contrast to the plaintive rejection that Herrick and Fuller derived from shining their moral-esthetic code on shabby Chicago, in contrast to the prim pieties that Upton Sinclair gained by countering socialist purity to capitalist corruption.

The first novel about Chicago to meet these demands was *Sister Carrie* (1900), which Theodore Dreiser wrote in a few months when he was twenty-eight years old. Born in Terre Haute in 1871, Dreiser shared in the rebellion waged by his many brothers and sisters against the life-thwarting rigidities of their German Catholic father. The sharing was fitful; the father's inability to support the large family caused it repeatedly to separate, reunite, separate again. Theodore was toted from one Indiana town to another during his boyhood. At fifteen, he moved to Chicago where he worked at odd jobs. After a year at Indiana University in 1889-1890, he returned to Chicago for two more years, becoming a newspaper reporter in 1892. For the next seven years he worked on papers and magazines in St. Louis, Pittsburgh, New York. By 1899 he was an established free-lance magazine writer in New York. He began *Sister Carrie* that autumn, and the next spring it was finished.

The plot is simple. A young woman named Carrie Meeber arrives in Chicago from a small town in Wisconsin. Frustrated in her search for a job and for pleasure, she soon becomes the mistress of a traveling salesman, Drouet. One evening Drouet brings to his home George Hurstwood, manager of a high-class saloon. While Drouet is on trips, the married Hurstwood begins to court Carrie. Drouet discovers it, quarrels with Carrie, and leaves her. Hurstwood, jaded with his work and entangled in a marital dilemma, steals a large sum from his employers and deceives Carrie into running away with him. Caught, he is forced to return most of the money but is not prosecuted. In New York, he becomes part owner of a shabby (to him) saloon. When the owners of the building refuse to renew the lease, he has trouble finding work. He drifts into being a bum. Carrie becomes a chorus girl on Broadway, then an actress. She leaves Hurstwood. The book ends as he commits suicide by turning on the gas in a Bowery flophouse.

To readers steeped in Victorian morality, the novel was shocking, so shocking that it was not really published for seven years after Dreiser finished it. Even then, its readers were so preoccupied with Carrie's amorality that they ignored the majestic theme of the book: the need of the individual for material security, satisfying work, and love. The theme controlled the flawless structure of the book, which is a complex web of inclined planes: Carrie's rise, Hurstwood's fall, the inching ahead in status of Drouet and Mrs. Hurstwood while their humanity sags. Every episode extends one or more of these planes a little further.

Only a little. Whereas life to Upton Sinclair was a congeries of smashing climaxes, to Dreiser it was a gradual accumulation of habits: the individual moves onto a new plane of existence by an almost imperceptible accretion of small developments. It was Dreiser's genius to perceive these almost imperceptible changes, to see them truly as they would happen to a specific person, and then to devise a literary form to contain and control his insights. In the world he wrote about, there are no equals and no stability. All is change, but the change is in identifiable directions. No man can stand still; he must rise or he will sink. These are the processes that Dreiser traced out.

In tracing them, he took man for what he is, a total organism, and constantly showed the interaction of mind and body, of sense perceptions with mind, of thought with emotion. Typical is the arc of Carrie's relations with Drouet. When they first meet on the train, as Carrie is going from Columbia City, Wisconsin, to Chicago, he seems to her the model of elegance: "a roll of greenbacks. . . . The purse, the shiny tan shoes, the smart new suit, and the *air* with which he did things. . . ." But from his business card, "Chas. H. Drouet," the reader knows that this is the false elegance of the uncultured fraud. Again in Chicago, after Carrie has lost her first job because of illness, she seduces herself into Drouet's bed by reflecting that he "rode on trains, dressed in such nice clothes, was so strong, and ate in these fine places."

But after she lives with him a while, her perceptions are educated to the level of his. Then she meets Hurstwood, who gives her a still higher standard of manhood. One day at dusk Carrie hears a piano being played in the apartment below. The sounds make her feel nostalgia and remorse. She is crying when Drouet comes home from work. He tries to comfort her by suggesting that they dance to the music. This is so dissonant to Carrie's feelings that she feels Drouet is insensitive. "It was his first great mistake." A few weeks later Hurstwood takes Carrie and Drouet to the theater; as he chats with them,

Carrie comes to think that Drouet is "a kindly soul, but otherwise defective."

But even after Hurstwood calls while she is home alone and makes his play, she remembers the kindness Drouet has done for her, and her desires are confused. Then Drouet returns from a sales trip and says that if certain business prospects work out right, he will marry her. She replies that she does not think he intends to ever marry her. "The recent protestations of Hurstwood had given her courage to say this," but she says it "ruefully"! Carrie for the first time senses that she must leave him, but she needs something to calm her conscience about her involvement with Hurstwood, and she finds it in Drouet's "light, airy disregard of her claims upon his justice."

Drouet thoughtlessly (as he does everything) gets Carrie her first part in an amateur theatrical. Even this benefaction widens the rift between them. When Carrie returns home from her first rehearsal, Drouet is thinking of something else and does not question her warmly about it. "She felt his indifference keenly and longed to see Hurstwood. It was as if he were now the only friend she had on earth. The next morning Drouet was interested again, but the damage had been done." Carrie's need for security, her inertia, still keep her with Drouet. At last the chambermaid tells him that Hurstwood has called many times while he was away (while she tells him, he is giving her the once-over). He upbraids Carrie for her deception "after all I've done for you," and tells her Hurstwood is married. She flares back: "What have you done for me?" She is angry at Hurstwood for *his* deception, but she is even more angry at Drouet for not having told her earlier that Hurstwood was married. "There he stood now, guilty of this miserable breach of confidence and talking about what he had done for her!" (This deft passage shows the difference between pamphleteer and novelist. If Upton Sinclair had heard of projection and reaction formation, he might have included a sermon about them in *The Jungle;* Dreiser shows them at work in a particular mind.)

Drouet and Carrie quarrel, and she starts to leave. He leaves instead. She is stunned when he actually goes, and half wishes he would come back, because she is dismayed by the thought of supporting herself. Her insecurity makes her vulnerable to Hurstwood's desperate game, and Drouet, halfway through the book, drops out of the story. The reason for this disappearance is obvious when he reappears briefly at the end—almost exactly the same man, slightly more prosperous, slightly more vulgar. Dreiser had the sense to know that a writer cannot continue for long merely to "reveal" a character: characters who do not change become boring quickly.

But it is essential for contrast with Hurstwood that Drouet should not change, and he would not. He is perfectly adapted to his society, living only for mercenary success and sensual pleasures. He thrives on the surface of life, kindly in his trifling way, but taking no responsibilities and making no commitments. Also adjusted is Mrs. Hurstwood, who is shown at the end of the book on her way to Europe with her daughter and a new, wealthy son-in-law. She wanted money and social standing, and both were attainable in the Chicago of 1890. But Hurstwood is a man of deeper feelings, of sometimes saner but inchoate wants, who acts out his passion and is destroyed by it.

The account of his disintegration in New York is one of the most moving portrayals in American fiction. For the first three years, while he is managing his own saloon, he seems to be going along on a level plane. He is not. He falls victim to his own values: New York is in part "an awesome place to him, for here gathered all that he most respected on this earth—wealth, place, and fame." As he compares the clientele at his saloon to the gallants he had known at Fitzgerald and Moy's in Chicago, he despises it. To heighten his feeling of insignificance, the top of society in New York is even higher than what he had known in Chicago. He is eaten by self-contempt, remorse, defeat. He is losing his identity, his sense of self, just as he has been forced to change his name to George Wheeler.

Because of his destructive emotions, "certain poisons . . . called katastates" are secreted into his bloodstream. "His step was not so sharp and firm. He was given to thinking, thinking, thinking." He sees occasional items in the paper about former friends in Chicago, "men whom he had tipped glasses with— rich men, and he was forgotten! Who was Mr. Wheeler? What was the Warren Street resort? Bah!"

Then he loses the Warren Street resort. No longer the figure he once was, without contacts, lacking money, he has trouble finding work. He continues to pretend to Carrie that he is looking for a job, when actually he spends each day sitting in hotel lobbies reading the newspapers. He gives up the pretence. Carrie begins sleeping alone. Hurstwood stops shaving, starts wearing old clothes. After Carrie gets a job, he is glad to live on her earnings. At last she protests, and one of her protests insults him. During a street-car strike in Brooklyn, he reasons that the companies will hire anybody. He sympathizes with the strikers, but his self-respect has declined so far that he becomes a strikebreaker. He is called a scab, beaten by a mob, at last scurries home to the warm stove and the newspapers. He has tried, and failed, for the last time.

Carrie leaves, and he becomes a beggar. He determines upon suicide and thinks of the rooming house where he can turn on the gas. But to rent the room will cost fifteen cents. He asks a man on the street for money. Having no smaller change, the man gives him a quarter. "Hurstwood moved on, wondering. The sight of the large, bright coin pleased him a little. He remembered that he was hungry and that he could get a bed for ten cents. With this, the idea of death passed, for the time being, out of his mind. It was only when he could get nothing but insults that death seemed worth while."

The passage illustrates one of the chief ideas that Dreiser used in writing: human experience is a continuous interaction between external reality and subjective response. In this he continued, along with Ford Madox Ford and Thomas Mann, in the great tradition of fiction that reached back to Fielding.

Dreiser has often been regarded as a heavy-footed "peasant," a man without subtlety or intellect, whose ideas were all foolish but who wrote fairly decent books because he had something called "compassion." This view contradicts itself: no foolish man ever wrote a good novel. In writing his best books, such as *Sister Carrie*, Dreiser was a good novelist and a wise man. As a writer he had one major fault: in common with many journalists, he often yielded to the temptation to set down ideas in the words that came readiest, rather than struggle for the exact phrase. He could be stilted, awkward, falsely "literary." In *Sister Carrie* there are words that should have been changed, phrases that should have been deleted. But in the entire book every page, every paragraph, is essential to the story—until the last three pages, when he added on some vapid rhetoric about Carrie and "the pursuit of beauty." Not until 1939, when John Steinbeck published *The Grapes of Wrath*, would another major American novel end on an equally embarrassing note.

IV

Apart from *Sister Carrie*, the outstanding works of art in these years in Chicago were buildings. The first of them was finished in 1885, a wholesale store for Marshall Field. By bringing Henry Hobson Richardson from Boston to design it, Field made his first nonprofit donation to Chicago. (The building proved to be far from nonprofit, in spite of Field's early pessimism about his ability to make profitable use of its half-million square feet of floor space.) A massive sandstone structure, finding its beauty in the size and placement of the stones and in the rhythm of arched and rectangular windows, with reduced cornice, it was a study of simplicity. Louis Sullivan paid it homage: "in a world of barren pettiness, a male," and in designing the Chicago Auditorium he showed how much he had learned from Richardson's stone arches—although not all he could have learned. The store also pointed up a major architectural opportunity: how to design a tall building. Only seven stories tall, it still required walls thick at the base to support the weight above. Sullivan attacked this problem directly.

Tall buildings were made possible by the invention of the elevator in the 1850's and its improvement in the 1870's. They were made desirable by the growing value per square foot of urban real estate which resulted from the growth of Chicago. But in John Wellborn Root's superb Monadnock Building, for instance, the sixteen stories required walls that were fifteen feet thick at the base. This wasted valuable space, and impeded use of the first-floor windows by stores for display purposes. Invention of structural steel had already created a new possibility—tall buildings in which the exteriors were thin sheathings hung from the hidden steel skeletons. This method had been used in Chicago by William Le Baron Jenney in the Home Insurance Building, 1884-1885, and by Holabird and Roche in the Tacoma Building, 1887-1888. But it remained for Sullivan to grasp the esthetic challenge.

His first eloquent statement was the Wainwright Building in St. Louis, begun in 1890. The first two of its nine stories were a sweeping horizontal of large windows. This band was broken by corner piers that soared unbroken from sidewalk to cornice. The vertical pillars were tied together by horizontal panels and the topmost frieze, all in terra cotta and decorated with Sullivan's free-flowing designs. Here was an integrated shell of red granite, brick, and sandstone which was worthy of the light but strong steel framework of the building. In the next eight years Sullivan did other office buildings in Buffalo and Chicago, but none was better than this. More impressive were two other and quite different creations in Chicago: a tomb and a department store. The Getty Tomb in Graceland Cemetery was an example of imagination restrained by discipline, with its lacy designs exhibited perfectly upon a plain arch. The store for Schlesinger & Mayer featured a daring array of horizontal windows, and a rounded bay at the corner. This was Sullivan's last important structure in his home city, and he was unable even to finish it. The company changed hands while the store was under construction, and the new owners, Carson, Pirie & Scott, commissioned Daniel Burnham to finish the work.

Four years earlier, in 1895, Sullivan had quarreled with Adler and broken up their partnership. It was a sad mistake for Sullivan, for he needed Adler's engineering genius and his ability to get along with clients. But Sullivan insisted on his right to make his own mistakes. Everything about him spoke his arrogance: his pointed beard, his immaculate clothes, his burning eyes that showed humor only occasionally, his strut that came from walking with a longer stride than his legs were made for. After 1900 he got a few commissions for homes or for banks in country towns, but not many—it was not only the hapless Hurstwoods who were separated from work, and Sullivan could not fit into an age that thought imitation was architecture. So he found comfort in liquor, and sat in his room in a third-rate Chicago hotel, and wrote wonderful books.

His verbal statement of his ideas was as searching as his architectural expression of them. He was the first American to consciously ponder the relations of architecture to society. He was just as concerned as Dreiser with exploring the relations of objective to subjective, but he came at it from a different angle. "What the people are within," Sullivan wrote, "the buildings express without; and inversely, what the buildings are objectively is a sure index of what the people are subjectively . . . the unhappy, irrational, heedless, pessimistic, unlovely, distracted, and decadent structures which make up the great bulk of our contemporaneous architecture point with infallible accuracy to qualities in the heart and mind and soul of the American people that are unhappy, irrational, heedless, pessimistic, unlovely, distracted, and decadent." Dreiser defined a man's character by describing his clothing; Sullivan, by describing his building; Veblen, by describing both.

Sullivan also wrote: "Form follows function," and the statement was used by others to justify buildings of an antiseptic and inhuman frigidity. Nothing could be a worse parody of

Sullivan's viewpoint, since it was his greatness to insist that buildings must be functional psychologically as well as technically and commercially, that their form must be beautiful as well as honest and efficient. "Instead of a 'form follows function' scientist," said Frank Lloyd Wright in his book about Sullivan, "I shall give you a great lyric poet," a statement suggestive of Sullivan's own ideals.

Although he repudiated the view expressed by Sir Gilbert Scott, chief figure in the Gothic revival in England, that "architecture is the decoration of construction," Sullivan was affected by it. His own training had been at the fountain of stylistic imitation in architecture, the École de Beaux Arts in Paris, and throughout his career he got many of his most cherished effects from applying designs to the surface of structures. He was not much interested in the differences between materials: he handled one about like another. He was not an engineer, and he was never captivated by the possibilities of the machine.

Wright brought to his work a training that Sullivan lacked, and he penetrated to insights that Sullivan never reached. When Wright, nineteen years old, joined Adler and Sullivan in 1887, he had spent three and a half years studying engineering at the University of Wisconsin. He was convinced that each material has its specific character, that the architect must discover that character and remain true to it, seeking the forms and the patterns that reveal its essence. (Thus he denounced classical architecture as an effort to use in stone the basic forms that had been appropriate to wood: the pier and the lintel.) He was also convinced that the machine and the products of the machine—especially glass, steel, and concrete—not only made new forms possible; they made new forms essential. Cantilevered steel and reinforced concrete opened the way for "plasticity" of which the essence was its quality of pull, or joint support, a quality that found perfect expression in John Roebling's design for Brooklyn Bridge. Glass opened the way for walls that would be mobile screens, so that inside and outside could flow into each other.

To these technical possibilities, Wright brought an emotional stance that had its origins in the Unitarianism of his mother's family: "Unity was their watchword, the sign and the symbol that thrilled them, the UNITY of all things!" He made this into an approach to his profession: "Organic building is natural building: construction proceeding harmoniously from the nature of a planned or organized inside outward to a consistent outside." Architecture is not a matter of volumes or cubes, as in houses or buildings where each room is a box; it is a matter of controlling the flow of space.

These ideas went beyond any that Sullivan had had, but they were stimulated by Sullivan's example as Wright worked with him, notably on the designs for the Chicago Auditorium. Wright has said of any master: "His function is not to teach but to inspire." This explains his statement about Sullivan: "He taught me nothing nor did he ever pretend to do so except as he was himself the thing he did and as I could see it for myself." One man cannot teach technique to another, Wright proclaimed, "each man's technique must be his own, his own way of getting his way with an idea."

From his five years with Adler and Sullivan, Wright got inspiration and experience. He also got clients. Since the partners preferred to design only large public buildings, they turned over to Wright many commissions for residences. Even with this added income, he could not support his growing family, so he started doing independent work in his spare time. Sullivan learned of it and was furious. Wright quit and set up on his own.

For Wright, the rupture was fortunate. His relations with Sullivan were so strained that they did not see each other for the twelve years from 1893 to 1905, and Wright was free to find his own way. In 1895 he gave his revolutionary lecture at Hull-House, "The Art and Craft of the Machine." Four years later, Sullivan was still joining with Clarence Darrow, Frank Lowden, Mrs. Potter Palmer, and others to organize such ventures as the Illinois Industrial Arts League, which, starting from the esthetics of William Morris, tried to revive handicrafts like stone-carving, furniture making, and the fine binding of books. Wright, like Veblen, regarded such activities with contempt. This was a new age, a time to look to the future, not to the past.

Wright had other temptations. As he was working with Sullivan on the Transportation Building at the Columbian Exposition, his last work as an apprentice, Daniel Burnham said to him: "Frank, the Fair shows our people the beauty of the Classic—they will never go back." When Wright quit Sullivan, Burnham offered to support Mrs. Wright and their children while Wright studied for two years at the Beaux Arts and for another two years in Rome if Wright would join his firm when he came back. Wright refused.

Already he had shown the direction he would take. His Charnley House in Chicago in 1892 was a daringly simple structure in which materials played against one another, solid forms interlocked with a geometric precision. The next year, in the Winslow House in a Chicago suburb, Wright used wide eaves, a cut-off roof top. Here was evidence that he had already found one of his main ideas: that architecture must be scaled to the human figure and must take account of human perceptions. On the Midwestern prairies, where men were accustomed to the broad sweep of landscape, all horizontals appeared shorter than they were, all verticals appeared longer than they were. Two years later he made himself a studio with solid rows of windows; in another design he wrapped the windows around the corners of the building; he made a country club shaped like a modified cross, with a chimney at its center. By the time he designed the Willitts House in 1902, his conception of the Prairie House was complete: the solidly interlocked planes, the use of windows and porches to fuse inside with outside, the hovering friendly roofs.

The early houses around Chicago were in suburbs; not until 1909 did he do his first mature house in the city itself. The Robie House, a short stroll from the University of Chicago, was a masterpiece in brick and cement on the outside, in brick and wood inside. Its main floor was one long room, with living room in front divided from dining area in back by an enormous brick fireplace. Space flowed around both sides of the fireplace, and over its top between the chimneys, and outside through the almost solid rows of windows divided by narrow brick piers. Wrapped around the living room was a broad porch, almost like the deck of a ship around an open stateroom.

Wright's early work in public buildings was equally revolutionary. His best office building was in Buffalo, but in the Chicago suburb of Oak Park he built Unity Temple, a church. When this Universalist congregation told him they wanted to spend only $45,000 to house four hundred persons, Wright said that they could do it only by using concrete as the material. Instead of a spire reaching toward God, he proposed to build a temple hugging the earth as was appropriate to natural, liberated men. The church accepted his plans, and he designed the first building in the world to be completed in the wooden forms into which concrete was poured.

He was not always so fortunate. Local building regulations forbade some of his projects. Banks were loath to give mortgages on such unorthodox structures. Manufacturers of building materials would not make parts by his prescriptions. Contractors misread his plans. Especially in the decade after 1925 he put up relatively few buildings; most of his ambitious projects were not carried out. One of the best of these was a superbly integrated conception in steel and glass for the National Life Insurance Building in Chicago, for which all the parts were to be manufactured in factories.

Wright carried the plans to the aged and neglected Louis Sullivan, nearing his death. Sullivan studied them and exclaimed: "I knew what I was talking about all these years— you see? I could never have done this building myself, but I believe that, but for me, you could never have done it." Wright has conceded it: "I should never have reached it, but for what he was and what he himself did."

Never did two great men see more truly, or acknowledge more generously, their relations to each other. Sullivan was the prophet of modern architecture; Wright was the first great modern architect.

CHAPTER 14

Philosophic Harvest

Here now stands in full light Man erect and conscious as a
moral power.

—Louis H. Sullivan *

I

IN DISCUSSING his debt to Louis Sullivan, Frank Lloyd Wright
concluded: "the flow of consequential ideas may persist, infinite in variety and great in effect." Both men, and many of
their contemporaries, sought to learn the relations of perma-
nence to change, the forms by which change occurred. Major
Jenney said that his pioneer skyscraper was not an invention
but an evolution. Sullivan contended that "in the process of
things we have called a flow, and which is frequently spoken
of as an evolution . . . the tall commercial building arose from
the pressure of land values . . ." In a striking passage in *Sister
Carrie*, Dreiser wrote of Drouet: "He had no mental process
in him worthy the dignity of either of those terms." Men had
long attached a dignity to the term *mental*, but never before
had they granted similar dignity to the idea of process.

Until Darwin published *The Origin of Species* in 1859, the
usual mode of thinking in science and philosophy was to set
up a certain number of airtight categories, to define the quali-

---

* *The Autobiography of an Idea* (New York: Peter Smith, 1949), p. 268.

ties that distinguished each, and to place each of the specific items in a single category. This static, taxonomic method was undermined by the discovery that even species were born, changed, and died. By 1908 Thorstein Veblen could truly say: "The sciences which are in any peculiar sense modern, take as an (unavowed) postulate the fact of consecutive change. . . . This notion of process about which the researches of modern science cluster, is a notion of a sequence, or complex, of consecutive change in which the *nexus* of the sequence . . . is the relation of cause and effect." John Dewey later wrote: "In science the order of fixities has already passed irretrievably into an order of connections *in process*." On this basis Dewey argued that an event is not "historical" merely because it happened in the past: the idea of history necessarily involves "a *direction* of movement."

Darwin's research underscored the need to study how change occurred, and so did the onrushing social change in the United States after the Civil War: the rise of industry and of great cities, of corporate monopoly, the first national strikes, the tramp problem and slums and prostitution. All these seemed to threaten the Lincoln ideal. The threat was emphasized by such upheavals as the railroad strike of 1877, the Haymarket bombing, the Pullman strike—three episodes that residents of Chicago experienced at first hand.

As Chicagoans used the idea of process to analyze varied segments of life, the meaning of the idea itself was clarified, until the essential core of propositions stood as these: (1) The universe in all its aspects is constantly changing. (2) But no change is total: in each change, elements of the past are preserved. As Veblen said, consecutive change "runs in terms of persistence of quantity or of force." (3) The changes are cumulative: term B is a modification of term A; term C is a modification of term B; and so on. Thus Veblen ridiculed Adam Smith's contention that events, if perchance they were diverted by "disturbing elements" from their "natural course," would return to it as soon as the cause of disturbance was removed. (4) These cumulative changes never reach an end.

In biology, Jacques Loeb applied these ideas in working toward his staggering goal of controlling the entire development of organisms. He learned how to artificially fertilize an egg by a variety of methods both physical and chemical. He found that some of these parthenogenetic animals could be raised to mature normality. He discovered ways to cross-fertilize so that he could produce hybrids not found in nature. In some species he was able to produce two-headed animals, Siamese twins, triplets. He learned ways to induce tropisms, to control the regeneration of organs, to force adaptations. He experimented with death, finding that in some animals it could be postponed by keeping the temperature low. (His brother Leo was able to keep ordinary cells alive indefinitely by transplantation and tissue culture.)

John Dewey's views on education began with his thinking about development: social and individual. Traditional methods of education erred in not seeing the new demands made by an urbanized industrial society; they also erred in not taking account of the biological and social processes in children. To Dewey, the structure and functioning of a personality at any time was linked to a continuous chain of development beginning at conception ("his life up to the point at which he stands," Veblen had said). In a sense the chain begins long before the individual is conceived, since he is shaped by customs that themselves have social histories. Thus he develops habits, which determine how he expresses the wide range of his native impulses. But one habit may conflict with another, or a habit may be frustrated by changes in his environment. To resolve these problems, the individual thinks. Dewey insisted that the individual and his environment act continuously on each other, and as a result, each is continuously being modified. Dewey's colleague at Michigan and Chicago, George Herbert Mead, took these theories as the basis of his own work in social psychology.

They were Veblen's theories, too, and he agreed with Dewey and Mead that "thinking" is an effort to solve problems, but he doubted that many people could identify the meaningful problems. *The Theory of the Leisure Class* traced the changes in the habit of thought that Veblen termed "invidious comparison" and in the institutions that expressed this habit of thought. These aspects of human affairs he ironically called the "higher range of theoretical explanations of phenomena": animism and religion, government and law, philosophy, and particularly, in the modern age, business. But alongside the development of institutions there occurred an accelerating growth of technical knowledge, in which each advance required as a starting point the accumulated knowledge of the past. Institutions and technology were in conflict: the progress of science stimulated a matter-of-fact viewpoint that undermined all mystical concepts, while the progress and use of technology were sabotaged by business, as in times of depression, and by patriotism, as in times of war.

Theodore Dreiser was concerned in his novels with a different sort of conflict: between persons, or between a person and his society. But he no less than Veblen made use of the idea of process: the plot of *Sister Carrie* is a thorough if implicit application of this notion. Besides the process within his story, Dreiser realized that the craft of fiction required a process external to it—the growth of insight and belief in the mind of the reader. *Sister Carrie*, like *King Lear*, is a fugue that states its themes, varies them, restates them.

Dreiser used trivial episodes to foreshadow climaxes. Early in the book he shows that Hurstwood is generally aloof from his home and family. The novel then explains a point in which Hurstwood does take an interest; he teaches each new maid an arrangement "which could not be questioned" for the objects on the sideboard in the dining room. "In his manner was something of the dogmatist. What he could not correct, he would ignore. There was a tendency in him to walk away from the impossible thing." Thus the reader is unwittingly prepared for the fact that Hurstwood, when his marriage becomes an "impossible thing," walks away.

After Carrie has begun to be disillusioned about Drouet, she meets Hurstwood, who sets a higher standard for her and thus hastens her disillusionment with her first ideal. After Hurstwood's disintegration begins, Carrie meets a young man named Ames, who gives her a higher perspective from which to view Hurstwood. Thus the theme is restated, but with a major variation. In the first statement, Carrie and Hurstwood are important to each other: they become man and mistress. But in the restatement, while Ames is important to Carrie, Carrie is never much more than a casual acquaintance to Ames, even though he greatly influences her aspirations. Here Dreiser added to the solidity of his story by touching again on another theme. Ames is like Hurstwood, he is also like Drouet. Drouet never has any deep emotional feeling for Carrie, but he enormously changes her life by educating her up to his level, by introducing her to Hurstwood who educates her to a higher level, by introducing her to the stage where she finds success.

Soon after Carrie meets Hurstwood, they go with Drouet to the theater one evening. As they emerge, a bum asks them for the price of a bed. "Drouet . . . handed over a dime with an upwelling feeling of pity in his heart. Hurstwood scarcely noticed the incident. Carrie quickly forgot." When Hurstwood becomes a bum, the reader recalls his earlier indifference. One evening he goes to the theater where Carrie is playing with the intention of begging from her. The doorman throws him out. He falls in the snow. A few pages later, Carrie is sitting in her expensive suite in a hotel. Her roommate is looking out the window. She laughs at a man who falls in the snow.

The richly worked texture of *Sister Carrie* is unostentatious, quiet in tone. These qualities are also combined in Clarence Darrow's jury arguments, which have elaborate structures but seem off-hand and wandering. In perfecting this mode of rhetoric, doubtless Darrow learned from the oratory of other lawyers, but he learned even more from literature. From childhood on, he participated deeply in the imaginary lives of characters in fiction, and he studied how writers got their effects. As early as 1892 he published a pioneer statement of the creed of the Midwestern writers, "Realism in Literature and Art." Darrow, wrote Brand Whitlock to a friend in 1898, "should have devoted himself to literature, but he has been under the awful compulsion of the age, to make money." Whitlock was wrong: Darrow lacked the type of creativity and discipline that a writer needs, and his efforts at fiction were not very good. What Darrow had was not the writer's genius but the actor's genius: to take the barest outline of a plot and character and then project himself into it so that its inner life was revealed. One night a newspaperman sat enthralled for hours, in an upper room in Chicago's ghetto, while Darrow "told the story of Waslova as drawn in 'Resurrection,' but as usual, with as much of Darrow as of Tolstoy." This was the quality that prompted William Dean Howells to say, when he read Darrow's final argument in the Kidd trial (1898), that it was "as interesting as a novel."

Just as Dreiser painstakingly etched the evolution of his characters, Darrow in his court arguments liked to describe the whole background to the crime. He always assumed that a criminal act has no "cause" other than the continuous growth of habits in the personalities of the participants. The common question: "Why did he do it?," was subtly rephrased into: "How did he come to do it?" In reply, Darrow offered a full-length biography, or a group of them. And just as Dreiser knew that the understanding of his readers was not static, Darrow wove his way back and forth across the facts of the case, trying to make the jury see each fact in the proper emotional light. Always he watched his audience. If he missed them once, he dropped the point, only to strike it later from another angle. He told the whole story, a rich fabric of the crime itself, and the events just before the crime, and things that had happened long ago. Until finally, far more often than not, the jurors understood the chain of events as he understood it.

"Knowledge is power," as John Dewey wrote, "and knowledge is achieved by sending the mind to school to nature to learn her processes of change." Clarence Darrow was a keen student of many parts of nature, including the human mind and emotions.

II

Man does research, he thinks, only when he becomes aware of a problem, and each problem involves only a limited part of his world. To succeed in their effort to understand certain processes of change, men found it essential to define and isolate a limited portion of reality. But the prominent thinkers in Chicago a half-century ago knew that processes interact with each other; that, in the language of philosophy, reality is composed of relatively isolated systems, not of absolutely isolated ones; that ultimately all lesser processes are parts of one great process, the changing universe. If the idea of process was central to their thought, the idea of context was hardly less so.

Henry Demarest Lloyd was not being facetious when he wrote: "Sometimes when I am asked to define myself, I say that I am a socialist-anarchist-communist-individualist-collectivist-cooperative-aristocratic-democrat, for . . . the very complicated thing we call society is rolling forward along all these lines simultaneously." Theodore Dreiser was pointing to the same complexity when he said that he was "not a propagandist" for anything. "Reform," he said, "has a tendency to put all but the biggest temperaments in a cocksure intellectual attitude—and that attitude puts one terribly out of harmony with the great underlying life forces. The gods take their revenge on the cocksure."

Sister Carrie is steeped in awareness of interactions. The cities of Chicago and New York are not merely the scene of the story; they are characters in the drama. They and the weather act on the other characters. It is not Hurstwood who soothes Carrie when she is most upset; it is the rain. Hurst-wood's basic failing is his inability to get along with the two cities, which have lives of their own. Carrie's success on Broadway is due, not to any great talent she has, but to outside factors: luck, the bandwagon nature of theatrical success, the barren lives of city folk that make them eager to glimpse vicarious lives that are slightly (but not much) richer emotionally than their own. By his detailed description of complex and fortuitous situations, Dreiser creates a superb sense that they are not detailed enough, that there is more to be understood, that he has not penetrated through the mystery and inscrutability of life. (Here again he stands in the great nineteenth-century tradition in fiction; when Herman Melville read *The House of the Seven Gables*, he checked the remark: "I begin to suspect that a man's bewilderment is the measure of his wisdom.")

A sense of context was basic to Veblen's work. Having declared that "habits of thought are an outcome of habits of life," he probed into the social environments that shaped such general modes of thinking as invidious comparison, mysticism, and the scientific viewpoint. Similarly Louis Sullivan, in discussing the early tall buildings in Chicago, emphasized the technology and commercial context. He emphasized too the contradictions that the commercial context created: "the tall steel-frame structure may have its aspects of beneficence; but so long as a man may say: 'I shall do as I please with my own,' it presents opposite aspects of social menace and danger." The profit motive and the tall building combined to produce over-crowding, inhuman noise and hurry, ugliness. "Our capitalism was a kind of piracy," Frank Lloyd Wright commented, "our profit-system tended to encourage low forms of avaricious expansion."

Such statements indicate that much of the new interest in context did not arise from intellectual concern so much as from emotional concern with the relations of the individual to society. In this, the Judeo-Christian heritage was a major stimulant. Much of Lincoln's appeal for the generation that followed him lay in his embodiment of many elements of the story of Christ: his humility, his mystical identification with "the people," the manner of his death with its overtones of vicarious sacrifice and atonement. But Chicago liberals in 1905 could not accept Lincoln's philosophy of individualism and self-help as an adequate solution of the problems they faced. Too much had changed in the forty years since his death.

Lincoln had meant his prescription for a rural society of small-scale, independent equals. It had involved far more than the right to accumulate property; it had involved also the idea that Walt Whitman put into "A Song for Occupations":

> Neither a servant nor a master I, . . .
> I shall be even with you and you shall be even with me.

Lincoln had said: "As I would not be a slave, so I would not be a master." But by 1905 Chicago was a city of giant organizations, and how could such organizations be run except by having superiors and inferiors? How could any kind of equality be established? How could a person maintain any independence of his context, of the dominant values and goals?

Jane Addams acutely pointed out that no individual could rise far above the level of his society. The only thing to do, then, if you want to become more human yourself, is to humanize your society. Then your society will humanize you. Man and society inch their way forward together. "Humanity sees its goal to be not perfection but progress," wrote Henry Lloyd, and the form of that progression is an endless dialectic.

It was his consciousness of this that controlled Clarence Darrow's approach to trials. He could have been a good book-lawyer, but he scorned this approach to the law. To rely on precedent was to accept the fetters of a savage past. And it was not the way to win cases. A trial is not won or lost in court, Darrow insisted; it is won or lost in the community. Judges and juries are moved by the currents of opinion that seep into the courtroom from the newspapers and the streets and the market place. A person accused of crime is instantly convicted in the headlines, and he must win his acquittal in the headlines.

In applying this approach Darrow, like the Bible, was accomplished at paradox. He believed simultaneously in salvation by grace and by works. In his jury arguments, he repeatedly called on the jury to love the defendant, to recognize that he was not responsible for his actions. But Darrow was not willing to forgive the jurors in advance. He assured them that if they were so evil as to punish the defendant, they and only they would be accountable. Here is one of the deepest Biblical insights into the requirements of a humane ethics. After a man has erred, we should recognize that all men are fallible, that each man always acts as he must act in view of the complex of pressures operating on the specific organism, and we should acknowledge the sinner as our brother and love him. But before a man has acted, while we can still alter by our actions the total complex of pressures on him, we should demand that he do his duty.

A similar sensitivity to total situations was the basis of Altgeld's greatness as a politician. Just as Lincoln in 1862 had encouraged the abolitionists while realizing that he could not act like an abolitionist, so Altgeld realized that no man can be elected to public office if his views are far ahead of the majority views. In 1899, when it seemed likely that William Jennings Bryan would again be the Democratic nominee for President, Henry Lloyd wrote Altgeld, expressing his doubts about Bryan's liberalism. Altgeld wrote a lecture in reply:

> In order to carry an election, you must have a man upon whom enough voters who differ somewhat in individual views will unite in order to give him the majority. . . . What we want is to get into the White House a man who is not necessarily radical to begin with, but whose sympathies are with the great toiling masses, who will not be controlled by concentrated wealth, and who will be ready to carry out any great reform just as soon as the country is ready for it.

Thus Altgeld affirmed the diversity of the American electorate, its competing interests, and the resulting wavelike nature of any reform.

Lloyd himself used a sense of context to denounce the philosophy of self-interest as "frontier morals," constructive perhaps in an economy of small-scale agriculture, but destructive in an economy of big organizations and interdependence. In a complex industrial society, the canons of self-help led "not to wealth but to that awful waste of wealth": unemployed men, idle machines, idle land. Private property, Lloyd declared, had become an obstacle to social welfare. But what to do? For a decade Lloyd wrestled with the problem of defining a social religion, in which private property would be democratized and regulated. Rejecting the doctrine of human depravity that he had learned as a child in the Dutch Reformed Church, he came to believe in the potential altruism of men, the solidarity of mankind.

In 1903, before he had worked out a systematic statement of his new religion, Lloyd died. His notebooks were edited for publication by Jane Addams, who found in them an affirmation of her own views about the oneness of the human race. And her ideas, like Lloyd's, had been shaped by the example of the Pullman strike. They both saw the sympathetic strike by the American Railway Union as a shining instance of the selfless love they advocated. They both saw the smashing of the strike as fearful proof of the conflicts and animosities that still existed. "The constant fear of slave insurrection proved that the relations of master and slave in the South were not those of love," Lloyd wrote; "the terror of industrial revolution disclosed . . . by the Debs episode gave the same information about the relations of employer and employed."

John Dewey thought the schools could play a major part in healing these social rifts and in developing habits of cooperation in children. He also thought education could train people to deal with problems in a rational and scientific spirit. But as his ideas spread into the glutted public-school systems of the cities, they had results that he had not foreseen. A half century later, the deputy superintendent of education in Florida could declare: "The training of our youth in sound practices in the operation of motor vehicles is as important as learning to read." And in the decade after World War II, the courses in the public schools of West Virginia that showed the largest increases in enrolment were driver education, office practices, and band.

These results would have horrified Dewey. He never supposed that other schools, dealing with great masses of students, could literally imitate what he did at his laboratory school at the University of Chicago. He knew that the methods used in his school depended on teachers familiar with the whole range of human knowledge. In emphasizing that education must take as its starting point the practical problems and the capacities of the child, he had not meant that education should end there. He knew that education must train people in abstract thinking, in logical analysis.

But he did not give enough weight to the social environment in which he was propagating his theories. The contempt of American society for abstract thought, its emphasis on practicality and its readiness to equate the practical with the profitable, made it certain that Dewey's ideas would be seized for the wrong purposes and turned to the wrong ends. School administrators came increasingly to demand teachers who were trained in little except "methods of education." Science courses neglected basic principles and taught applications. Where Dewey had emphasized the internal growth of the child, schools came to emphasize external utility. Education deteriorated into learning a trade, and wealthy donors hurried the process along. Philip D. Armour in 1892 founded the Armour Institute of Technology and gave it a million dollars a year for five years. George M. Pullman in 1897 willed a million dollars to found a manual-training school for boys.

Dewey's theories of education were to some extent vulnerable to this sort of corruption because he did not take enough pains to make himself clear. He could be magnificently lucid, as when he explained the idea of process: "One thing, as common speech profoundly had it, led to another." But his books became increasingly labored and ambiguous, and the ambiguities occurred with alarming frequency at crucial points in his argument. He also overestimated the capacity of the schools for independent action. Education, he declared in 1897, "is the fundamental method of social progress and reform." More realistic were the views of Clarence Darrow, who argued that the school system in every community "has no independent initiative of its own, but is a reflection of the dominant forces, which shape it to their own image." In one age, the schools train for war; in another, for religion; "now it is typically education for producing and getting wealth."

Just as Dewey failed to face up to the full context, so Veblen came to a distorted view of the effects of factory labor on the habits of thought of workers. Most of the industrial workers in Chicago had been peasants in Europe, where their universe had been thoroughly animistic: even rocks and rivers had been endowed with individuality and some capacity for conscious action. But at least the peasant was in touch with the total process of production, from seedtime to harvest. In a Chicago packing house or reaper works he did one small repetitive job, day after day. He came slowly, if at all, to think in terms of mechanical cause and effect because he did not come in contact with the over-all process. Few industrial workers lived in the context that Veblen created for them.

At other times Veblen concentrated so completely on the context, on "the massive forces working obscurely in the background," that he lost sight of the individual actors in the foreground. He argued as if society did everything; individual men, nothing; as if the exact course of technological progress were foreordained and independent of the acts of individual men. Certainly the invention of the Pullman car, for instance, depended on a long course of previous inventions; it also depended on George M. Pullman's determination, and his skill, and his fevered desire to make a profit. The interactions of business and industry were more complicated than Veblen made them out to be.

III

Veblen's research also raised the ancient theological dispute about free will and determinism. By emphasizing the effect of social environment in shaping the habits of thought of individuals, he seemed often to deny that individuals can exercise any choice at all. Jacques Loeb, Dreiser, and Darrow urged variants of this determinist view. Henry Demarest Lloyd, Louis Sullivan, and Frank Lloyd Wright insisted that individuals do make choices, but they also agreed that objective circumstances limit and define those choices. At the other extreme from determinism was the pragmatism of John Dewey and George Herbert Mead, which tended to overemphasize the freedom of the individual by overlooking how the external context makes certain goals unrealistic.

Dewey wanted to use the schools to inculcate better goals into the community, when nearly always it is the community that prescribes what goals and attitudes the schools should teach. Similarly, in 1917 Dewey, supporting the declaration of war by the United States against Germany on the ground that it might lead to "a world organization and the beginnings of a public control which crosses nationalistic boundaries and interests," urged also that the government should not resort to "conscription of thought" in its efforts to win the war. But an appraisal of the total situation at the time would have eliminated both of these goals as impossible. (Three years later Dewey himself would comment: "To profess to have an aim and then neglect the means of its execution is self-delusion of the most dangerous sort.")

One road that led Dewey into such difficulties was his denial of the validity of any distinction between "the critical" and "the gradual." When he took over from Darwin the idea of adaptation, it became almost synonymous with the idea of conciliation. Conflict might occur, but it resulted always in harmonious resolution, never in the destruction of one or both contestants. Human history, for Dewey, held no analogs to the dinosaur. Man, he thought, was a rational animal, who would use his powers to arrive at a scientific solution of problems.

Jacques Loeb agreed that man should do so. "What progress humanity has made, not only in physical welfare but also in the conquest of superstition and hatred, and in the formation of a correct view of life, it owes directly or indirectly to mechanistic science," Loeb wrote in 1915. Motivating his own research were not only idle curiosity and an urge to investigate but also his profound ethics and his belief that ignorance was responsible for most human ills. But in contrast to Dewey's stress on voluntary choice, Loeb's chief contribution was to prove that many actions seemingly resulting from free will actually are involuntary mechanisms.

Having found a way to show this experimentally, Loeb in 1890 announced his tropistic theory. Certain caterpillars, for instance, had been assumed to have an "inherited instinct" that prompted them, upon emerging from the ground in the spring, to crawl up trees to the tips of the limbs where the opening buds served them as food. But what was this instinct? How did it operate? Loeb proved that the caterpillars were heliotropic, attracted by light. He then found ways, by subjecting some species to chemicals, to produce tropisms. This led him to think that certain psychological phenomena in man could be reduced to physico-chemical causes. He pointed, for instance, to a possible relation between glandular secretions and sexual attraction. He suggested that "what we call an idea" could "bring about chemical changes in the body."

Loeb suggested several fruitful paths for psychology to follow: the importance of external stimuli in motivating behavior, the physiological bases of learning and other psychological phenomena, the recognition that man is an organism of complex interactions. He tackled the problem of the regeneration of organs, long a fount of mysticism, and showed that regeneration occurs, not because of any "directive force," but because specific substances accumulate where the organ is to be formed. He undermined the hypothesis of some "directive force" behind evolution by emphasizing that many "adaptations" arose before the species had any conceivable use for them and that they can often be explained on a physicochemical basis.

But Loeb went beyond his experimental results to try, prematurely, to construct a theoretical system that would explain all behavior. In order to include human beings, he stretched the meaning of "tropism" until it encompassed actions far different from a caterpillar climbing toward the source of light. He argued that the true source of human ethics is human instincts, that altruism is instinctive in man just as tropisms are instinctive in lower animals, that we are instinctively driven to eat, sleep, reproduce, work, "to see our fellow beings happy." He then invented the term "associative memory" as the criterion of consciousness and said that only the lowest animals were truly conscious; a term that was thus overgeneralized to the point of bluntness, and that was later subverted by the discovery that even the lowest animals learn a little from experience.

When Loeb's ideas were first announced in the 1890's, they were a sensation, and his books rated full-page reviews in Chicago newspapers. It was inevitable that his research and philosophy would be seized by Clarence Darrow and Theodore Dreiser as evidence for their own determinist views, for their conviction that the universe is without meaning. "As I see him," said Dreiser, "the utterly infinitesimal individual weaves among the mysteries a floss-like and wholly meaningless course —if course it be. In short I catch no meaning from all I have seen, and pass quite as I came, confused and dismayed."

The central image in *Sister Carrie* is of "drifting." The first chapter ends with the statement that Carrie, at her sister's home, is "a lone figure in a tossing, thoughtless sea." Carrie leaves, and her sister Minnie has a dream in which Carrie is on something that "is sinking" into the water, and "the strange waters were blurring everything." When Hurstwood breaks with his wife, he is "rolling and floundering without sail." Carrie, suspended between Drouet and Hurstwood, is able to do "absolutely nothing but drift." Later she "is drifting" out of Hurstwood's life while he is "drifting farther and farther into a situation which could have but one ending." Near the end of the book, the men around a flophouse are "of the class which simply floats and drifts."

Clarence Darrow used the same image repeatedly. In a court argument: "We are tossed on the sea of fate. We are driven here and we are driven there. . . . We die and no man knows where he is bound, or whether there is a port." In a speech: "Look at man. I like to think of them all together on a raft floating on a bottomless sea. Nobody knows when they are going to be pushed off, and while together on this raft we all should be considerate and show sympathy for the thoughts and the ideas of the individual."

Just as Dreiser came to describe love in terms of "chemisms," so Darrow could write a friend that, although life was a "damned humbug, and not worth while," yet he knew that he would resist dying: "It is instinctive in the organism and we cannot help it." Darrow professed to be sure that "one's thoughts and philosophy have nothing whatever to do with his conduct. His reactions are purely mechanistic and cannot be changed." But he could not hold to this view, and at other times he professed a thorough idealism: "It may be that only the ideal really is," he wrote. "All the facts of life are not what are, but what seems to us to be." Dreiser could be similarly inconsistent. Neither he nor Darrow was a systematic thinker; when either of them tried to state his own philosophy he was prone to be vapid and contradictory.

But while the ideas that they explicitly stated were often shallow, the ideas that implicitly guided their work were far from it. Darrow's court arguments and Dreiser's novels rest on firm insight into process and context, and also on a deeper understanding of what causation is than either John Dewey or Thorstein Veblen, both formally trained in philosophy, came to. If we induce Dewey's views from his analyses of specific situations, it seems that he held a loose conception of causality in human affairs. Veblen maintained that the idea of cause is "unproven and unprovable," a "metaphysical" postulate—a position that collapses as soon as theory is subjected to the test of practice.

In contrast, Dreiser faced squarely the question of what causes Hurstwood to steal the money from his employers and flee with Carrie to New York. His answer was: the total situation, including the specific characters of all the actors, causes it. Hurstwood is a success in Chicago, but he gets no satisfaction from his work; as he tells Carrie: "If you were to meet all day with people who cared absolutely nothing about you, if you went day after day to a place where there was nothing but show and indifference, if there was not one person in all those you knew to whom you could appeal for sympathy or talk to with pleasure, perhaps you would be unhappy too." (Dreiser's gift for ambiguity was great: since Hurstwood says these words while he is trying to seduce Carrie, they may be part of his sales talk—but the reader knows that Drouet could never have said them.) Hurstwood's son and daughter have grown away from him. His wife is threatening him with divorce because of his liaison with Carrie. Mrs. Hurstwood will get all his property because, when their marriage was happier, he rashly put it all in her name. He may lose his job too because of the divorce action; Fitzgerald and Moy's is a reputable place which will hardly approve of his involvement in scandal. Floundering in this impasse, he gets drunk. The safe in the saloon has been left open by accident. By accident also, it contains an unusually large sum. Hurstwood considers taking the money. In chaos and inebriation, he mentally shuffles to and fro. While he is holding the money in his hand, the safe door swings shut and locks. (Again Dreiser is ambiguous:

he leaves it unclear whether Hurstwood closes the door, or whether the wind blows it to.) The entire episode manifests Dreiser's conviction that human experience involves the interplay of external stimulus and personal response, that personal response depends on physiology and habits as well as on external stimulation, that chance is a quality that really exists in the world, and that the cause of any change is the total situation in which it occurs.

Dreiser in *Sister Carrie* was writing about characters with slight capacities for sustained, purposeful action. He saw that man has a power that beasts do not have, the power of self-consciousness, and that an essential problem of man is to learn how to live with this power. But Dreiser was hobbled by his belief that beasts are "wholly guided by instinct," whereas when man becomes truly "human" he will be "wholly guided by reason." In fact, human action is a matter of perception, and emotion, and thinking, all at once. It is distinguished, not by any pure rationality, but by efforts to solve problems. The more complex and serious the problem, the more human the action. The greater the obstacles and temptations that are overcome, the more human the action.

Consider the career of Henry Demarest Lloyd. His father-in-law was William Bross, who owned a quarter interest in the Chicago *Tribune*. Soon after Lloyd's marriage to Jessie Bross, he was given 5 percent of the *Tribune* stock. He and his wife could look forward to inheriting the other 20 percent. But his activities in behalf of the Haymarket defendants so outraged Bross that, when he died in 1890, he left his estate to his grandchildren and cut off his daughter and son-in-law from the guardianship. Lloyd had been warned that he was running this risk, but he went his own way and followed his own purposes. ("Do you suppose any such consideration will stop Henry Lloyd from doing what is right?" Mrs. Lloyd had asked.) He had an exalted sense of his own role on earth. It was the proper role for any man. "The creator will never stop creating—and the creator is man," Lloyd wrote. To him the

conception of Christ seemed valuable "only as a symbolical figure portraying the possibilities of humanity."

These possibilities—the potentialities of human beings—absorbed Louis Sullivan even more than the possibilities of
inorganic materials did. In his autobiography, written in the
third person, Sullivan described "his aggressive research in creative architecture, and, simultaneously . . . his studies in the
reality of man":

> In childhood his idols had been the big strong men who *did*
> things. Later on he had begun to feel the greater power of men
> who could *think* things; later the expansive power of men who
> could *imagine* things; and at last he began to recognize as domi-
> nant, the will of the Creative Dreamer: he who possessed the
> power of vision needed to harness Imagination, to harness the
> intellect, to make science do his will, to make the emotions serve
> him—for without emotion nothing. . . . There lies another power
> in man. That power is MORAL: Its name is CHOICE! Within
> this one word, Choice, lies the story of man's world. . . . Need
> we know man's thoughts? View his works, his deeds; they tell
> his choice. . . . Now the real man begins to shape within our
> vision. Consider his primary powers: He, the *worker*, the *in-
> quirer*, the *chooser*. . . . While . . . we shall find all men to be
> alike in native possession of essential powers, we are at once
> confronted by the paradox: That all men obviously are differ-
> ent, that no two are alike. In plain words we find each human
> being unique. . . . Without Ego, which is Life, man vanishes.
> Ego signifies Identity. It is the free spirit.

Thus Sullivan came to a new and deeper statement of the
nature of freedom of the will. Perhaps we will learn, some day,
that Jacques Loeb was right in his hunch; perhaps when we
know enough about human nature and about external reality,
we will be forced to realize that every specific choice made by
an individual is utterly predictable on the basis of his total
character and the situation in which he must choose. But what
Sullivan asserted, and what his own career demonstrated, is
that a man need not be the pawn of external circumstances,

that he can sometimes find ways to assert his own needs, his own understanding, his own purposes, that he can to some extent shape the world in accord with his visions.

Sullivan's career also demonstrated how a man can do this. Sullivan could not create the possibilities that confronted him. They existed outside him and independently of him, technical processes that had progressed only so far, commercial processes that made their own demands, esthetic traditions that had reached specified points. He had to work with these existing realities. But his context was not a monolithic mass; countless processes were going on, and he could select certain ones from among the many that were available to him. By understanding, by inquiry that led to understanding, by desire, and by imagination, he could snatch up certain possibilities that his context with its interacting processes created. He could fuse those possibilities into a new unity that met the commercial requirements and simultaneously realized his own technical and esthetic conceptions. Thus Sullivan showed how a man exercises choice by finding an answer to the question: What are the existing possibilities that, when guided and stimulated by my personal, unaided force, will become a new and worthy reality?

The answers found by Sullivan resulted in the Chicago Auditorium, the Wainwright Building, the Getty Tomb, the store for Schlesinger & Mayer. By finding these answers, he stimulated and extended the processes that seemed to him to lead forward, resisted the processes that seemed to him to lead backward. But in spite of his resistance, the wrong processes surged ahead; in spite of his stimulation, the right processes shriveled for a time. His context changed, and he could no longer find the answers he needed. Then he bitterly realized that a man of creative imagination, a Louis Sullivan, cannot work out of anybody's understanding but his own; if the world demands hack work, hacks must do it. So Sullivan and the world of architecture parted, and both parties were poorer for the separation.

But the world lost more than Sullivan did. At least he never forgot that every man owes his ultimate loyalty to the entire human race, and he found incisive and resounding words to express his realization:

> Our dream shall be of a civilization founded upon ideas thrillingly sane, a civilization, a social fabric resting squarely on man's quality of virtue as a human being; . . . created in the likeness of his aspirant emotions, in response to the power and glory of his true imagination, the power of his intelligence, his ability to inquire, to do, to make new situations befitting his needs. . . .
>
> Such dream is the vigorous daylight dream of man's abounding power, that he may establish in beauty and in joy, on the earth, a dwelling place devoid of fear.

In these words, Sullivan stated the vision of his generation of humanists in Chicago: of Altgeld and Jane Addams, of Debs and Darrow, of Veblen and Dewey, of Loeb and Dreiser, of Theodore Thomas and Henry Lloyd. It was a vision that moved men and women to great deeds, a vision of individual responsibility for the welfare of mankind.

Epilogue: From Altgeld to Our Time

What aim do you wish to achieve, where are you going, what
is in your soul? In a word, who are you? What are you?
—Anna Sergeevna Odintsova, in *Fathers and Sons* *

ALTGELD WAS ONE of the first to die, but none of the founders of
Chicago's great corporations survived him long: George Pullman died in 1897; Armour, in 1901; Potter Palmer, the next
year, and Gustavus Swift, the next; Yerkes, in 1905; Marshall
Field, in 1906. Their companies are still dominant in their re-
spective industries, and, if their methods have been modified,
their aims are still to earn a profit and to grow as organizations.
Of the entire generation of reformers who tried to counter
these aims with more complex and humanistic goals, only
Frank Lloyd Wright is still alive. Not only alive, but still
working, and still in the vanguard of his profession.

The sole survivor of an earlier generation, Wright is a bench-
mark against which to measure the present. The perspective
is sobering. In the United States today, where is the governor
to rank with Altgeld? the social critic to rank with Veblen? the
lawyer to rank with Darrow? the educator-philosopher to rank
with Dewey? the social worker to rank with Jane Addams or
a half-dozen of her associates? the novelist to rank with Dreiser?
the architect to rank with Wright?

* Ivan Turgenev, *Fathers and Sons*, trans. by Harry Stevens (New York:
Alfred A. Knopf, Inc., 1950), p. 256.

Although some of these specific questions might be answered, the general point is not likely to be shaken: when we compare the single city of Chicago a half-century ago with the entire country today, it is the country today that suffers by the comparison. Only in the natural sciences are men and women now able to achieve the self-realization that comes from expending one's full powers on a worthy task. In spite of the diversions that exist even in these subjects (the military orientation of much research, the emphasis on applying basic principles to create immediately useful machines rather than on extending our grasp of the basic principles, bureaucracy and fretwork), at least in them the dedication to a search for truth is deep enough, and the standards of achievement and verification clear enough, so that the fakes are found out, and the best men usually find ways to indulge their disinterested curiosities and so to benefit us all. But in Chicago two generations ago, humanists were pursuing their own goals in a far greater variety of fields than seems possible today.

We are often told, and we tell ourselves, that others of our contemporaries are great thinkers, great leaders, great artists and composers and writers. But the thinker who inflates his own reputation by gibing at Veblen or Dewey—is he half as creative as the men he mocks? The executive who studies the public-opinion polls before choosing goals for the country or policies for himself—is he another Altgeld, another Lincoln? The writer who is so submerged in our own time that he can only reflect its confusions, the composer who can only play back the cacophonies he hears and feels, the painter who can find nothing to do with a canvas except to paint the left half of it black and the right half of it red—are these great artists? Have we all, including our artists, tried to make our peace with discordant and impoverished lives?

In many respects, life is less impoverished now. Severe physical want, of the sort that occupied Jane Addams and Florence Kelley, still exists, but it is less common. Output per capita in the United States has increased about six times since 1900, and social legislation and trade unionism have served to distribute the increased output to an increasing proportion of the population. The results achieved by the big corporation in producing goods have won public acceptance for it, so that the erstwhile clamor against the trusts has become a whisper. American firms have tried to extend their dominance over most of the world, as Henry Lloyd predicted in 1901. They have cleaned up their methods: the flamboyant John W. Gates and the unscrupulous Yerkes have been succeeded by smooth talkers who speak of business responsibility to the community, of human relations, who have a keen ear for public response to business policies.

Thus it has come about that most families, at least in northern cities, have risen above the level of material need. The whole logic of industrialization—together with the countervailing forces that were spawned by the early humanists to help equalize the distribution of the fruits of industry—has been to displace human workers altogether, except as consumers. But the escape from dire poverty has not brought happiness. Having no experience with, or no hope for, any satisfactions other than the sensual pleasures and the status that a high income can yield, many persons are trying to use goods as an adjustment to the frustration of other needs. This type of compensation is pathetic, but understandable. At a haunting moment in *Fathers and Sons*, the young nihilist Bazarov is packing his trunk, and he turns to his friend and says: "Do you know what I am doing? There's some room left in my trunk, and I am putting hay into it; and that happens in our life's trunk too; we'll fill it up with anything rather than have an empty place in it." The hay may muffle our needs temporarily, but it does not appease them, and we grow increasingly confused and anguished for reasons that we do not understand.

Some early reformers warned of this impending emptiness. Eugene Debs, in the speech at Canton, Ohio, that sent him to prison in 1919, told of a man whose conscience said he should join the Socialist party, but whose fears said he would lose his job if he did. He decided not to. That night in his sleep, said Debs, the man had "a terrible dream. He awoke, and at midnight he bounded from his bed in a state of terror, for he said: 'My God, there is nobody in this room.' (Laughter.) And he was absolutely right. (Laughter and applause.) No one! He was terror-stricken. . . . It is an awful thing to be nobody."

Here was a warning that we might well become a "lonely crowd." If the audience had understood Debs better, probably nobody would have laughed.

Robert Herrick had underscored the danger even before Debs gave this speech. In his last novel about Chicago, *The Memoirs of an American Citizen* (1905), Herrick traced the career of Van Harrington, who first makes a fortune in meat packing, then spends a big slice of his fortune to buy himself a seat in the United States Senate from the Illinois legislature. But in the process of winning his success, Harrington lops off or stifles one piece of himself after another. At last he can find no pleasure in the present, because his center of gravity is gone. He cannot think about his own past without deceiving himself about it. He has stopped being a coherent, identifiable personality. This, Herrick implied, is what must come of abandoning your Self to make a full-hearted acceptance of things as they are.

The most important of these external realities, so far as the individual is concerned, are the goals that society sets for his own life. In Chicago in 1890, one goal threatened to swallow up all others: men would do anything to make money, and their prestige depended solely on how much money they made. When Veblen wrote his ironic depreciation of this way of life, he did not deride the quest for status—all men everywhere need to be respected so that they can respect themselves. What he derided was status based on the false standards of pecuniary emulation, for he knew that those standards blocked the satisfaction of other needs and thwarted the full and balanced development of personal character.

The goal of personal wealth has persisted to our own time,

and the highest repute commonly goes to the biggest fortune. But other aims have become even more pervasive than they were in Veblen's time, and the new ones are even more conducive to insanity than the old. In addition to trying to make money, men aim increasingly at consuming goods. The well-to-do in New York (who, as Veblen observed, influence the standards of the whole country) try to eat in the best restaurants, live in the best suburbs, drive the biggest cars, go to the most plays. But the best restaurants are too noisy; the best suburbs are devoted to shallow ways; the highways are jammed with the biggest cars; the plays are stale. Men try to find pleasure by reaching out like amebas to incorporate sensations, but the sensations bring no pleasure, and the men find that they are walking the road to boredom and that it ends in a psychiatric ward.

Equally self-defeating are the efforts of a person to be liked, not for what he genuinely and specifically is as a human being, but by being all things to all men, by altering his personality at will to meet what he imagines to be the requirements of each situation, until at last he has no personality, but only a set of masks, and behind the masks he seems as undefined and free-flowing as any fluid. Yet, he is not a fluid, but a man, and in the end the needs he shares with other men may assert themselves, and he too may lose his psychological balance.

These are some of the problems that confront us now, and the Chicago reformers left guideposts toward solutions. Implicit in their activities was the recognition that all human beings have certain basic needs, and these needs arise in a fixed order. If a person lacks food, or warmth, or sleep, all his faculties will be focused on ways to remedy these deficiencies. But when the physiological needs have been met, the other needs assert themselves. Now the person seeks a sense of safety and security. He wants to understand the world he lives in. He wants to feel that he belongs to some group, to identify himself with it, to know that others accept him and that he accepts them. He wants to be loved, and to know that others need him to love them. He wants to know that he is making a reality of the potentialities that he was born with, that he is developing his own best powers by using them. He wants to know that he is a personal force in the world. He wants to know that by his efforts to alter the world he is also changing himself into a better and richer person.

Jacques Loeb explained why no single, simple goal in life would suffice for a human being: "We eat, drink, and reproduce . . . because, machine-like, we are compelled to do so. We are active, because we are compelled to be so by processes in our central nervous system; and so long as human beings are not economic slaves the instinct of successful work or of workmanship determines the direction of their action. . . . We seek and enjoy the fellowship of human beings because hereditary conditions compel us to do so. We struggle for justice and truth since we are instinctively compelled to see our fellow beings happy."

Here Loeb stretched the notion of instinct until it became almost meaningless. The need of a man to see other men happy is not the same as the heliotropism of the caterpillar; the caterpillar has no choice, the man has. Loeb recognized this: "Economic, social, and political conditions or ignorance and superstition may warp and inhibit the inherited instincts and thus create a civilization with a faulty or low development of ethics." Men are born not with instincts—total patterns of need, goal object, and behavior—but with innate needs, and they must learn after birth what objects and what behavior will satisfy those needs. The needs can be thwarted, or they can be muffled by false goals that do not really satisfy; but only a truly appropriate satisfaction can preserve the health of the individual.

The tragedy of our society is that these appropriate satisfactions are often impossible to come by. The ability of a person to live an adult life—sometimes, to live at all, as Dreiser showed in writing about George Hurstwood—depends on his success in two basic quests: for love, and for work he finds satisfying.

Work is satisfying to the extent that it yields material comfort, security, and continuous growth of understanding. From work and from love the individual comes to believe that he belongs in the world, that he has a proper place, that the world would be, in some sense, for some people, a worse place if he should die. But we conduct these basic quests today under terrifying circumstances.

We search for love in a world inhabited largely by Drouets, people frightened of deep commitments, incapable of wholehearted acceptance of another, saturated with false images by the mass media, ashamed to expose their own needs and wants and sensations and ideas, desperately trying to skim along on the surface of life. As Bessie Smith sang it:

> Gee, but it's hard
> To love someone
> When that someone don't love you.

More than hard. Impossible.

The search for satisfying work is, if possible, even more difficult. Men can rise high today, but few men rise so high that they reach the point of security. Veblen was misleading when he argued that the chief effect of contact with modern industry is to train men in matter-of-fact thinking; this is true to some extent for scientists and engineers, but work on an assembly line trains men in boredom, educates them hardly at all, and stimulates them not a whit, preparing them only for their evening of stupor in front of the television screen. Many jobs that should be satisfying turn out otherwise: editors spend much energy competing for manuscripts they detest, written by men they hold in contempt, on the theory that the author's neuroses are shared by five thousand or more book buyers who will be lulled to sleep by the wish-fulfilments he has packaged. And certainly a sizable number of advertising copywriters doubt that composing radio jingles to sell soap flakes is a fitting activity for a grown man. In spite of the earnest efforts being made to persuade them, they may increasingly realize that their roles in life are not only smaller, but are less human, than those played by Altgeld and Darrow, by Jane Addams and Florence Kelley, by Veblen and Dewey, by Dreiser and Sullivan.

It is the vitality of this past generation that contrasts so strongly with our own confusions and lethargy, and their vitality came from the intensity and exaltation of their purposes. Men like Altgeld and Darrow had some ambitions that were far from noble, and they had more conflicts than the typical man. But in most situations they ultimately faced up to the question: What is right? The question has gone out of style. Nowadays an effort to reach a decision is likely to begin and end with the query: Am I covered? In this shift lies the collapse of a civilization, and we still do not realize exactly what has happened or how.

This collapse is the theme of *Parade's End,* by Ford Madox Ford, published thirty years ago, and perhaps still the last major novel by an Englishman or American in which the hero and heroine are likable adults pursuing sane goals with intelligence and decency. In a climactic scene, set early in World War I, Chris Tietjens explains to Valentine Wannop that he can no longer keep his job as second secretary in the Statistics Office because he is fed up with faking statistics for propaganda purposes, and that he intends to enlist in the British Army. She tries to dissuade him; then she reassures him by saying that he will be able to get his job back after the war. He replies: "But no! They'll never let me back. . . . They'll pursue me, systematically. . . . You see in such a world as this, an idealist—or perhaps it's only a sentimentalist—must be stoned to death. He makes the others so uncomfortable. He haunts them at their golf. . . . No, they'll get me one way or the other." They do. After the war, Tietjens, a brilliant mathematician, goes into the used-furniture business.

This cuts close to the core of the dilemma. Chicago fifty years ago was already a city of organizations. Although forceful individuals could fit their own purposes into the purposes of some of those organizations—Altgeld and the Democratic party, for a time; Dewey and the University of Chicago—the alliances were uneasy. Veblen was forced out of the University of Chicago and lived out his life as a marginal man in the academic world. The other reformers lived in the fissures between organizations, and life there was hard. They had to supply what the market wanted, but they catered to small and specialized markets. Darrow needed only individual clients, and he could ignore what most people thought of him. Sullivan and Wright sold their designs to single men or to small groups, and the time came when Sullivan could not do even that. The women at Hull-House had independent incomes, and their activities were financed by a few wealthy donors. Dreiser's inability to get *Sister Carrie* published is an instance of what happened when these early humanists tried to penetrate the mass market.

In our day, the situation has developed much further. All activities face toward the big market. Men even try to shuffle their personalities to meet the contradictory demands of different buyers. The range open to lone wolves has become smaller; the fissures between organizations are fewer and narrower; and the market covers them all. So the organizations set the purposes, and the man who cannot or will not yield up his life to the service of some organization is apt to find himself outside society altogether, unable to earn the simplest sort of livelihood. The dilemma arises because no man can find sanity or fulfilment in serving the purposes of most of our organizations.

The most important ones, the big corporations, are what no person (not even Marshall Field, although he tried hard) could ever become: The Economic Man. They seek to survive and to expand, and their ability to achieve those goals is dependent on their profits. They seek to make money by giving the public what it wants, even if what it wants is shoddy or destructive. More, they seek to persuade the public that it wants what it clearly does not need. Before the employees can persuade the public, they must persuade themselves; nobody is more gullible than a salesman or an advertising man. Thus members of the supposedly privileged classes spend their lives making money so that they can suffer the inconvences of owning a Cadillac in New York, or taking a mid-winter trip to Miami where they find little except the resentments and discontents that they carry with them from Dubuque.

For most people, this outcome is inevitable. As society is now organized, it is certainly easier to make money and to get ahead (for those who abandon themselves to the effort) than it is for anyone to achieve a more balanced and constructive set of goals. So men try to adopt as their personal goals the purposes of the organizations that employ them and to compensate for the deficiencies by getting ahead and living high. The trouble with this effort is that it cannot succeed; men cannot exorcise their innate needs merely because their employers expect them to. Men continue to be men, but malformed ones, and they will remain so until they achieve a more developed and healthy set of purposes. "Principle alone is defense and refuge," Frank Lloyd Wright has said, "—from chaos and utter defeat."

Purpose must be personal, or it is meaningless to the individual. Each person must find his own way to be creative, but the final test of what is creative is the one that Louis Sullivan set: "Are you using such gifts as you possess for or against the people?" In his final book, *Man, the Social Creator*, Henry Lloyd came to the balanced paradoxes of human existence:

> There must be independence as well as interdependence. Every citizen must have his field, his home, his separate things, to be administered by himself alone. His personality, his self-reliance, his sense of private power must be more than kept intact, must be cultivated and developed, if he is to be fit to meet his fellows in the co-operative activities. . . . We must be men as well as members.

Which is perhaps only to spell out the much older injunction in Matthew (X:39): "He that findeth his life shall lose it; and he that loseth his life for my sake shall find it."

But for whose sake, for what cause, should a man live? We have tried to live for personal status and sensual pleasure, or for the security and status of our children, and the effort has failed. Causes so narrow and selfish do not breed the richness and happiness that Chicago humanists found two generations ago by devoting their lives to the advancement of all humanity. If the human race is now in danger of exterminating itself, part of the explanation is that the natural curiosity and involvement of many men and women has been stifled, so that their days are ruled by lethargy and boredom. As a result, they have never found satisfying reasons why they should go on living. Nor will they, it seems, until they extend their search to areas of experience they have never explored, and rediscover the paths that some of our predecessors blazed.

Sources and Acknowledgments

In doing research for this book, the most useful sources were the daily newspapers of Chicago; I have examined at least one of them, usually the *Tribune* or the *Record-Herald*, column by column, day by day, for the entire period from 1892 to 1906. Another periodical that proved very valuable was Louis F. Post's weekly *The Public* (1898-1919).

The richest collections of manuscripts that I found were Jane Addams Papers, Swarthmore College; Theodore Dreiser Papers, University of Pennsylvania; Richard T. Ely Papers and Henry Demarest Lloyd Papers, Wisconsin Historical Society; Henry George Papers, New York Public Library; Robert Herrick Papers, University of Chicago; George A. Schilling Papers, Illinois Historical Library; and the Papers, all in the Manuscript Division of the Library of Congress, of the following men: Grover Cleveland, Clarence S. Darrow, Richard Olney, Louis F. Post, Theodore Roosevelt, Elihu Root, and Brand Whitlock.

By the time I began working on this study, the relevant records of the Altgeld administration in the Illinois State Archives had deteriorated so badly that they had been withdrawn from use. This fact further increased my dependence on three fine works: the unpublished dissertation by Harvey Wish, "The Administration of Governor John Peter Altgeld of Illinois, 1893-1897" (Northwestern University, 1936), Chester McA. Destler's *American Radicalism, 1865-1901* (1946), and Harry Barnard's *"Eagle Forgotten": The Life of John Peter Altgeld* (1938). Unfortunately for me, the three volumes thus far published (1937, 1940, 1957) of Bessie Louise Pierce's detailed *A History of Chicago* carry the story only to 1893, so that they overlap only slightly with my own study, but I am indebted to them for many background facts. I have also profited from the books about Chicago by Lloyd Lewis and Henry J. Smith (1929) and by Emmett Dedmon (1953).

The generation that forms the subject of this book was addicted to writing autobiographies and memoirs of friends; Jane Addams, Alice Hamilton, Darrow, Dreiser, Sullivan, Wright, and Whitlock all did so. While such books are notoriously inaccurate about objective facts, they can still, if used carefully, give an intimacy and immediacy that would be impossible otherwise. I have relied on them especially in writing about the women at Hull-House.

Without Florence Kelley's reports as chief factory inspector of Illinois, the books of Edith Abbott and Sophonisba Breckinridge, and particularly the volume from Hull-House, *Maps and Papers* (1895), I could never have tried to re-create the living and working conditions of Chicago's lower classes.

The two chapters about the Haymarket bombing and the pardon rely especially on Barnard's biography and on the excellent study by Henry David, *The Haymarket Affair* (1936). Altgeld's papers were published in various editions under the title, *Live Questions*. The sources for Chapter 6, about the Pullman strike, are cited in detail in my earlier biography of Debs, *The Bending Cross* (1949).

Before writing my discussion of the works of Veblen, Dewey, Dreiser, Fuller, Herrick, and Sinclair, I of course read the views of them held by many other commentators. I cribbed wherever I could, so that I have more debts than I could acknowledge, and doubtless have many that I do not even recognize. But in every instance I have been guided by my first-hand reading of and response to the original work itself. Similarly, so far as the buildings that I have discussed still exist, I have seen them with my own eyes; if the structure had been torn down, I tried to get the best photographs available.

I have benefited from several extremely generous contributions, of money, time, energy, and wisdom. The late Mrs. Clarence Darrow, the late Mr. Paul Darrow, Judge William H. Holly, and William Carlin, Esquire, shared with me their memories of many of these events. The present study grew out of research begun in 1950-1951 under a grant from the Committee on Midwestern Studies of Michigan State University and the Rockefeller Foundation. Two friends, Dr. A. Theodore Brown of the History of Kansas City Project and Dr. Irvin G. Wyllie of the University of Wisconsin, and my wife Evelyn have all read the entire manuscript, with great sympathy for and insight into my intentions, but with no patience for my mistakes and excesses. They have done all that a person can do to improve another's work, and, since I have sometimes rejected their suggestions, they are blameless for the deficiencies of the published work. Mr. Herbert Gutman of Fairleigh Dickinson University was kind enough to lend me his voluminous notes about labor in Illinois during the 1873 depression. Mrs. Sylvia Shipp did an exceptionally quick and conscientious job of typing the manuscript for the printer.

R.G.

New York City
June, 1958

Index